What Others Are Saying

"Tracy and Peter have successfully pulled off two major challenges, bike riding huge distances and writing a book. They achieved success at both efforts. You may not enjoy riding thousands of miles, but you will enjoy reading about those who do."

- Jeff Pagels, author of "Always Climbing Higher"

"Coast to Coast on a Tandem *should be read cover to cover by anyone interested in the details of cross-country bike touring."*

- Seth Portner, Executive Director, Warmshowers.org

"Getting two perspectives on the same sequence of events was both different and quite entertaining. I wanted to keep reading to find out what Tracy thought about Peter and vice versa!"

- Andy Clarke, internationally recognized bicycle policy and planning expert

"A fascinating read for anyone who has ever dreamed big."

- Jacob VanSickle, Executive Director, Bike Cleveland

"You will find yourselves drawn into their traveling adventure. This is just fun."

- Tom Huber, former Wisconsin Bicycle and Pedestrian Coordinator

"Peter and Tracy take you on adventure! Along the road, you can't help but get caught up in the highs and lows of the journey. You anticipate what's around the corner as they colorfully tell their story as individuals and as a couple. Don't be surprised if you find yourself longing to explore!"

-Christian Jensen, Executive Director, myTEAM TRIUMPH WI Chapter

Coast to Coast on a Tandem

Our Adventure Crossing the USA on a Bicycle Built for Two

Tracy and Peter Flucke

M&B Global Solutions, Inc.
Green Bay, Wisconsin (USA)

Coast to Coast on a Tandem

Our Adventure Crossing the USA on a Bicycle Built for Two

First Edition

Disclaimer
The views expressed in this work are solely those of the author and do not necessarily reflect the views of the publisher, and the publisher hereby disclaims any responsibility for them. In the event you use any of the information in this book for yourself, which is your constitutional right, the author and the publisher assume no responsibility for your actions.

Front cover photo:
Peter and Tracy Flucke pose at Marine Park on Bellingham Bay in Washington State at the outset of their journey across the United States.

Back cover photo:
In accordance with tradition, Peter and Tracy Flucke hoist their tandem in celebration of reaching the Atlantic Ocean in Bar Harbor, Maine.

Map graphics courtesy of Sydney McNeill

Printed by Seaway Printing Company, Green Bay, Wisconsin

ISBN 10: 1-942731-28-0
ISBN 13: 978-1-942731-28-3

Published by M&B Global Solutions Inc.
Green Bay, Wisconsin (USA)

Dedication

To Tracy my love, my partner, my wife, my "stoker."

To Peter my "captain" on our journey through life.

To our daughters, Melissa and Alexandra ...
Thank you for supporting us on our adventure.
We love and respect you both more than you will ever know.

Contents

Preface 1
Introduction 3
1. Getting Ready to Go 9
2. Our Trip Begins 23
3. Combining Work and Play 45
4. Glacier National Park and the State of Montana 61
5. North Dakota - A Windy State 93
6. Minnesota - Great Trails and Family 109
7. Wisconsin - Friends and Family 115
8. Michigan - A Challenge to Travel Through 135
9. Indiana and Amish Country 147
10. Ohio and the Ohio Byway 157
11. Northeast Ups and Downs 173
12. Vermont and New Hampshire 197
13. We Made it to Maine! 203
Epilogue - Recovery and Return Home 213
Acknowledgements 219
About the Authors 220

"If you can't be riding your bicycle, write about it."

- Fred Meredith

Preface

The purpose of this book is first and foremost to entertain you. If you are anything like the thousands of people with whom we have already shared our adventure, you will enjoy this journey. Secondly, and not surprisingly for those who know us, our goal is to educate. We never could have completed this ride without the collective knowledge and wisdom of those who came before us. Now it is time for us to give back.

Finally, our hope is to inspire you; not to ride across the country on a bicycle built for two and test your relationship – unless you want to – but rather to get out of your comfort zone and push your boundaries ... even just a little bit. You won't regret it!

This book is based on our 2014 unsupported cross country bicycle trip across the Northern Tier of the United States, recorded in the daily blog that Tracy wrote and my daily Facebook posts. We have supplemented our story with tidbits of information about training, the bike, gear, navigation, bicycling in traffic, nutrition, mechanics, etc.

Why two points of view when we are on the same bike? Surprisingly, Tracy and I often had very different experiences during each day's ride, even though we were only six inches apart. From my position in front, I have almost complete control over the bicycle (starting, steering, interacting with traffic and stopping). Tracy has to follow my lead. I can see the road directly ahead, but Tracy cannot. Conversely, from Tracy's position behind me, she has the freedom to look around, but she is also responsible for navigating and checking behind us for traffic. These different perspectives and responsibilities meant we very seldom had the same experience on the ride. If we did not put those experiences together, you just wouldn't get the whole picture.

We came together many years ago because we were in love and wanted to make a life together. But life is hard! The pressures of work, family, and growing as individuals can strain any relationship. This trip was an opportunity to celebrate making it this far in life and push our boundaries. Many of the experiences we had over our fifty-plus years of life prepared us well for what lay ahead, but we were not prepared for many of the trials we faced and had to figure things out along the way. It was fascinating to see how life had prepared us for this adventure and how the adventure, in return, prepared us for life.

Tracy and I enjoyed planning our trip and we loved the adventure itself (usually). But now that we are home and the trip is complete, the journey in many ways continues. We still reminisce about the adventure, share our stories, and practice the bicycling and life lessons learned. This book allows us to continue to share an adventure we will never forget.

Thank you for joining us. We hope you enjoy accompanying us as we bicycle across the Northern Tier of the United States.

Peter Flucke

Introduction

I rolled over in bed and said to Tracy, "I think we should bike across the country. I don't want to wake up some day when it's too late and wish we had done it." She looked at me and said, "Okay!"

The fact that we were going to ride across the northern part of the United States (the Northern Tier route) on our tandem (a bicycle built for two), and on our own were all consent items. We had been talking about and training for this for years – now we just had to do it! Both of us had led active lives and loved being outdoors since we were kids. We were in a better position physically and mentally to embark on a major adventure than most people, but we also realized we would have to ramp up our fitness to safely achieve our goal. Here is a little bit about how we arrived at this point.

I learned how to ride a bicycle growing up in a suburb of Minneapolis, Minnesota, and later was a three-sport athlete at Shorewood High School near Milwaukee, Wisconsin. I participated in football (badly), wrestling (okay) and track and field (better). I didn't ride much until I started training for my first triathlon when I was in college at the University of Wisconsin-Stevens Point. I majored in Recreation and Forestry and minored in Environmental Law Enforcement.

After college, I went to work as a manager for a membership campground company and worked at resorts in Michigan, Wisconsin, and Illinois. I met my future wife while working at a resort in Wisconsin Dells. I would take long bike rides (25-50 miles) on my days off, and sometimes I would ride out one way and

Tracy would meet me at the end. Back then, I knew nothing about training or nutrition and would regularly ride myself to exhaustion. Occasionally, Tracy would wake up to find me switched end for end in bed, on my back with my aching legs up against the headboard and wall so I could sleep. It scared the heck out of her the first few times it happened.

Tracy grew up in Wauwatosa, Wisconsin (near Milwaukee). She played center on her school's first ninth grade all-girls basketball team and continued to play through her high school years. She also played volleyball and participated in track and field. At five-foot-nine, she wasn't the tallest player, but she had springs. Once upon a time, Tracy could slam dunk a volleyball in a regulation ten-foot basketball hoop. Damn, girl! Tracy is the one on Team Flucke with the natural athletic ability. I'm the average recreational athlete who is, usually, in really good shape. Tracy graduated from the University of Wisconsin-La Crosse with a degree in Recreation Administration. We were married in Milwaukee in May 1987.

I became a park ranger for the Suburban Hennepin Regional Park District (now the Three Rivers Park District) near Minneapolis in December 1987. I was a full-time, licensed law enforcement officer (gun, bulletproof vest and all) and EMT (Emergency Medical Technician) for the Park District. While at Hennepin Parks, I started one of the first police bike patrols in the state. Tracy became the first Parks and Recreation Director for the City of Savage, Minnesota.

The first of our two daughters, Melissa, was born in November 1990. The following spring, Tracy, Melissa and I took our first, supported, multi-day bicycle trip. The event was a three-day ride along the Mississippi River organized by the American Lung Association. They transported all of our camping gear and extra clothes. I was riding a Trek 560 road bike and pulling six-month-old Melissa in a Burley d'lite bike trailer – not the ideal setup for tackling the hills along the river. Tracy was riding an average Trek hybrid. We had no clue what we were getting into. Just as we started the ride, the sky let loose with thunder and lightning, striking a telephone pole maybe fifty yards from us. In minutes we were soaked, but fortunately, Melissa was warm and dry in her trailer. Beautiful scenery, warming baby bottles in the microwave at convenience stores, sleeping under the stars ... we were hooked! We did this ride three more times.

We moved to Ashwaubenon, Wisconsin (a suburb of Green Bay), in March 1993. Tracy became the Director of Parks, Recreation and Forestry and I started our family consulting business, WE BIKE. Our second daughter, Alexandra (Alex) was born in March 1995.

In 1996, I became a nationally certified League Cycling Instructor with the League of American Bicyclists. We also bought our first tandem bicycle, a Trek T-100 ($1,200). We outfitted it with a second-hand kiddy crank in the back so Melissa could pedal and ride with me while Tracy pulled Alex in the trailer. This setup served us well. Melissa's longest ride on the tandem was seventy miles, and except for falling asleep once and almost falling off, it worked great. For a number of years, we did an overnight trip with another family to Shawano, Wisconsin.

We would ride the Mountain-Bay State Recreational Trail west from Green Bay to Shawano (forty-one miles). We would stay at a hotel, swim in the pool, go out to dinner, and in the morning, have breakfast and ride home.

In the late 1990s, Tracy decided she would like to do the Door County (Wisconsin) Century, a one-day, 100-mile, organized ride for the first time. I had already done the ride several times. Not wanting to try and ride that far on her own, we decided to do it together on the tandem. Even though the T-100 is more of a hybrid design and isn't really made for long road rides, we completed the ride and discovered that we really liked riding the tandem together, me in front and Tracy in the back. We continued riding the Trek together for the next several years.

By 2001, we had decided that we wanted to try unsupported bike touring together on the tandem. Since the Trek wasn't really designed for serious touring and it didn't fit us all that well, we decided to buy a new bike. Now, road touring tandems are not cheap! We justified the purchase ($6,000) by saying it was an investment in our marriage. By now, Melissa was ten, Alex was five, Tracy was working on her Master's degree in Public Administration, and we were starting to get really busy with the kids. Somehow, we knew we needed something that was just ours to keep us going as a couple. We bought our first tandem to keep our family strong. We bought our second tandem to keep our marriage strong!

After much research (aka obsessing), I decided on a 2000 Santana Arriva. As is my custom to save money, I bought "last year's model." We had two choices of color, black or purple. Tracy chose purple and named the new bike "Violet."

I had a blast buying all of the racks, bags and gear for the bike. Being a bike nut and having done lots of camping and some backpacking as a teenager, I was like a kid in a candy store looking through all of the catalogs.

Our first unsupported, fully-loaded, overnight trip on Violet was to my brother's hobby farm in Fond du Lac, Wisconsin, about eighty-five miles to the south. We biked down on a Saturday, camped near the creek in the heat with the mosquitos, and biked home the next day. We loved it and were hooked again. We did almost 25,000 miles of biking and touring on Violet over the next thirteen years.

We would talk about bicycling across the country from time to time, but we had no idea if we could do it. So, kind of as an experiment, we started taking longer and longer trips as time permitted – three days, four days, one week, two weeks. By the time we did our first three-week trip from Green Bay to Minneapolis to Prairie du Chien (Wis.) and back to Green Bay, in ninety-plus degree heat, we figured we could do it – bike all the way across the United States. We would just do three-week trips, back to back to back, until we got there.

Now that I had Tracy's okay, the only things stopping us were two children, jobs, money, and time. That's all!

Bellingham, Washington, to ...

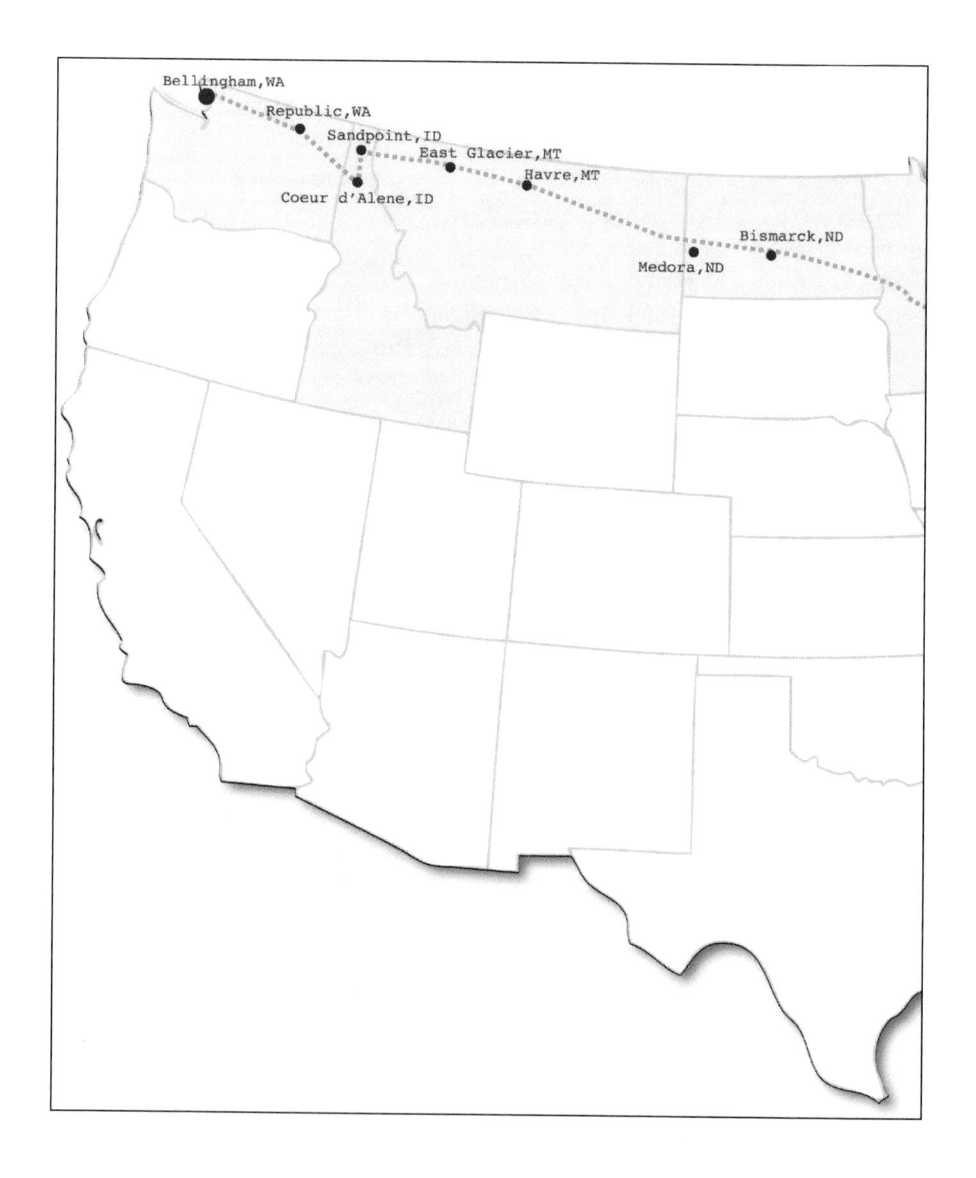

... Bar Harbor, Maine

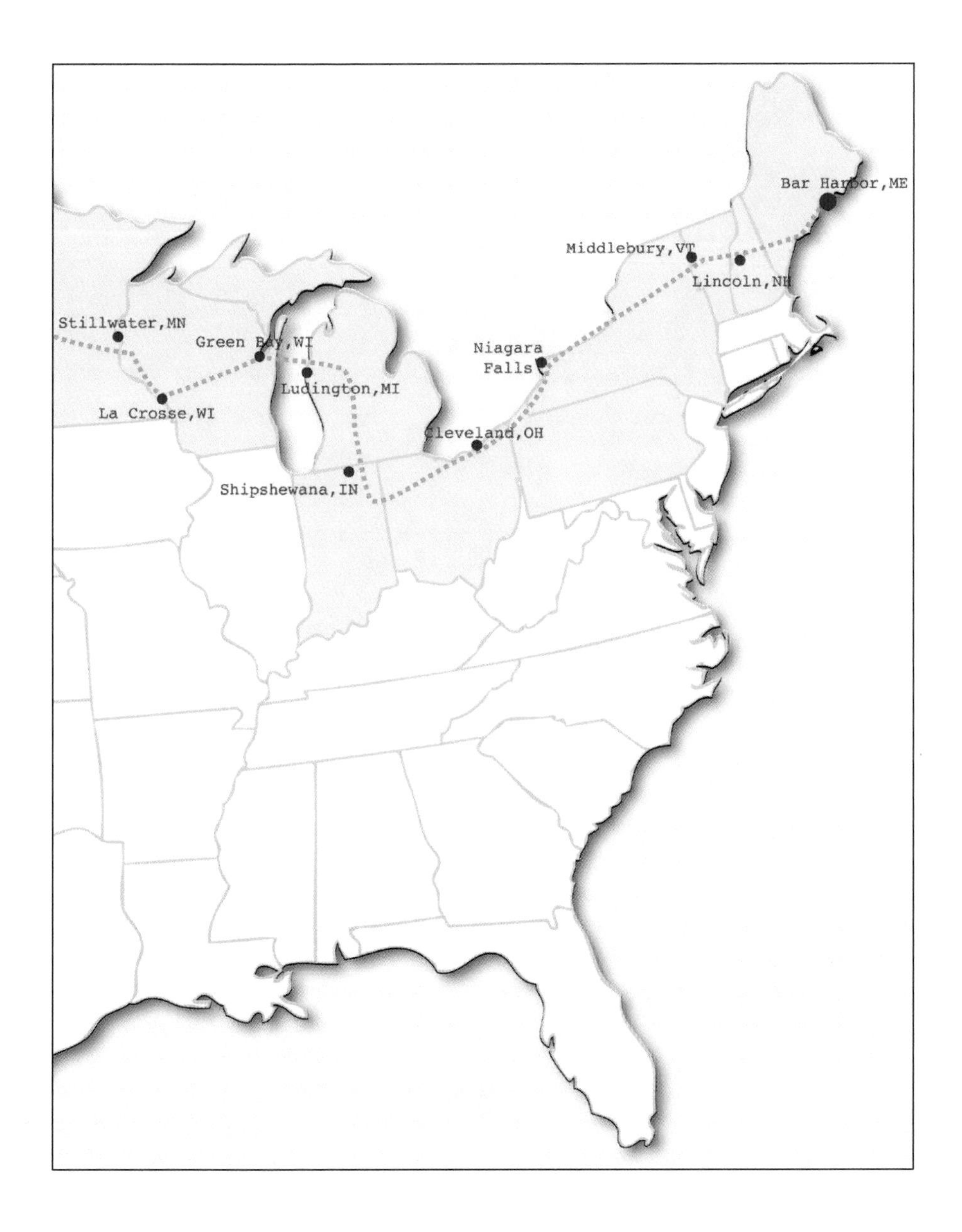

Peter works on preparing the bike for the demanding adventure ahead.

Chapter 1

Getting Ready to Go

Before we could seriously consider an adventure of this magnitude, we felt we needed to ask our daughters for their permission. We were working on the major logistics, finances, jobs, training, etc., but we wouldn't go without the girls' blessing. Individually, and without knowing what the other had said, we asked both girls if it was okay for us to "leave them" for an entire summer – even though neither one would be home – and bicycle across the country. When asked, they both laughed and told us they didn't know anyone who was more qualified and would enjoy the trip more – and that was that! There was no way we could miss this once-in-a-lifetime opportunity.

We had been building our family business, WE BIKE, etc., LLC for twenty years and it was at a point where it could support us – we

Our Virtual Support System

Peter

Before we left on our adventure, we decided we would post to social media daily. This required extra technology in the form of a smartphone and a tablet computer. I would post to Facebook and Tracy would blog. We felt these were good ways to keep family and friends up to date on our progress and document the adventure. What surprised us was how much our following grew and how reliant we became on our followers' support to keep us going. You will see some of those comments in shaded boxes like this one throughout the book.

hoped. The business was founded in 1993. We specialize in the areas of engineering, education, enforcement and encouragement for walking, bicycling and healthy communities. Our cross-country trip would become a key part of our bicycling encouragement initiative. It is not that we want everyone to bicycle across the country, we simply want people to see bicycling as a legitimate form of both recreation and transportation. We also want, and need, motorists to be aware of bicyclists on the road and give them the space they need. Peter's mom has the right idea. She says, "When I am driving and see a bicyclist, I always think of Peter or someone else I love and give them lots of space."

Before we placed things irrevocably into motion for the trip, we needed to make sure we could really afford to do this. We met with our financial advisor of more than twenty years, Dan Balch of Woodman Financial Resources in Green Bay. Our question we had for Dan was pretty straightforward: Could we afford to have Tracy quit her job and take three months off to bicycle across the country? Were we nuts? Peter had crunched the numbers and was fairly certain we could do it, at least for a while. Tracy was less certain. Dan's response surprised us both. He said we had saved well, and as long as we only wanted to maintain our current, moderate lifestyle, we could afford to go.

"What is nuts," he said, "is when one of my clients drops dead at age sixty-five and never gets to spend any of the money he saved. Go."

Now that we had the go-ahead from our girls and Dan, it was time to figure out what to do about Tracy's job as the administrator for the Village of Allouez, a Green Bay suburb. She had been working in Allouez for four years and had spent almost thirty years working in municipal government. Tracy considered asking for a three-month leave of absence, but it seemed unlikely she could get that much time off. Besides, it was time for a change. While we pondered our options, we started to train. It was a good stress reliever.

Bicycling across the country obviously is no easy task. Therefore, we really wanted to be in the best shape possible for the challenge. We began training six months prior to the trip and slowly, but surely, built up our strength and endurance. Unfortunately, the atypically cold and snowy spring weather did not allow us to get out on the tandem much – only three times. Oh no! We were also training in Wisconsin, which meant we had no access to mountains or altitude. The first week of our ride was to be over the Cascade Mountains, and Tracy, especially, was nervous about climbing over the mountains.

Peter

We were already training to run the Green Bay Cellcom Half Marathon in May. If we were going to even consider bicycling all the way across the country, we needed to ramp up our training immediately or we would run out of time to train. So how do you train for a cross-country bicycle trip?

I had trained for and completed four marathons (including the Boston Marathon) in the past several years, so I was already familiar with following a rigorous training plan. However, those training cycles were only three months long. Our bicycle ride alone would take that much time. Training for a three-month bicycle tour is much more like training for an Iron Man Triathlon (2.4-mile swim, 112-mile bike, 26.2-mile run) than a long, single-day, run or bicycle ride. We would be bicycling an average of seventy-five miles per day. Our bodies need to be finely tuned machines.

We decided to work with a personal trainer to help us develop a plan and coach us through the process. Christian Jensen is a personal trainer who works for Bellin Health Fitness Center in Green Bay. Because he was going to ask us to train like we had never trained before, it was important that we trusted him. Christian came highly recommended, was a collegiate athlete like both of our daughters, had a background as a fitness professional, and was an endurance athlete himself. He understood what we were trying to do and was the perfect match.

Because we would always be on the tandem together, Tracy and I always trained together. Not only did we need to strengthen our bodies, but we needed to strengthen our team as well. It was critical that we could sense each other's movements and energy levels. Training side by side would help us do that.

Our training formally began in November 2013. The overall plan included and progressed through flexibility, strength, and endurance training. We typically trained six days per week. In November and December, our training focused on improving our flexibility and building strength, with an emphasis on flexibility.

For January and February, we emphasized the strength training, but added endurance training as well. We continued our flexibility training throughout, but it often had to take a back seat to our other training. I love yoga and continued my practice. Tracy, not so much. She just can't seem to sit still, relax, and doesn't like to hum.

The training emphasis in March and April shifted to building our endurance, while trying to maintain as much strength as possible. When we started training in November, we trained for up to eight hours per week. By April, that figure was as high as twenty hours per week. Toward the end of our training, we were doing workouts that lasted as long as six hours.

If the weather wasn't too bad, which it was most of the time, we would run for an hour, bike for four hours, and then finish up with another one-hour run. If we were stuck inside at the fitness center we would do half-hour rotations on the exercise bike, treadmill and elliptical trainer for a total of one and a half hours, and then repeat that circuit four times. Voila! A six-hour workout. On our long training days, I would walk into the gym with a stack of six energy bars. - I eat one per hour just to keep going and wouldn't leave until they were all gone. Work, train, eat, sleep, repeat – there wasn't much time left for anything else.

A lot of our training was geared toward building our endurance. The long hours we spent training not only strengthened our bodies, but they strengthened our minds as well. There is a fair amount of chronic pain that goes along with endurance sports. Training for long hours increases your body's ability to handle the work load as well as your mind's ability to tolerate the pain. Your body and mind are designed to conserve energy. When the going gets tough, your mind tries to get you to stop. Hours of training makes it easier to keep going.

Tracy

All the training gave me time to think and make a decision regarding my job. I decided to submit my letter of resignation to the Allouez village president on March 24, 2014, and we officially announced our plans to bicycle across the country shortly thereafter. My last day of work would be May 2. We planned to fly to Bellingham, Washington, on May 23 and start our great adventure from Bellingham Bay June 1.

We were now past the point of no return and needed to complete the preparations for our adventure. It is a lot like planning for any vacation or outing, but this one was definitely different because we would be gone for almost three months and traveling unsupported on a tandem bicycle.

May is always a busy month for Peter and our business. But this year, due in part to our delayed spring, it seemed to be in overdrive: three project proposals; Enforcement for Pedestrian & Bicycle Safety trainings in Boise and Idaho Falls, Idaho, for a week; Bike to School Day; Bike to Work Day; two project interviews and four invoices; his regular work;

and we needed to close up the business for three months.

Alex, our youngest daughter, finished her first year at the University of Minnesota-Twin Cities. She did well in her studies and transitioned to collegiate pole vaulting for the Golden Gophers after a very successful high school career. She would be in Fiji over the summer working on a shark conservation program through Projects Abroad.

Melissa, our first born, finished her first year of graduate school at the University of Wisconsin-La Crosse to become a school psychologist. She would spend the summer in La Crosse working, taking classes and caring for our two cats.

Peter

We decided to buy a Microsoft Surface Pro tablet computer and a GoPro® video camera to take with us on the trip. We felt the extra weight would be worth it. The tablet would make it easier for us to use the internet for email, paying bills, blogging, searching the web, and watching videos. We hoped to capture some of the sights and sounds of the trip with the GoPro to keep as memories and share with others via Tracy's blog, my Facebook posts, and presentations after the trip. All we had to do now was learn how to use the new technology.

Since we were going to be away from home for three months, we needed to figure out how to keep the electricity hooked up and not default on our mortgage. We pay most of our bills electronically, so we could do this with our smart phone as long as we had connectivity. We aren't sure we always will, although Verizon assures us they have the best network in the nation.

We discovered while working through this process that our world is not designed for people to just check out for three months. For example, it seemed simple enough to us that we could pay our mortgage three months in advance. Apparently not. If you send the mortgage company a check for three months of payments, they automatically apply the entire payment to the first month's interest, then principal, and you are subsequently late on your second and third month's payments. Fortunately, Tracy caught this before we left and set up electronic monthly payments instead.

I wasn't excited about letting our house sit empty for three months. What if the water heater sprung a leak or we had a storm and there was roof damage? Who would cut the grass? Fortunately, one of Melissa's friends since elementary school, Tracy Devroy, was living with her parents and more than happy to have a house to herself for the summer. Picking up the mail and cutting the grass was a small price to pay for having her own place. She even agreed to make bank deposits for WE BIKE, etc., LLC as needed. For us, it was like having one of our children watching the house – but maybe safer.

Shipping the tandem turned out to be way more of a pain than we thought it would be. First, we had to estimate the weight of the bike and packaging, and the size of the shipping container. This turned out to be two old bicycle boxes telescoped together and secured with rolls of packaging tape. Although the bike is fitted with S&S Bicycle Torque Couplings™, that allow it to be broken down and placed in a special, oversized suitcase, we don't ship it that way anymore.

Prior to the attack on the World Trade Center on September 11, 2001, the tandem, in its suitcase, could fly with us for free as standard baggage and was never searched. Post-9/11, the Transportation Security Administration (TSA) requires us to open the suitcase and remove all bike parts for inspection. It is a really tight fit to get the bike in the suitcase. I even have to let the air out of the tires. Packing the disassembled bike takes about an hour. The last time TSA made me unpack the bike, we almost missed our flight. Never again.

After we had the weight and dimensions needed, we called FedEx, which is just down the road from our house, to see what it would cost to ship the bike to my mom's house. We had plenty of time, so we decided to ship it FedEx Ground to save some money, or so we thought. "$1,000 what?"

Apparently, the bike boxed is oversized and overweight, too – even for FedEx Ground. After many phone calls to other shipping companies and finally to our bicycle shop, we discovered the only practical way to ship a tandem was from bicycle shop to bicycle shop. They get special business-to-business pricing and exemptions on the size restrictions. Okay, we can do that. I had already decided to let my friends at JB Cycle & Sport in nearby Howard package the bike for shipping. Although I could have probably figured out how to package it, we were really busy with other things, and the "boyz" pack and unpack bikes all the time.

Fairhaven Bicycle, less than a mile from my mom's house, agreed to receive and hold the bike box for us at no charge. The cost to ship the bike from shop to shop was $500. It still seemed like a lot to us, but it was half of the original estimate from FedEx. Two weeks before our trip departure date, the bike was on its way. I bet I checked the tracking number for the bike twice a day until it arrived.

It is not every day someone decides to bicycle across the country, and it is even more unusual for a couple to do it on a bicycle built for two. Estimates are that approximately 2,000 people bicycle the Adventure Cycling Association's Northern Tier bicycle route every year. Maybe 1 percent of those bicyclists attempt the route on a tandem – even fewer with their spouse. Ha!

The local media was very interested in our trip, and the week before we left we were busy doing lots of TV, radio, and newspaper interviews in response to a news release we sent out. One of the television stations wanted to get some footage of us riding the tandem. Unfortunately, we had already shipped the (purple) Santana road tandem to Washington. Fortunately, we still had our old (green) Trek hybrid tandem. We rode the Trek and no one ever noticed the difference. The coverage was great and allowed us to get the word out about our trip, as well as encourage people to follow us on our blog and Facebook page.

Friday, May 23 – Saturday, May 31

It was finally time for us to fly to Bellingham. Our flights from Green Bay to Minneapolis, Seattle and Bellingham were uneventful. We couldn't help but marvel that soon we would be retracing much of this very same route, but at fifteen miles per hour rather than 500. Things started to get real when we crossed the Cascade Mountain range on our approach to Seattle. There was still snow on the mountains, and a lot of it.

In my last year of college, my parents "abandoned" me and moved to Seattle, Washington, where my father had been hired as the head pastor for University Congregational United Church of Christ. My parents divorced in 1993, and eventually my mother (Ruth) connected with an old friend, Rod MacKenzie, and she moved to Bellingham to live with him.

Rod is a retired pastor and pastoral counselor, and has lived in Bellingham since 1970. He loves to hunt, fish, backpack hike, or simply be in the woods or mountains. He knows Whatcom County, seemingly everyone in it, and the North Cascade Mountain Range like the back of his hand. Mom calls Rod a "mountain man." It was Rod who put us in contact with the owner of Fairhaven Bicycle, John Hauter, who agreed to receive and store our shipped bicycle. Rod is my ace in the hole. In addition to his love for and knowledge of the outdoors, he loves and restores old cars. He has most tools known to man in his garage in the alley behind their house.

The Green Bay and Bellingham airports are small and easy to negotiate. Ruth and Rod met us at the Bellingham Airport. They took us out to dinner at their favorite restaurant, Boundary Bay Brewery. A great meal and beer (oatmeal stout) were just what we needed. We spent Saturday relaxing, catching up with Ruth and Rod, picking the bike up from the bike shop, putting it back together, and checking the gear boxes to make sure we had everything.

The reality of bicycle touring is that things break, and they often break when you are nowhere near a bicycle shop. If you have a breakdown, you need to be able to fix it out in the middle of nowhere by yourself and with limited tools. The tandem is designed and built specifically for touring. Almost everything on the bike can be assembled, disassembled, and repaired with a multi-tool that fits in the palm of your hand. I have very little innate mechanical ability. I am definitely not a bike mechanic or a "wrench," as they are referred to in bicycle shops. Fortunately, I have a pretty good sense of logic. There are only so many ways something can go together. If I have long enough, I can usually fix it. The reassembly of the bike went well.

Bicycling is a minimalist sport. The weight of the bicycle and the gear you carry is directly related to how hard you have to work to make it move and how fast you can go, particularly uphill. You don't want to carry any more weight than is absolutely necessary. This means you try to bring with you only what you absolutely need. It also means that if you forget something, you are screwed. Forget a full water bottle and you don't ride very far. Forget a shoe and you don't ride at all.

Everything we will need for the trip has to fit on the bike. Violet is equipped with both front and rear racks. The front rack attaches to the bike via the bolts that secure the front brakes and the front axle. Two small panniers (baskets) attach to the sides of the rack by hooks and straps. They sit low to the ground to lower our center of gravity and increase stability. The front panniers carry our camping stove, cook kit, emergency survival kit, head lamps and candle lantern, and extra food.

The rear rack and panniers attach similarly, but they are much larger. The rear panniers hold our clothes, extra shoes, first aid kit, toilet kit, sleeping pads, and our down sleeping bags. On top of the main compartment on each pannier is a large pocket that holds the emergency repair kit, jackets, hats, glasses, sun screen, and extra food. Two extra tires are secured behind the bags by compression straps that hold the whole thing together. There is a small bag behind my seat which holds snacks, my wallet, glasses cleaner, and gum. The bags are all black. We have a high-visibility, slow moving vehicle sign on the left rear pannier to make us more visible.

Tracy

We need to rest our legs before the start of the trip, but because our bodies had become so accustomed to the long hours of exercise through our training, we also need to get some exercise so our muscles won't tighten up. So, we ran into downtown Bellingham on Sunday morning on the old railroad grade trail adjacent to Bellingham Bay. It is beautiful! We return inland to Ruth and Rod's house, which sits on top of a hill overlooking the bay.

Later in the day, we had the pleasure of watching the final (sea kayaking) leg of the 100+ year-old Ski to Sea race on Bellingham Bay from the balcony of Ruth and Rod's house. We used a spotting scope that once belonged to Peter's grandparents. The relay race is approximately 123 miles. It starts at the Mt. Baker Ski Resort with a cross-country ski

Peter (and the bike) pose with Rod and his Model A.

leg, followed by downhill skiing, a downhill run, road biking, canoeing, Cyclocross, and the final leg, sea kayaking. The race ends at Marine Park on Bellingham Bay, the starting point for our upcoming adventure. The race has approximately 3,000 participants of all shapes and sizes.

On Monday, we have the privilege of previewing the first ten miles of our bicycle trip along historic Chuckanut Drive in Rod's 1934 Model T Ford. The weather and views are spectacular. Ruth took me to a spa later in the day to get our nails done. I'm pretty sure this isn't going to happen again for a while.

The next day, Peter and I took the bicycle on a twenty-mile shakedown ride south on Chuckanut Drive to the Skagit Valley. It gave me the opportunity to test the GoPro camera. The camera is small and fits easily in the palm of my hand. It has a weatherproof housing and several mounting options: handle bars, chest, or helmet. We decided I would wear the camera on my helmet for this trip. I cannot see to the front of the bike very well because I am so close to Peter and his head is in my way.

The GoPro, however, works perfectly mounted on the top of my helmet. From this position, the high-definition camera with its wide-angle lens has a commanding view to the front and a surprisingly good field of view to the sides as well. Peter's head and back can be seen is the shot, but they don't block the view. This gives the viewer a real sense of what it is like for me to ride on the back of the bike. This is important, because I am writing our blog and the videos I shoot will accompany it. We couldn't wait to get back to the house and watch the videos on our tablet.

Peter

I grew up hearing stories from my mother and grandfather about my great-grandfather, the "Singer Sewing Machine Company," and Chuckanut Drive. Great-grandpa (Otto Charles Reinhardt Wiechmann) sold industrial Singer sewing machines along the west coast of the United States in the 1920s and 1930s. Since great-grandpa never learned to drive, my grandfather (Robert Otto Wiechmann), did the driving from the time he was twelve years old. They would travel from their home in the San Francisco Bay area as far north as Vancouver, British Columbia, Canada, making sales calls.

Chuckanut Drive was completed in 1896 and runs from Burlington, Washington, and the Skagit Valley Tulip fields twenty-one miles north along the bluffs overlooking Bellingham Bay to Bellingham. For years, "The Chuckanut" was the only way to get to Bellingham. This is the road my forbearers traveled, and the very road on which we will begin our trip. Pretty cool.

We stopped at Taylor's Fish Market (site of a *Dirty Jobs* episode with Mike Rowe) on the way back and bought five live Dungeness crabs for dinner. A trip to Taylor's followed by a hand cleaning of the crab and a crab boil, following the directions in an ancient Whatcom County cook book, has become a family tradition. When Ruth asks what we want for dinner, we always say, "Crab." It is hard to get good seafood where we live in the Midwest. Here, we can easily drive or bike to the ocean to pick it up fresh at a market. There is not much better than fresh crab. A man wearing rubber boots and a large white apron filled two medium-sized plastic bags with ice and the five crabs. We had fitted the bike with our two small panniers. One bag of crab fit perfectly in each pannier. This was the first time we hauled crab, dead or alive, on the bike. We mused that we probably would be hauling lots of unique items on our bicycle during the upcoming months.

Tracy

Wednesday was a fun day in Seattle. We spent several hours exploring the Pike Place Market and watching the crowds of people. We stopped at the first Starbucks for coffee and later lunched on humbows (a bun filled with good stuff - BBQ pork, vegetables, chicken, etc.), another family tradition. We soaked in the sights, sounds, and smells, knowing that in a few days we would be mostly on our own.

We took an easy run into downtown Fairhaven on Thursday via the back roads and returned on an old railroad grade trail along the bay - still beautiful! Later in the day, we drove the sixty miles to Vancouver, British Columbia, to visit Peter's father, Paul, and his wife, Noralyn. Paul is a retired United Church of Christ minister. After he and Peter's mother, Ruth, divorced in 1993, Paul eventually married his high school sweetheart. Noralyn had moved to Vancouver with her first husband and still lived there. Paul moved to Vancouver to be with Noralyn and they were eventually married.

This is an easy trip unless the border crossing is slow. One never knows how long it will take (ten minutes or three hours). We were lucky this time and made it across the border in about an hour. We toured the University of British Columbia and the botanical garden, where we experienced the spectacular Greenheart TreeWalk canopy walkway. We went out to dinner on Granville Island and enjoyed watching the busy harbor. Vancouver is a spectacular city for bicycling. With miles of trails and bicycle lanes, it is easy to get almost anywhere you want by bicycle. As we toured the city by car, we wished we were on our bike. Soon enough.

We returned to Bellingham on Friday and went to the rental shop on Saturday afternoon to pick up the RV. Ruth and Rod rented the RV to travel the first week with us over the Cascade Mountains and into Idaho. They will serve as our support crew (sag wagon) and not only haul our gear, but also provide us with a comfortable place for sleep, great snacks and meals, clean laundry, and good company.

> "I get tired just thinking about your trip. Good luck!"
> ***- Ramona Hennen***

The RV is twenty-four feet long and has everything we need. In the back is a double bed for Ruth and Rod, and plenty of storage. Moving forward there is a very small bathroom with a shower (if you are a contortionist), and hot and cold running water. Next comes the kitchen with a two-burner gas stove, microwave, refrigerator, and hot and cold running water. Two bench seats flank the RV forward of the kitchen. One of them has a kitchen table that can be converted to a small bed – too small for either of us.

Above the cab there is a small double bed where Peter and I will sleep. We climb a small ladder behind the passenger's seat to access the bed. There is only about two and a half feet of clearance between the bed and the roof of the RV; not enough room to completely sit up in the bed. I think I will feel too cramped and confined to sleep on the side of the bed near the small front window over the hood of the RV, so I'm going to make Peter sleep there. He can sleep anywhere. The RV is equipped with lights and electricity throughout. This is luxury compared to what we will have once we are on our own.

Peter

It will be great to leave most of our gear in the RV and not have to lug it over the mountains. We will still need to carry basic supplies with us such as the repair kit, food, water, and extra clothes, just in case. We

Tracy with Peter's father, Paul, and his wife, Noralyn

Tracy with one of the iconic Pacific Coast fish market displays during our final days of preparation.

will use our small panniers just like we did with the crab. While we bicycle during the day, Mom and Rod will explore, run errands, and relax.

We have only done the RV thing twice before, probably because we love tent camping. The first time was when the girls were about five and nine years old. Tracy and I shipped our single road bikes to Bellingham, Washington. In Bellingham, Mom and Rod rented an RV and drove with our bicycles to Portland, Oregon. Tracy, Melissa, Alex and I flew to Portland to meet Mom and Rod, and from Portland, Tracy and I biked, and the elders drove with the girls down the Pacific Coast Highway to Northern California. Our goals were the Redwood Highway in Humboldt County, California, where my maternal grandmother grew up and my mother played as a child, and Santa Rosa, California, where Rod grew up.

While Tracy and I biked each day, the girls, grandma, and grandpa would explore the sea shore and countryside. We would meet at a campground each night for dinner. It was tight with all of us sleeping in the RV, but we loved it. A couple of years later in the fall, Tracy and I rented an RV and took the girls camping at Rib Mountain State Park near Wausau, Wisconsin. It was cold and even snowed one night, but the heater in the RV kept us all snug. The girls still talk about these trips.

Tracy

Tomorrow we begin our bicycle adventure. We are both a bit nervous, but also excited to get going. We spent today getting the bicycle and RV ready to go. The bicycle was already road worthy, but Peter rechecked every nut and bolt, literally. Even he is now satisfied that it is ready to go.

Loading the RV was a bit of an experience. Ruth and Rod live on a hill fifteen blocks above Bellingham Bay. The view is spectacular, but the roads leading to their house are almost too steep for us to bicycle up. The house fronts on Fifteenth Street, but we almost always use the alley behind the house as the entrance because that is where the garage is and it is mostly level with the house. It is a steep climb along a retaining wall from the street in front to the house.

Unfortunately, the RV is too big to park in the alley, which means we have to park it on Fifteenth Street and hike up and down the hill to load it. The other problem is that the sidewalk is a good five feet above the road surface. We had to place a ship-like gangplank from the sidewalk to the side door of the RV just to get in the body of the RV. The severity of the climb to and from the house and the questionable stability of the gangplank made it only logical that Peter and I do most of the loading. It wasn't an easy job, but we got it done.

We will leave early tomorrow morning for the first day of our cross country trip!

Chapter 2

Our Trip Begins

"I see you dipped your rear wheel in the Pacific and hope to see the front one in the Atlantic in a few months. Best of luck to both of you."
- *Roger Schmitt*

It is bicycling tradition to start your cross-country journey by dipping your rear wheel into the ocean. Here we are doing just that at Bellingham Bay in Washington State.

Rod and Ruth pose with us and the bike before we set out.

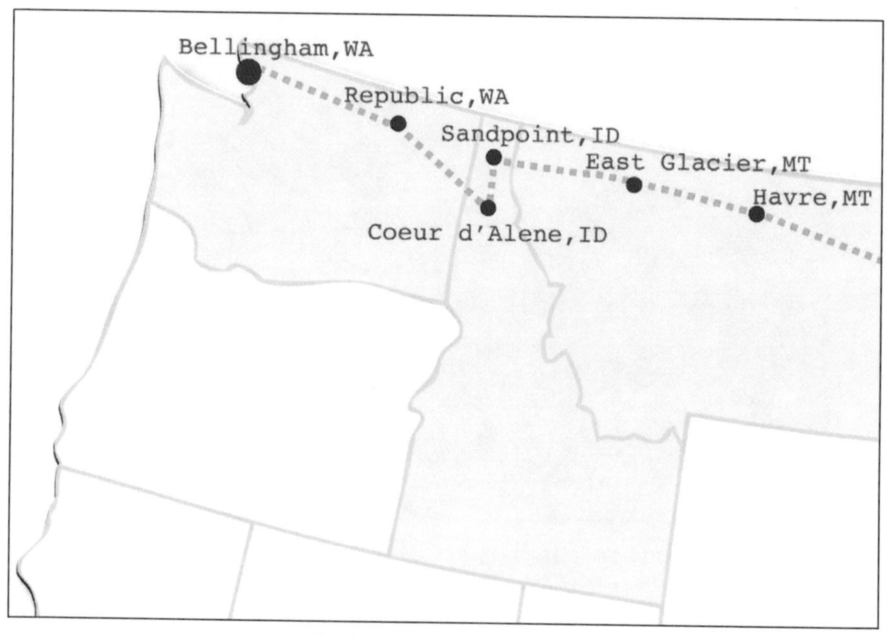

The beginning of our route

State of Washington
June 1-6, 2014 – Total Miles 457/457 total

Day 1

June 1 - Bellingham to Nehalem, Washington
94 miles (total mileage - 94)
Beautiful day, 67 degrees with a tailwind

Tracy

After all our preparations, we are ready to start our cross-country bicycle adventure on the Adventure Cycling Association Northern Tier Bicycle Route. We are up by 7:30 a.m. and put on our cycling clothes: high-tech bicycling socks, bicycling shoes, padded black shorts, and brightly colored bicycle jerseys. We will carry one extra set of cycling clothes throughout the trip, so every third day we really need a washing machine or at least a sink to hand wash our clothes.

We have a good breakfast and load the bike for the first time. Loading the bicycle is easy today because Rod and Ruth will carry most of our gear in the RV. Besides the two panniers (bags) on the back rack, we will also carry the tent. Normally we will not carry the tent when traveling with Rod and Ruth. However, Rod plans to take his Model A pickup truck to a car show in Canada this morning. They will leave from Bellingham late in the afternoon and arrive at the campground after us. We want to make sure we have somewhere to go if it rains or they do not show up for some reason.

We mount up and coast the one mile downhill to Marine Park on Bellingham Bay (the Pacific Ocean). We put our rear wheel into the bay and officially start our adventure. It is a tradition for cross-country bicyclists to put their rear wheel in the ocean at the start of their trip and their front wheel in the ocean at the end of the trip.

At this point, it is hard to imagine what we will experience before our front wheel meets the Atlantic Ocean in Bar Harbor, Maine. We are

> **Adventure Cycling Association (ACA)**
>
> "A nonprofit organization, Adventure Cycling Association's mission is to inspire and empower people to travel by bicycle. Established in 1993 as Bikecentennial, we are the premier bicycle-travel organization in North America with more than 35 years of experience and 50,000 members." https://www.adventurecycling.org/

definitely ready, but nervous for the adventure. The weather could not be better for the start of our trip – sunny, upper sixties, with a nice tailwind. The forecast for our first week is more of the same, lucky us. After lots of pictures and hugs from friends and family, it's "Pedal up" and we are on our way.

Starting the tandem is not an easy task, and to be successful we need to follow certain steps. It would be very embarrassing to begin the ride by falling over. I ride on the back of the tandem and need to make sure Peter is ready for me to get on the bicycle before I mount up. This is done through the use of various voice commands: "Ready for me," "Go ahead," "I'm in," "Here we go."

> "Safe travels! You guys are amazing!! :)"
>
> ***- Kathryn Kroll***

We also have to make sure we are balanced when starting. I get on before Peter, so it is important for me to remain as still as possible and stay centered so he can get up and get us moving. We do it this way so only one of us is trying to get settled at a time and I can put power to the pedals as soon as Peter gets on. Normally we have no problem with this, but on one training ride it didn't go so well. We were getting ready to leave a friend's house to head home and Peter was talking to them and not paying attention to me getting on the bicycle. He responded to me, but really wasn't ready for me to get on. I got on and the bicycle tipped and down I went - onto the top tube – ouch. I think I was more embarrassed than hurt.

The beginning of our ride is on the beautiful and historic Chuckanut Drive, which we have traveled many times. It is more relaxing to ride on a road we have been on before because we know what is coming around the next corner. The road is popular with local bicyclists and the motorists know this and naturally share the road.

Chuckanut Drive is chiseled into the western side of Chuckanut Mountain some 100 feet above Bellingham Bay. The road itself is a narrow two-lane that twists and turns along the edge of the mountain with barely enough room to pass and many blind corners. To the east is the jagged side of the mountain with steep cliffs, beautiful cedar trees, and an occasional waterfall. Looking west presents a commanding view of the Bay and the San Juan Islands.

At the end of Chuckanut Drive, we cross the Samish River and drop into the flats of Skagit Valley. The valley is literally ablaze with color when the tulip fields bloom in the spring. We are too late for the color this year. We travel through the valley with snow-covered mountains to the east, knowing that tomorrow we will begin climbing those mountains.

About twenty miles into our trip, we see our first touring cyclist in the distance. He is easy to identify as a bicycle tourist because of his panniers.

We are excited to catch up to him and hear his story. He is a grizzled, middle-aged guy from Scotland, heading to Boston, Massachusetts. We can tell he and his bicycle had put on many miles. They both looked weather-beaten and well-used. His body, particularly his legs, are honed from bicycle touring and I wondered if we will end up looking like that. It was nice to meet him, but also a bit deflating when he told us he had just finished cycling through Africa. We think we are doing something amazing and the first cyclist we meet has toured all over the world.

He asks if we had run into the "big group" of cyclists who are traveling on an Adventure Cycling Supported Tour. We had not. He explains the group left Anacortes, Washington (the official starting point for the Northern Tier Route), that morning with him. We chose to leave from Mom's house in Bellingham and got on the official route about thirteen miles into our ride. I am sure we will run into the group sometime during our trip.

The maps we are using throughout the adventure are produced by the Adventure Cycling Association. ACA also offers supported tours for cyclists who want to do the ride, but not on their own. This particular group is on a van-supported tour traveling the entire Northern Tier Route. The tour provides camping and shared group cooking. All gear is carried in the van and two experienced guides provide all the support needed.

> "I just found this blog this morning and will be following it from now on. My husband and I ride tandems and single bikes, and your trip is a dream of ours. Can't wait to hear about all of your adventures. Good luck!"
>
> ***- Colleen***

We ride with our new friend for several miles and then take off at our own pace. We have discovered on previous trips that our typical touring pace is between thirteen and fifteen miles per hour and is usually much faster than other cyclists. This can make traveling with them difficult. We cross paths with him again about twenty miles down the road in the City of Sedro-Woolley. Would we see him again?

We come upon our first detour in Sedro-Woolley. The city is building a new roundabout and we end up hopelessly lost as we try to get through the city. I finally convince Peter to stop at a convenience store to get directions. The journey continues with us enjoying the beautiful views, flat terrain and a tailwind.

I serve as our navigator, mainly because I ride on the back of the bicycle (the stoker) and it is much easier for me to be responsible for this task. I am definitely not the best choice for this, since reading a map does not come naturally to me. Even knowing what direction we are traveling is a challenge. Peter would be a much better choice to navigate, but with him on the front of the bicycle (the captain), it would be difficult for him to navigate because he already has lots of jobs to do. He is responsible for making sure we do not hit anything on the road, i.e. potholes, glass. etc., interacting with motor vehicles, positioning us properly on the road, and responding to traffic control devices, etc.

Knowing directions are an issue for me, Peter has attached a small compass to my handle bars. Now at least I know what direction we are going when we get lost. The fact that I struggle with navigation adds stress to our trip. Peter gets aggravated when I get us lost and I get upset when he gets mad at me. We have to be aware of this, because it puts a lot of pressure on our relationship. The bicycle does not move unless we are working together.

Our maps are specifically designed for bicyclists and provide us with a lot of helpful information. They are printed in sections, eleven of them for the entire route covering approximately 500 miles each. Section maps include an overview map and around fifteen individual detail maps, which typically cover about thirty miles each. The detail maps have written directions for both eastbound and westbound travelers. Each section map contains field notes, route elevations, average weather, service directory, and emergency contacts for each community we will be traveling through.

The field notes are great because they give us an idea of what to expect as we travel through various areas, as well as a history of the area. For example, the Cascade Mountains area is described as follows: "Jungles, Volcanoes and Icy Rivers – Past the coastal plain and rolling hills are the mountains of the North Cascade Range. Drenched in rains from the wet Pacific winds, the Cascade's western slope is a veritable jungle." The maps are even waterproof.

Adventure Cycling Association had put out a call on their website looking for cyclists traveling the Northern Tier Route to beta-test their first version of electronic maps. We applied and were selected. It will be interesting to see how helpful they are.

Later in the day we encounter our second group of touring cyclists, two women and a man. We come upon them standing in the middle of a bridge taking pictures. We continue across the bridge, believing that stopping in the middle of a narrow, two-lane bridge is not a great idea, and wait for them on the shoulder of the road. We find out they are from Indiana and traveling as far as Fargo, North Dakota, on their first cross-country ride. It is apparent already that we will meet touring cyclists with a wide range of abilities and experience.

We enter North Cascades National Park toward the end of the day and stop at the visitor center to gather information about the area we are about to bicycle through. North Cascades National Park is massive at 504,781 acres (about three-quarters the size of Rhode Island). Managed by the National Park Service, the park consists of northern and southern districts that are separated by Ross Lake National Recreation Area.

We are traveling on Washington State Route 20, also known as the North Cascades Highway and the only road which bisects the park complex. The information at the visitor center warns park users about the lack of services in the area. Our bicycle maps also include a warning that we will have very limited services for seventy-six miles from the visitor center, and to carry extra food and water. We definitely heed the warning, but luckily have a safety net with Ruth and Rod sagging us.

Our average speed on relatively flat terrain of about fifteen miles per hour would take us about five hours to ride seventy-six miles. But with the mountainous terrain we will be riding tomorrow, we will probably average closer to seven miles per hour on the uphill section. It will take us a lot longer to cover the miles, and therefore our margin of error is much slimmer.

> "Good luck and be safe!!"
> ***- Matt Trahan***

As we pull into our home for the night, Colonial Campground in Nehalem (unincorporated), we agree it was a good first day and look forward to telling Ruth and Rod about our journey so far. They pull into the campground with the RV about an hour later. It is a beautiful campground located right on Diablo Lake and surrounded by the Cascade Mountains, which will be tomorrow's challenge.

This National Park Service campground is nice, but lacks the one amenity we really want/need at the end of a long day: a shower. If you haven't been in this situation, you probably can't imagine how dirty we get during the day being out in the elements for seven to eight hours, sunscreen covering every inch of exposed skin, sweat, dirt, dust, and bugs. We really need a shower at the end of the day, not only for us, but for anyone within five feet of us. Since there are no showers at the campground, it's into the restroom I go to take a sponge bath and change clothes. I clean up the best I can and hope for a shower the next night. The RV does have a shower, but unfortunately it is full of supplies for the trip and not usable right now. There is a hose bib on the outside of the RV, and we can set up a shower curtain if we really need to have a shower.

We are hungry and badly need to refuel for the next day. It is a challenge to make sure we have enough food on the bicycle to make dinner. We typically carry at least two days' worth of dehydrated food with us and supplement that by picking up fresh supplies at a grocery or convenience store close to our ending point. The first week of our trip we will not have to worry about this, since Ruth will be providing meals at the end of the day and she is a great cook.

Peter

We started our adventure at sea level on the edge of Bellingham Bay, and already by the second day we'll need to cross Washington Pass at 5,477 feet above sea level. Our home in Green Bay, Wisconsin, is at an elevation of 581 feet. We are more than a bit apprehensive about making this climb and those that will follow. Can we climb that high? Tandems are notorious for going up hills like a brick. Will we get altitude sickness?

The greater Green Bay area is basically flat, with the exception of the Niagara Escarpment. "The Ledge," as we call it, is a limestone bluff that rises approximately 200 feet above the Fox River and the bay. The river runs right through Green Bay. Normally we would have spent countless hours climbing the ledge. Unfortunately, our delayed spring would not make that possible. We were only able to ride the tandem three times before we left for the trip. All we could do was turn up the resistance on the exercise bike and hope our conditioning would see us through.

There was not much we could do, realistically, to prepare for the altitude. We just couldn't simulate the decreased atmospheric pressure and resulting thinner air. There are a couple of factors working in our favor though: we are in excellent shape and most people do not get altitude sickness until they are above 8,000 feet. Factors working against us are how quickly we will be ascending to elevation and our age (both fifty-two). The faster you climb and the older you are, the higher your risk. We are concerned about how the elevation will affect our bicycling. Only time will tell.

Day 2

June 2 – Newhalem to Winthrop, Washington
80 miles (total mileage - 174)
Beautiful day, 40-70 degrees

Tracy

This is the toughest thing I have ever done! I wake up not feeling well (headache, upset stomach) and continue to feel worse all day. I am having trouble eating or drinking anything, so I am not able to get the energy I need to climb over the passes. We spend a total of eight hours on the bike with six and a half hours of climbing. It is definitely a character-building ride.

Rod got up early and made us his famous Scottish Oats to start the day. Unfortunately, it takes longer than planned in the RV and we get a later start then we want. As we eat breakfast and get organized to leave for the day, we see two female touring cyclists heading out of the campground.

We load the bike, exit the campground, and immediately start to climb. There is no resting or coasting, just a steady seven to eight mile-per-hour pace on a 3 to 8 percent slope – manageable, but no joke.

About two hours later, we catch up with the two cyclists who had headed out about an hour before us. They are standing under a small waterfall trying to cool off. They appear to be struggling with the climb more than us. Hopefully they will make it to their ending point today.

Most of our day is spent climbing forty-one miles over Rainy and Washington passes on Highway 20 through North Cascades National Park. As promised, there are no services between Newhalem and Winthrop; just beautiful, snowcapped mountains, cascading streams, waterfalls, and evergreen trees. The route is difficult, but gorgeous. Thanks to Ruth, we have lunch and snacks on board to get us over the passes. Unfortunately, I feel so badly I am not able to eat any of it.

We have three twenty-four ounce bottles of water each on the bicycle, and under normal conditions, we drink one bottle per hour. But this is not normal. Due to the constant climbing, our slow pace, the heat, and altitude, we are using water much faster than usual. We are almost out of water about halfway up the mountain. So now what? We have to fill our bottles from a stream near the road, but we can't drink the water directly from the stream because we don't know what is in it. So into the bottles go water purification tablets from our emergency kit. They work well, but make the water taste like iodine – terrible. I am not able to drink the water after we refill the bottles.

Now, I am feeling worse. We have only covered about twenty miles in three and a half hours, averaging a very slow six miles per hour. Peter and I have not been talking much. I am using all my energy to make the pedals go round and just focusing on getting to the top. Because I have not been eating or drinking anything, the power in my legs continues to drop off, which requires Peter to work even harder.

Peter

Although Tracy is suffering, I am not. The beautiful views, the fresh mountain air, and even the rhythm of the climb are a joy for me. Feeling good and with Tracy's decreased power output, I try to increase my effort to compensate. Unfortunately, the speed of the tandem is a function of the output of both riders, and I eventually have to back off to avoid blowing up.

Tracy

Ruth and Rod show up in the RV with fresh water about five miles later. We dump out the water from the stream and refilled our bottles with fresh water. Unfortunately, the nasty taste from the purification tablets does not go away and I am still struggling to drink it.

Ruth and Rod continue on with plans to meet us at the top of Rainy

Tracy gathers herself during the climb toward Rainy Pass.

Pass (4,855 feet). As I watch them drive away, I am scared I will not be able to get to the top and wish I would have called it quits. Not a good feeling. I climb back on the bicycle with tears rolling down my face. My inexperience in the mountains has added to my fear of tackling this climb. Peter has spent time in the mountains and assures me we will be fine. Ruth and Rod know if we do not show up by the designated time, they will simply drive back down the mountain to find us. North Cascade Highway is the only road, so it will not be hard to find us.

We stop at a vehicle pullout for a break five hours into the ride and about three quarters of the way up the climb. Peter takes a great picture of me sitting on the edge of the pullout with my head between my hands, trying to figure out how I am going to make it to the top. At this point, I am not sure if I can go any farther. I just have no energy left. Peter promises me that someday this picture will be funny. Sure it will.

Then I think about how much work we have put into doing this and it is only our second day out. I can't just quit and climb into the RV. I eat a bit of a PowerBar, drink some water, and say "Let's go." The rest of the climb is still tough, but mentally I get on top of it and continue to eat and drink in small amounts as much as possible.

After forty-one miles and six and a half hours of climbing, we finally make it to the top of Rainy Pass – 4,855 feet. The RV is waiting for us along with three feet of snow on the side of the road and in the parking lot. Peter wants some pictures of us by the Rainy Pass sign, so I take a deep breath and stumble over to the sign for the shot. I am sure the view is beautiful, but I don't take the time to enjoy it. Instead, I climb into the RV to recover, warm up, and relax. I drink some water out of a clean water bottle and Rod suggests I eat some salt to boost my electrolytes. The salt really helps, and I start to come around and have a bit more energy.

Peter and I are back on the bicycle after the brief rest to climb the last 600 feet of elevation on the five-mile uphill to reach Washington Pass at 5,477 feet. Leaving Rainy Pass, we travel downhill to cross the Porcupine River and then start climbing again. After coasting downhill, I peek around Peter to see an intense uphill and just close my eyes and start singing my mantra: "One elephant went out to play ..." I get back into the rhythm of the ride and enjoy the views. We make it to the crest of the pass about fifty minutes later and Rod takes some pictures to document and celebrate our accomplishment.

> "Looking forward to traveling with you via this blog!"
> ***- Kathy Rohde***

We put on more clothes for our downhill ride, including tights, long-sleeve jersey, jacket, and gloves to hopefully keep us warm. We know we will be flying down the mountain and not generating any heat, so the extra layers are needed. Back on the bike, we drop like a stone into Winthrop. We don't even pedal for twenty miles. It is great to be traveling down the mountain and not climbing, but it still is a challenge. I am anxious about the speeds we are reaching on our first big downhill.

The aerodynamics of a tandem are very different from a single bicycle. While we have the weight of two people pulling us down the slope, we only have the wind resistance of one person, with me tucked behind Peter, to slow us down. This is why we have an auxiliary drum brake on the rear wheel of the tandem to help slow the bicycle down. It would be difficult to control our speed with just two standard rim brakes; we could even burn them out. Peter has almost total control of our speed with the brakes, although the straighter I sit up on the back of the bicycle, the more wind resistance I create and I can actually slow us down a little.

The downhill ride is great with spectacular views that I want to try and capture. I turn on the GoPro camera on my helmet and get what I hope is some amazing video of the cascading streams, waterfalls, and mountains we are buzzing by. It is a wonderful way to end a tough day and a chance to recuperate a bit.

The Pearrygin Lake State Park is our home for the night, and Ruth and Rod are waiting for us when we arrive. As we roll into the campground, everything is unfamiliar until we spy the RV. Ruth and Rod get stinky hugs upon arrival. They were great help throughout the day and definitely a factor in us completing the ride. After a snack, shower, and dinner, we are glad to climb in for the night.

Day 3

June 3 – Winthrop to Omak, Washington
48 miles (total miles - 222)
Warm and sunny, 50-80 degrees with a nice tailwind

Tracy

This morning I feel better, but still a bit under the weather. I am able to eat breakfast. Luckily, we have fewer miles to cover today, but still have to tackle our second mountain over Loup Loup Pass (4,020 feet). Our ride begins with a ten-mile downhill into the small town of Twisp (pop. 919). With all this climbing, we are burning a lot of calories (5,000-7,000 per day) and always hungry. Although Twisp is small, it has all the services we need and we stop for breakfast number two. Then we begin the twelve-mile climb, straight up, to the top of the pass.

About halfway up, we meet the two women cyclists again. Vivien and Abbie are sisters from Chicago, Illinois, and just graduated from Baltimore University. They decided to bicycle across the United States to celebrate. They obviously made it over Washington and Rainey passes, and are well on their way to finishing Loup Loup. We all agree yesterday's ride was tough and hope the rest won't be as difficult, but we know the highest pass – Sherman – is yet to come.

We reach the top of the pass an hour later and are glad to take a lunch break. We visit with Ruth and Rod, enjoy the view, and pull on our extra clothes for the downhill section. The downhill is quite steep and Peter has to keep the auxiliary drum brake on for much of it. We reach speeds of forty-five to fifty miles per hour even with the auxiliary brake on.

We have about twenty-three miles of downhill to Omak (pop. 4,845), our ending point for the night. At mile twenty, we arrive at the City of Okanogan (pop. 2,552) and take a break at the local coffee shop to watch the world go by and eat an early dinner. We find if we do not eat something before we meet up with the RV for the night, we are starving when we get there. It takes a bit for Ruth to make dinner and we tend to get grumpy as we wait. So to make it easier for all, we stop and eat an early dinner before we arrive at the RV. Eating dinner twice is not a problem.

The last three miles to Omak are along a quiet country road adjacent to the Okanogan River, beautiful. We are staying at the Omak municipal campground, Carl Precht Memorial RV Park, located right along the river. The campground is pretty bare bones, but has everything we need in water and restrooms with showers.

Shortly after we arrive, Vivien and Abbie show up. We bring them a bowl of fresh raspberries Ruth had purchased earlier in the day and take some time to get to know them better. Vivien is a fiber artist and received her degree from the Maryland Institute College of Art in Baltimore. Abbie is her twin sister. They are trying to get to Minneapolis to attend a contra dance. Peter and I have never heard of a contra dance, which Vivian is kind enough to explain.

Contra dance is a traditional American folk dance that is becoming popular in the United States. Similar to square dancing, the dance involves a band, a caller, and dancers that dance in couples along lines. The dance is social and enjoyable, with most attendees finding haven in the pastoral clip clop of contra. What was once an activity of an existing community, contra is now an activity that creates a community. Contra culture considers what might be a style of dress for contra dancing and incorporates the Spirograph design into each garment. The outfits are designed for couples; a full skirt or dress for the lady and a button-down shirt for the gent. Vivien designs and makes contra clothing. Very interesting. We never know who we will meet and what we will learn on the road.

We wish them luck and return to the RV to get organized for the next day's adventure.

Day 4

June 4 – Omak to Republic, Washington
80 miles (total miles - 302)
Beautiful weather, sunny, tailwind and 55-75 degrees

Tracy

We leave the campground by 7:00 a.m. due to the anticipated climb to Wauconda Pass (4,310 feet). Our first stop is in Riverside (pop. 280) about ten miles into our ride. We stop at the local coffee shop/convenience store where all the locals meet to drink coffee and catch up on the local goings on. Of course, we are of great interest as we walk into the shop clad in our bright-colored, Lycra bicycling outfits. First we receive stares, then a brave soul walks over to talk, and soon everyone is asking questions and introducing themselves. The patrons are kind and provide us with some great local information. All too soon, we need to hit the road again. They wish us luck and off we go.

We continue toward Stone Mountain, which is a much smaller mountain at 2,011 feet. Our ride over this mountain seems easy, and fairly quickly we are bicycling down the other side sixteen miles downhill to Tonasket (pop. 1,032). The views here are very different. The mountains are older and flatter, and the vegetation is mostly pines. We are riding through the Okanogan Valley with mountain ranges on both sides and the Okanogan River on our right.

From Tonasket, we start our climb to the pass. It is a much easier climb, less steep and with some flatter sections, but still twenty-four miles of uphill. We get to the top of the pass and the one convenience store/gas station in Wauconda (pop. 226) is closed. Not good. Thank goodness we planned to meet Ruth and Rod at the top, and they are waiting when we crest the pass. We are able to take a break in the RV, replenish our water and have something to eat.

The end of the ride is an amazing downhill of nineteen miles into Republic (pop. 1,073). The road has great sight lines, sweeping turns, and little or no traffic. We are able to cruise into Republic in less than an hour and are excited to see the Republic Brewery, a microbrewery. We decide to stop for a beer.

Peter

Tracy bought me the book *Wisconsin's Best Beer Guide*, by Kevin Revolinski, for Christmas in 2011. I have never been much of a drinker, but I do like craft beer. A perfect day for me consists of a long bicycle ride that ends at a microbrewery with a great stout, porter, or better yet, Scotch ale. The idea of putting bikes and beer together appealed to me, and I immediately hatched a plan to bicycle from our home to all seventy-four establishments listed in the book. We would need to improve both our bicycling and navigation skills to achieve our goal. Breweries are seldom located based on how easy they are to reach by bicycle. We would buy a commemorative pint glass at each brewery. Our plan was to continue the practice on this trip.

> "Luv seeing the pics of your adventure! Stay safe and have a great time!"
>
> ***- Kathy Lukes Faust***

Please note that I am neither endorsing, nor am I a fan of drinking and driving. Bicycling requires balance and good judgement, and alcohol can mess both up. Everything in moderation.

Tracy

We have a snack, a couple of beers (Peter had a stout and I had a porter), and buy the first pint glass of our trip. As we are enjoying our break and learning more about the brewery and Republic from the bartender, she keeps reaching up to the ceiling with a long hook and pulling down beer mugs. She then writes on a small piece of paper and puts the slip of paper in the mug and hangs it back up. After a while, I just have to ask what she is doing. She laughs and explains the mugs belong to her regulars and several have beer tabs to pay. She puts the tab in the mug and they pay up the next time they come in. Sounds like a good system to me.

We ride the last three miles to the campground on the first bicycle trail of the trip. It is a nice trail located on an old logging railroad line. We arrive at the campground, get cleaned up, and then decide to drive into town for dinner. This is a nice break for Ruth, who has been cooking for us since our trip began.

But first, we need to find out if the tandem will fit in the RV. We take off the bags, and Rod and Peter easily slide it into the side door of the RV. We do carry a lock for the tandem, but it is pretty lightweight and we did not feel it would be secure enough to leave the tandem at the campground. We return to the Republic Brewery for a second beer and then walk down the street for dinner. It is a nice, relaxing evening, and fun to explore Republic. It is a small town with a great downtown area that has lots to offer. The town is nestled in a valley between Wauconda and Sherman passes at the intersection of Washington State Highways 20 and 21. Peter likes to say, "Travelers from the east or west get over the passes, fall into Republic, and never leave."

Tomorrow we tackle the highest climb of the trip, Sherman Pass, elevation 5,575 feet. Hopefully it will go well. I think our climbing legs are getting stronger!

Day 5

June 5 – Republic to Colville, Washington
59 miles (total miles - 361)
Beautiful weather, sunny, tailwind, 48-75 degrees

Peter

In the mountains, our uphill speed can be as low as five miles per hour. Downhill we routinely hit forty-five miles per hour, and that is with the drum brake on. We recently talked to a tandem couple that hit seventy-one miles per hour coming down these same mountains. Nuts!

Tracy and I both have mantras we use during especially long and difficult climbs. If we lose our concentration, we simply stop. Getting going again on a steep climb is tough. My mantra is singing the *100 Bottles of Beer on the Wall* song over and over. My record is five times. Tracy's song goes, "One elephant went out to play, up on a spider's web one day. He had such enormous fun, that he asked another elephant to come. Two elephants ..." I'm not sure how many elephants she has played with at once.

Tracy

Today we are on the road by 7:00 a.m. for the last big climb in the Cascade Mountains, Sherman Pass (5,575 feet). We climb 2,500 feet of elevation in eighteen miles at an average speed of eight miles per hour. We make it to the top by 10:00 a.m., stop to eat an early lunch, and wait for our sag vehicle to put on more clothes for the cold downhill ride. It

Conquering Sherman Pass was a major accomplishment on Day 5.

The RV (and Ruth!) was a welcome sight during the first portion of our trip.

is cold and windy at the top of the pass, and we put on all the clothes we have along, which is not a lot, to wait for the RV.

While eating lunch, we hide behind the "Sherman Pass Scenic Byway – It is all Downhill from Here" sign to get out of the wind. Peter finds a handmade cardboard sign that says, "Sherman Pass." He tucks it in into his jacket for extra warmth. An older RV pulls up, not ours, and a family from Delta Junction, Alaska, piles out. We ask them if they have brought us coffee. No such luck.

We talk for quite a while and discover the woman (Judy) is involved in the Delta Junction Trails Association, and they are looking at contracting to have a bicycle and pedestrian plan completed. What are the odds that a potential WE BIKE, etc. client would show up at the top of a mountain pass? They are at the end of a three-week vacation and are heading home.

Just before our new friends from Alaska are about to leave, our sag wagon shows up with warm clothes, water, and food. We head down the other side of the mountain, which has a 6 percent slope for six miles. We easily hit forty-five miles per hour again on our way down. Fortunately, the bicycle actually gets stiffer and more stable at higher speeds, it is nothing like those old tandems that wobble all over the place, thank goodness. I do not have any control over our speed and just need to relax and lean the way Peter does. Our running joke is when I ask him how fast we are going he always says, "twenty-five."

This downhill is very steep. We drop from 5,575 feet to about 1,300 feet in thirty-one miles before arriving at the Columbia River, Lake Roosevelt, and the small town of Kettle Falls (pop. 1,595). From Kettle Falls, we follow the Colville River to Colville (pop. 4,673) and the Stevens County Fairgrounds, our campground for the night. There are lots of other campers from all over the United States, including a gentleman from town who is really into bicycles. Peter has a good conversation with him.

It is time to get our laundry done and a laundromat is located right down the road. We give Ruth and Rod our laundry to get started while we head into the restrooms for a shower. When we come out, a couple of chairs and two beers are waiting for us at our campsite. We enjoy the beers, talk with our new neighbors, and relax until the RV returns. Not a bad way to end the day.

Peter

We have found the drivers in Washington State to be quite pleasant. They routinely slow down and move over to pass us. They seem to understand we have just as much right to be on the road as they do, but we are vulnerable. If they hit us, we will lose!

According to the National Highway Traffic Safety Administration, there are about 700 bicyclists killed in crashes with motor vehicles in the United States each year. There are about 33,000 motorists killed.

We are well-trained cyclists. Heck, we teach the stuff. We know what the most common mistakes are for both bicyclists and motorists, and how to avoid them. We use proper lane position, follow the law, and wear bright-colored clothing and helmets.

How the roads are built and maintained in Washington has been to our favor. The road surface quality is excellent, which makes holding a straight and predictable line easy. Also, we often have a wide shoulder when we need it.

The three main factors that affect what we call the bikability of a road are curb lane width, speed, and traffic volume. A wide lane (greater than fourteen feet) allows us to stay out of traffic most of the time, as does a paved shoulder (five feet or greater). On narrow roads, speed can be an issue. Sharing the road becomes more difficult when traffic is traveling more than fifteen miles per hour faster than we are. Of course, the more cars there are, the faster the speeds and the narrower the roads, the more difficult and dangerous bicycling becomes.

Rumble strips can be a blessing or a scourge for bicyclists. If they are constructed and placed properly (narrow, on the fog line, and with gaps for moving left and right) they can create a buffer between us and traffic, and make us feel a lot safer. If, however, they are placed on a narrow shoulder, they can actually force us into the travel lane where we have to take our chances with the motor vehicle traffic approaching from behind. This can be downright terrifying.

Day 6

June 6 – Colville to Newport, Washington
96 miles (total miles - 457)
Weather beautiful, but cooler - 50-70 degrees, tailwind most of the day

Tracy

Today we are up early because we potentially have a long ride ahead. We are not sure where we will end today, but we would like to get as far as Newport, which is almost 100 miles away. We will meet up with Ruth and Rod several times during the day, so we can adjust accordingly depending on how we feel.

We leave the campground by 7:00 a.m. It typically takes about an hour of riding for our legs to warm up and be ready to pedal all day. It is difficult when we hit an uphill climb first thing in the morning, because our legs are just not ready for it. Unfortunately, the first part of our ride today is over some small mountains just outside of Colville.

Several years ago on a bicycle trip in the San Juan Islands (located off

Washington State in Puget Sound), we had a tough climb on Orcas Island. Our lodging for the night was a resort at sea level and we had a very steep climb to continue our journey the next day. We actually rode around for about fifteen minutes in the parking lots to wake up our legs before we took on the hill. I am proud to say we made it up the hill without having to push the bicycle. The funny thing was someone had glued a bunch of change to the side of the road where we were riding. Peter and I wondered if they thought it would distract a struggling bicyclist and help them keep going. It worked for us with Peter yelling out "dime," "quarter," "penny," etc., as we climbed the hill.

The climb out of Colville is about eighteen miles long followed by a ten-mile downhill. The downhill is steep, the road is narrow and twisty. It is a technical descent with two fifteen miles-per-hour hairpin turns. Now remember, I have little control over our speed and just need to lean the way Peter does. But, of course, I am able to see the hairpin turn warning signs, and I feel we were going way too fast to make the corner and should slow down. We take the first corner at thirty miles per hour. Peter uses the maneuverability of the bike to negotiate the curve faster than a car can. He sets us up for the left-hand curve on the far right side of our lane, dives to the inside as we enter the corner, then drifts to the right side of the lane again. We make it through just fine.

> "You two are crazy and amazing! Sorry to hear about not feeling well. The downhills sound like great fun, though 45 on a tandem sounds scary as all get out! Happy riding."
>
> ***- Tom and Barb***

However, as Peter sets us up for the second turn, again at thirty miles per hour, an RV comes around the corner in the opposite direction and we have to swing the corner much tighter than expected. My natural impulse is to sit up when I get scared, because I know that will slow us down. But this time I have to override that impulse, and with Peter yelling "Lean! Lean! Lean!" we make it through the corner.

Once we get through the corner, I ask Peter to stop so I can quit shaking and yell at him to never do that again. He apologizes and promises he will not try a fifteen-mile-per-hour hairpin turn at thirty miles per hour again. He'd better not.

Peter

In my defense, I have only crashed us out once in approximately 25,000 miles of riding this tandem. Several years ago, we were riding home at the end of a twenty-mile day ride. As we transitioned from the country to the city, the road widened from two lanes to four, and then narrowed back to two lanes again. When the road widened, I kept us near the curb until a parked car forced me to move left into the main travel lane.

I had ridden this particular stretch of road hundreds of times before and knew there is a wide joint line which runs parallel to the curb between the parking lane and the travel lane. To avoid getting the front wheel trapped in the joint, which would almost certainly cause us to crash, I cut left sharply across the joint and we were fine.

Then, for some reason, I decided to move back to the curb lane even though the road was going back to two lanes in about 200 yards. This time the front wheel caught in the joint. We went down so quickly I didn't realize we were going to crash until our right side was about a foot off the ground. I didn't even have time to let go of the handle bars. We hit hard and slid about twenty yards. We were both dazed and had road rash on our right sides from head to toe, but were otherwise unhurt.

"I am enjoying vicariously and recalling my ride there. Ride on!"

- Jim Baross Jr.

Within three long weeks, all of our road rash healed. I learned a valuable lesson that day: It is really bad form to crash out the mother of your children. Actually, Tracy was really good about the crash. It was one hundred percent my fault, but she never blamed me. She knows I am a very careful cyclist and accepts that fact that no one is perfect. She loves riding the tandem and accepts the risks that go along with bicycling.

Tracy

We stop briefly a short distance down the road at a rest stop along the Oreille River. As we pull in, we see two other bicyclists and ride over to say hello. The young men are from Washington State and have just started their trip to Washington, D.C. John is attending Western Washington State University and Grant is a recent graduate from Duke University. Grant has a job starting in September and talked John, after a few beers, into bicycling across the country with him. Grant figured he would probably have to wait a long time to get ten weeks off, so he decided to do it now – a very smart young man. They are stopping at a local campground for the night and John's mom is planning to bring them dinner. We wish them luck and continue on our way.

After the downhill, we bike a mile off route to the small town of Ione (pop. 447), where we meet Ruth and Rod for lunch. After lunch, we decide to meet up thirty miles down the road to see how we feel and decide how much farther we want to go. We head out, leaving Ruth and Rod in town to pick up more supplies.

We bicycle along the Oreille River for the rest of the ride. It is beautiful, with the wind at our backs, downhill, and amazing views of the river to our right. The thirty miles fly by and before we know it, Ruth and Rod drive by for our meet-up just down the road. With the wind at our backs and the downhill ride, we decide to continue to Newport, fifty-one miles away, and the Old American Kampground. Once again we set up a meeting point thirty miles down the road, just in case we decide we have had enough or need anything.

We spend about eight and half hours on the road today and finally make it to the campground about 3:30 p.m. after a stop in Newport for an early dinner. The campground is located in two states, Washington and Idaho. Our campsite is actually in Idaho, so we have officially made it to our second state.

We saw our first American Bison (buffalo) today, and Peter was giving me a hard time because a couple of days ago I thought I saw buffalo, but they were only large cows. This time they are the real things. I am sure there will be more to come.

Peter

I'm still laughing. Seriously, Tracy grew up in Wisconsin.

Tracy

Tomorrow we will be leaving the Northern Tier route, which continues to Sandpoint, Idaho. We will detour slightly to Coeur d'Alene, Idaho, where Peter will teach a two-day law enforcement class.

Chapter 3

Combining Work and Play

State of Idaho
June 7-12, 2014
Total Miles 193/650 total

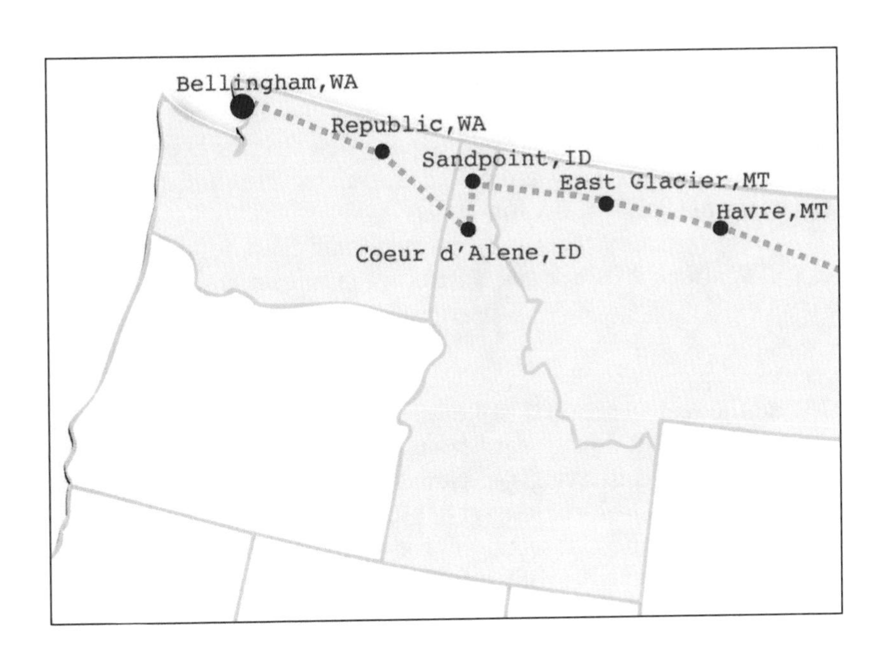

Day 7

June 7 - Newport, Washington to Coeur d'Alene, Idaho
43 miles (total miles 500)
Beautiful, 45-70 degrees, slight tailwind

Tracy

Today will be a short ride for us, which we planned for after hitting it hard yesterday. The shorter day allows us to leave later. I like the 10:00 a.m. starts better than the 7:00 a.m. starts. The ride officially takes us into the state of Idaho, although we actually camped in Idaho last night. It is rather odd, as our campground is half in Washington and half in Idaho.

The ride begins on Highway 41, a quiet two-lane country road. We enjoy the views of the adjacent forests and farms, which remind me of roads we have traveled in Wisconsin. We pedal through a gentle bend in the road and move left to prepare for our next turn. As we navigate our turn, Peter spots a couple of touring cyclists ahead and we speed up to catch them. We reach the two men a couple of minutes later. They are from Washington State and are on the last day of an eight-day loop ride that started in Spokane. One guy is retired and the other is a doctor. We ride together for about twenty miles. They are experienced cyclists, easy and fun to ride with, and travel at a speed that works for all of us.

We stop for a break at a local park with our new friends. There is a boys' baseball tournament going on, so we head toward the concession stand to get a snack. The tournament is huge and many little boys are playing ball and running around. Interruptions are frequent as we eat our not-so-healthy snack and get to know are new friends better. The boys and their parents are very interested in our bicycles and gear, and we catch questions like so many foul balls.

We leave the park together, but eventually part ways. The last ten miles to Tamarack RV Park and Vacation Rentals are uneventful and the ride flat.

Peter

My mother called me on the phone several months after we completed our trip to say she had just heard from Dorothea Nelson, a family friend from when we lived in Syracuse, New York, back in the late 1960s and early 1970s. The Nelsons belonged to our church and we were very close – I even lived with them at one point for several months when my family was out of the country. Dorothea followed our trip through Tracy's blog and had just realized something amazing. One of the cyclists, the doctor, was her daughter Sara's husband, Cy. She hadn't put two and two together until now. I haven't seen Sara in more than forty years and we ran into her husband on a bicycle tour in Washington State. Wow.

Tracy

We will be spending the next three days in Coeur d'Alene, Idaho (pop. 44,137), where Peter will be teaching a two-day "Enforcement for Pedestrian & Bicycle Safety" course for northern Idaho law enforcement officers. I will hang out with Mom and Rod, relax, and organize our gear for heading out on our own without our sag support.

Day 8

June 8 – Coeur d'Alene, Idaho
0 miles (total miles 500)

Tracy

We spend the day exploring Coeur d'Alene with Ruth and Rod. Everyone else had been to "CDA," as it is known locally, but I had not. It is a beautiful city with lots to do and see. Later in the day, we check into the Coeur d'Alene Resort on beautiful Lake Coeur d'Alene, renowned for its sport fishing, including Chinook Salmon, Smallmouth Bass, Largemouth Bass, Northern Pike, and Kokanee Salmon. The resort has its own marina with a floating boardwalk, and a nationally ranked golf course that features a hole where the green is an island in the lake that you must reach my boat. The hotel is world class with very comfortable rooms, shops, several restaurants, and a conference center.

Ruth and Rod are perfectly happy to spend the night in the RV at the Tamarack RV Park. It will feel a bit strange to sleep in a king-sized bed rather than the loft of the RV. I cannot even imagine how it will feel a month from now after spending most of our nights camping.

We finally have reliable internet at the hotel and I am able to post the first videos of the trip: Sherman Pass climb (6 mph) and descent (45 mph) to our blog

Day 9

June 9 – Coeur d'Alene, Idaho
0 miles (total miles 500)
Peter taught – Ruth, Tracy and Rod shopped

Peter

I awake before the two alarms I had set for 6:00 a.m. go off. After a cup of coffee, I shower, shave, and dress in highly buffed black dress shoes, tan khakis, and a slate gray long-sleeved dress shirt with a WE BIKE, etc. logo on the left chest. We had shipped my dress clothes to Bellingham and they had been waiting patiently in the RV for the past week.

I put the jump drive containing my presentation in my right front

During our visit to Coeur d'Alene, Idaho, Peter taught a two-day "Enforcement for Pedestrian & Bicycle Safety" course for northern Idaho law enforcement officers.

pants pocket and am ready for breakfast. It feels strange not having my laptop computer with me, but I am traveling light. I quietly open and close the hotel room door behind me so I don't wake Tracy, and head to the main floor and the most casual of the hotel restaurants for breakfast. I know there will be food at the police department, but I want that to be my second breakfast. Even though I'm not going to be biking today, my body is still burning a lot of calories trying to recover from the biking we had already done.

After breakfast, I collect Tracy from our room and we head down to the lobby, where Rod and Mom are waiting for us with the RV. The police department is only four miles from the hotel, but I'm not exactly dressed for biking on the tandem today. It is kind of funny arriving at the police department in an RV and then having my family wave goodbye and wish me luck. What, am I twelve?

It is actually kind of nice to have them here. Teaching should be old hat to me by now, but I still get nervous. Every time.

Tracy

After dropping Peter off, Mom, Rod and I head to breakfast at a café in downtown Coeur d'Alene before driving to the mall located on the outskirts of town. I am in need of shorts to wear when we are not on the bicycle. I do have jean shorts, but they are pretty heavy and don't dry quickly. Mom and I leave Rod in the RV with a good book and hit the mall. Of course, the mall has a fishing store. It has everything a fisherman/

woman could need, including lightweight fishing shorts. They turn out to be ideal for touring cyclists also – who knew? Mom buys me a pair.

I think Mom is nervous about leaving us on our own for the rest of the trip across the country. She keeps asking me, "What else do you need?" I assure her we are all set and do not need anything else, although she insists on buying food for us.

Truthfully, I am also nervous about being self-supported, but do not share that with her. It has been great having them along and will be tough to say goodbye tomorrow. Can Peter and I do this on our own? We are certainly in good shape and know what we are doing, but will that be enough? Let's hope so.

Ruth and I finish shopping and wander back to the RV. After a snack with Rod, we head back to the resort where we transfer our supplies to the hotel room, double-check what we will leave with Ruth to mail back to Green Bay, and relax a bit before picking up Peter.

Peter

I originally developed a course called "Enforcement for Bicycle Safety" back in 1995 for the Wisconsin Department of Transportation. The course was the result of my background in parks and recreation and law enforcement. As a former parks and recreation professional, I understand the benefits of bicycling, but as a cop I understand the potential dangers. Fortunately, most of the dangers are predictable and, therefore, preventable – but only if you know how they happen, and most cops don't. I am in a unique position to train law enforcement officers about bicycle safety and I love doing it. I added pedestrian safety to the course in 2006.

> "Omar asks every day to see your bike photos!! You're inspiring the masses to open their Facebook, not to ride 700 miles on a bike."
>
> ***- Barbara Ali***

The "Enforcement for Pedestrian & Bicycle Safety" course I am teaching today and tomorrow provides law enforcement officers with the additional training they need to identify and correct behaviors that most commonly lead to pedestrian and bicycle crashes and other related issues. This two-day training is a complete pedestrian and bicycle safety educational experience with classroom and on-the-road activities. The course contains information in the following areas: What, Where, When, How, Who & Why of walking and bicycling; components of the Highway Safety Triangle; Bicycle Environment Audit; How Pedestrian & Bicycle Crashes Happen; Pedestrian & Bicycle Laws; Crash Investigating & Reporting; Potential Law Enforcement Partners; and more.

I feel confident after the course that officers have the knowledge and skills needed to improve pedestrian and bicycle safety. As a recreation professional, law enforcement officer and a bicyclist, I see this as a win, win, win. I teach this course all over the country.

The first day of the course goes well. It usually does, but I always feel better when Day One is done.

Tracy

We pick up Peter at the Coeur d'Alene police department and meet some of the officers from his class. Several of them introduce themselves and tell me they enjoyed the first day and are looking forward to learning more tomorrow. The class just seems to work everywhere he teaches it because, as Peter says, "Cops can't enforce laws they don't know and won't enforce laws they can't defend."

Dinner is at an upscale restaurant in downtown Coeur d'Alene. Since it is our last night together, we want to celebrate and thank Mom and Rod for all their help over the past week. We reminisce about our week together and learn more about what they did while we were bicycling. They explain that while their days were relaxing, they definitely had enough tasks to complete each day to keep them busy.

Normally after we left, they got up, had breakfast, cleaned up, got dressed, reviewed the route to confirm our meeting places and times, figured out what they wanted to see or explore that day, and prepared the RV to move. Then they did laundry, picked up groceries, gassed up the RV, picked up supplies, etc., as needed. They did a great job of sagging and we thoroughly enjoyed their company and our last night together.

Day 10

June 10 – Coeur d'Alene, Idaho
0 miles (total miles 500)

Peter

Rod and Mom are taking me to the police department in the RV again this morning and then heading back to Bellingham. What took them a week to drive on the way here will only take them two days on the way back. It must be quicker because they have less weight in the RV. Ha! Special thanks to Mom and Rod for all their help the last week. It is much appreciated and we will truly miss them.

The course continues to go well, but I am really looking forward to getting back on the road – this time with nothing to do but bike with Tracy for the next two and a half months. As a class, we go to a restaurant called Melts Gourmet Grilled Cheese for lunch. This place has taken the grilled cheese sandwich to a whole new level. In my normal life, I would never even consider ordering a Reuben grilled cheese sandwich, given the exorbitant calories, fat and cholesterol. However, these are extenuating circumstances. I polish off my sandwich in record time and almost order another one, it was so good. I sure hope Tracy wants to come back here for dinner. No joke.

Because Mom and Rod are no longer available to chauffer me, I arrange for one of the officers in the course to give me a ride back to the hotel. I bet we won't get a speeding ticket – of course because we won't be speeding. Speeding motor vehicles can be dangerous for pedestrians and bicyclists.

Tracy

I am on my own today for the first time since we started the trip. I plan to spend the day relaxing, checking out downtown Coeur d'Alene, and getting organized to head out tomorrow. Packing all our gear into four bags is a challenge, but everything has its place. Although, as I am looking at everything I need to get in the bags, I am not sure it is all going to fit. Mom seemed worried about leaving us on our own, and her way to feel better about it was making sure we have enough food. She certainly did that. Thanks, Mom. I think we have enough food to hold us for several weeks. Now I just have to figure out where to put it all.

Peter gets back to the hotel about 3:30 p.m. After changing and relaxing, we decide to walk to a local brewery, Tricksters, for a beer and to purchase a beer glass for our collection. We use the Google Maps function on Peter's phone to get to the brewery, but get lost. Our three-mile walk becomes a four-mile walk to the brewery, which is located in the middle of an industrial park; strange place to locate a brewery.

We enjoy our beers and conversation with the other patrons and get directions to dinner. Luckily, Melts (Peter gets to go again) is less than a mile away and we arrive just before they close. The grilled cheese sandwiches are amazing and well worth the walk. I hope we find more Melts on the trip.

Day 11

June 11 - Coeur d'Alene to East Hope, Idaho
68 miles (Total miles 568)
Weather nice, 60-70 degrees, sunny and a tailwind from the south

Tracy

Today is our first day back on the bike after taking the last three days off for Peter to teach. The ride is mainly on U.S. Route 95 and Highway 200. Route 95 is not too bad to bicycle on, even though it is a four-lane divided highway with lots of high-speed traffic, including many trucks. This is the main route between Coeur d'Alene and Sandpoint, fifty-eight miles away. There is a nice, wide shoulder and the motor vehicle drivers are really good about moving over when they pass us. Thank goodness.

Peter

That is until we hit the construction. As we crest a hill, I start to see "Construction Ahead" and "Road Narrows" signs, and call these out to Tracy. From her position behind me, Tracy often can't see what is right in front of us, so I have to tell her, especially if it is something we might have to deal with quickly.

We continue forward, knowing this is the only practical route to Sandpoint and East New Hope beyond that. Now we are seeing orange construction barrels. Thousands of orange construction barrels. At first they are only on the shoulder, but then they start to angle across the shoulder we are riding on and ultimately across the first traffic lane. They are forcing us onto the inside lane of a freeway. There is no way we can share this single lane with trucks at freeway speeds.

With no other option, I dive us between two orange barrels and come to a stop in the closed lane. It is at times like this that I can literally hear my own voice in my head like I am teaching a bicycle safety class, "One of the great things about riding a bicycle is that if you get in trouble, you can always pull to the side of the road, gather yourself, and figure a way out."

There is no space for us in the travel lane. The closed lane is an option for a few hundred yards, but then it is all torn up and unrideable. We check our map, but there really is no alternative route. After watching the traffic for a few minutes, we discover that from time to time there are periods with little to no traffic. We decide to try and use these gaps in traffic to leapfrog our way through the construction.

We will ride as far as possible, with Tracy watching behind for overtaking traffic, and then slide off the road again when necessary and wait for traffic to clear. Ready? Go! We make it through the construction without incident, but the highway construction folks really should keep bicyclists in mind when doing road work. This was not cool.

Tracy

We survive the construction and enjoy biking into Sandpoint on a bicycle and pedestrian path. The path is mostly located on an abandoned bridge crossing Pend Oreille Lake and running parallel to the highway. It is great to be off the road for this long lake crossing.

We stop in Sandpoint for lunch and to shop a bit. It is a cool town with lots of nice places to eat and shop. Sandpoint, Idaho, (pop. 7,365) is described as a "hippy enclave." We agree and enjoy this very hip city. Lunch is at a local brewery, McDuff's, and the food and beer are both good. We purchase a pint beer glass and now have two beer glasses packed on the bicycle.

Back on the bike, we only have twenty miles to go to our campground in East Hope (pop. 210). We are on Highway 200 for the rest of the ride to the campground. It is not the best road to ride on – narrow with very little shoulder – but at least the drivers are good about giving us the space we need. The ride is flat with a few small climbs. We stop in Hope (pop. 86), which is at the top of one of the climbs, at the little store, bakery, ice cream shop. We sit on the deck and enjoy our ice cream and the view of Lake Pend Oreille.

Our overnight is at a beautiful and spotless national forest campground, Sam Owen Campground, located on Pend Orielle Lake. The thick duff of pine needles will make for soft sleeping in our tent. This is our first night of camping on our own and it takes us about an hour and a half to set up and find everything. We have no rhythm yet. I am sure, or I least I hope, we will get better and better at setting up camp as the days go on.

Unfortunately, this campground is primitive and has no running water except for a hand-pumped well for drinking water. So, no shower tonight.

> "Hope you get sun for Glacier, looking forward to pics. So beautiful there."
>
> ***- Carolyn Jones***

Then there are the bears. Well, at least the campground signs and hosts say there are bears. One had been spotted just a day or two earlier near a campsite. I have never been around bears before and I am, frankly, scared. Peter has camped in bear country before and he is not scared. This is of little comfort to me.

Peter

I have had some experience with bears in the wild. My parents met while working at Sequoia National Park in California. There were lots of bears in Sequoia, and I grew up hearing bear stories aplenty. Bears were not feared in these stories, but they were respected.

One summer when I was five or six years old, my family visited Sequoia and we had a bear wander into our cabin – probably should have locked the door. Fortunately, we were outside at the time – still probably should have locked the door. The summer after my freshman year in high school (I was fifteen), I took the Greyhound bus with two buddies to North Carolina and Tennessee, where we backpacked 150 miles of the Appalachian Trail and had several bear encounters. Once, while picking wild blueberries, we discovered that bears and their cubs like blueberries, too. Another time, we had a hungry bear come into our camp in Great Smoky Mountains National Park and try to get into our cyclone fence-protected shelter, with us in it. Thwarted by the fence, she ultimately settled for licking out our cooking pot which was outside of the shelter.

The following year in Kings Canyon National Park (near Sequoia

National Park) with the same two buddies, we had a bear come into our camp while we were sleeping under the stars. The bear sniffed our backpacks, which were no more than ten feet away from our heads while we cowered in our nylon and down sleeping bags, trying to decide if blowing our "bear whistle" would make the bear mad or go away. Luckily, we had put all of our food in a bear bag and run it up a tall tree some distance away from us. With no food to keep the bear interested, she ultimately left our camp on her own with us madly blowing the bear whistle behind her. Unfazed, she lumbered to the next campsite and destroyed a cooler with one swipe of her massive paw.

My experience has been that if you respect bears and store your food properly at night, they are seldom a problem.

Tracy

There are very few campers, but we do have a young couple car-camping at the site right next to us. As we struggle to set up camp and make dinner, I feel them watching us and think this must be as good as TV.

Peter

After dinner, I pull a coil of orange paracord out of our emergency kit and start packing all of our food, sunscreen, lip balm, gum, and anything with a smell into one of our sleeping bag stuff sacks. I tie one end of the cord around the end of the bag.

"What are you doing?" Tracy asks.

"Making a bear bag," I reply.

"Why?"

"Would you rather have a bear looking for food in our tent in the middle of the night or in a bear bag thirty feet up in the air between two trees 100 yards away from camp?"

"Got it," she says.

I sleep like a baby, knowing I have done everything possible to avoid being a midnight bear snack. I'm pretty sure Tracy didn't sleep all that well. There were no bear sightings while we were at the campground, only a few deer.

A rather basic sign welcomes us to Montana and doubles as a promotional board for a local inn. The gravel road, however, was an unwelcome surprise.

Day 12

June 12 - East Hope, Idaho, to Libby, Montana
82 miles (Total miles 650)
Weather cooler, but sunny – 50-70 degrees

Peter

Tracy is NOT a morning person, and between yesterday's hard ride and every noise sounding like a bear last night, I'm sure she is extra-tired this morning. No worries, I am a morning person and almost always up before the sun. No alarm clock needed. I boil water for my instant coffee and start Tracy's tea to steeping.

Our MSR Firefly backpacking stove is unavoidably noisy and this is Tracy's signal to start waking up, although I still have to roust her. Tracy starts to pack up the tent from the inside out while I make breakfast.

Breakfast consists of two packets of instant oatmeal each with an added tablespoon of peanut butter for protein, some trail mix, and a couple of apples we brought from the hotel. Yum.

Tracy

I run into the young man camping next to us as I head to the outhouse. He asks me many questions about our trip and tells me it was very interesting to watch us set up camp last night. He and his girlfriend were amazed at the amount of gear and supplies we were carrying and how quickly we set up camp. I laughed and explained it was our first night camping and we felt it took us forever to set up. He wished us luck and told me to enjoy the adventure. I assured him we would.

We cross into Montana about twenty miles east of New Hope. We are greeted at the state line with a gravel road and a very basic "Welcome to Montana" sign. There is no indication of this gravel section on our map and I wonder if we took a wrong turn. What to do?

Peter

We are running 700 mm x 28 mm, 115 pounds per-square-inch (PSI) Continental Gatorskin tires on the tandem. These are the same type of tires that originally came with the bike. They are very durable and have a low rolling resistance, which allows us to go faster with less effort – on smooth, well-paved roads that is. Gravel is another story.

I pretty much hate driving the tandem with these tires on gravel, even more so when the bike is fully loaded. Because the tires are narrow and high-pressure, they tend to sink into gravel instead of floating over it. When the front tire sinks into the gravel, it becomes incredibly hard to steer and wants to plow sideways instead of going straight or turning. It can be a real fight to keep the bike, our gear, and Tracy upright.

Under certain conditions, the back tire will actually slide as much as six inches from side to side. This is a disturbing feeling from my position on the front of the bike. From Tracy's position almost directly over the rear wheel, this has got to be terrifying. We have never crashed on gravel, but we have gotten so bogged down a couple of times that we literally came to a dead stop and had to bail off.

Tire choice is a tradeoff and highly debated at all levels of cycling. I have bet that we will have more good roads than bad by choosing these tires.

Tracy

We stop to take a picture of the "Welcome to Montana" sign and I pull out the map to double-check we are on the correct road. We are.

I keep the map in a clear plastic Ziploc bag in one of the back pockets of my bike jersey. It would be easier for me to keep the map in one of Peter's rear pockets, but it drives him nuts when I take it in and out of his pocket. I do it a lot because I don't want to get us lost. The plastic bag protects the map from tears, dirt, rain, and sweat. I can read the map through the bag if it isn't too trashed. We carry extra bags with us.

I need to go to the bathroom, so I put the map on top of the rear bike bags and tent, and head into the woods. I return to the bike and mount up. We will see if the gravel is ridable.

Peter

Luckily, the gravel on the road is relatively fine, hard-packed, and therefore ridable. There are several issues on gravel roads for the tandem.

Thankfully, we were able to find our missing map after only a few minutes of backtracking. Disaster averted.

The size of the aggregate on the road can range from dust to over one inch in diameter. Anything up to one-quarter inch is pretty ridable. Sometimes the road surface becomes like a washboard from uneven wear. This wash boarding can cause us to bounce uncontrollably.

Finally, gravel can build up in low areas or to the left or right of the wheel ruts. We can sink into the deep spots and slide out or simply come to a stop. I have to constantly change our line on the road to avoid these hazards. We are only able to average about ten miles per hour, but it is still way faster than pushing the bike.

After about a mile of riding, Tracy yells, "I lost the map!"

"What?"

"I LOST THE MAP!"

"SHIT! Where?"

"I don't know."

We stop.

Without the map, we are kind of screwed from a navigation standpoint. There are few roads out here, fewer signs, and even fewer people. We haven't seen a car for hours. Also, we don't have any cell service, so the GPS on our phone is useless. We kind of need to find the map. Our discussion isn't pretty, but we eventually figure out that Tracy probably forgot to put the map back in her pocket and it must have fallen off the bike when we started to ride again. We turn around and start to retrace our route. Our tire print in the dirt makes it easy to know exactly where we had ridden. God, I hope the map is still there, I really don't have a plan B at this point. We ride for about five minutes and there it is. The map is sitting in the middle of the road right where it had fallen. I make Tracy pose for a picture picking up the map as her penance.

The gravel portion of the road was only three miles long, but it took us almost an hour to ride.

Tracy

I just about shit when I realized I had lost the map and really did not want to tell Peter. I am relieved that we found it and will keep better track of it in the future.

We are back on a paved road again, but are still out in the middle of nowhere. We come around a bend, see a restaurant, and decide to stop in for a snack and fill our two bright green, empty water bottles. We enjoy chatting with the very nice middle-aged woman who owns the restaurant.

She happily fills our water bottles and sets them on the counter. Peter heads to the restroom and tells me he will grab the water bottles on his way out. I head back to the bicycle to put everything we pulled out back in its place – the wallet, sunscreen, hats, map, reading glasses, phone, etc. Peter comes out and we continue on our way to Libby, fifty-one miles down the road.

We didn't notice the water bottles were missing until we were about five miles down the road. We were not going to return for them.

Peter

I had one job to do and I blew it. Without a map, you are lost. Without water, you are dead. We agree that water, food, money, map, reading glasses, and cell phone are all essential to our trip and survival, and we pledge to never start riding again without all of them.

"Ready?"

"Ready."

"Water?"

"Yup."

"Wallet?"

"Check." ...

Because I lost the water bottles, we need to find another way to carry an adequate amount of liquid. Unfortunately, we cannot find replacement water bottles. We decide to grab a couple of bottles of Gatorade and strap them on the back of the bike on top our rear panniers. This should work.

Why the water bottles are green

We decided to order water bottles with our WE BIKE, etc. company logo on them for the first time a couple of years before this trip. The idea was to give them away to clients, friends, and family. We worked with our main bicycle shop, JB Cycle and Sport, to order the bottles. People loved them. With our supply of bottles running low, we placed another order the year before our cross-country trip. The order was for 200 clear bottles, 100 large and 100 small, with the WE BIKE, etc. logo on them. I got a call from Jeff Wentworth, the owner, the day the bottles arrived at the shop.

"How do you feel about green water bottles?" he asked.

"Green?" I replied with disappointment.

The bottle manufacturer apparently had mixed up the shop's order for green bottles with our order, and printed all of our bottles on green. I really did not like the color of the bottles, but the discount we got because of the error made them too good of a deal to pass up.

When it came time to pack up the gear boxes for the trip, I asked Tracy what color bottles she wanted to take with us, clear or green.

"Green," she said. "I think they will look cool."

"On the purple bike?"

"Yeah," she said, and that was that.

Now here's the funny part. Invariably, when people spot us on the tandem for the first time, dressed in our biking gear, with all of our gear. What do they notice first? You guessed it, the six green water bottles. Nice job, Tracy.

Tracy

It is only the second day carrying all our gear and my legs are still getting used to the extra weight. We are also battling the wind and the hills to Libby. I poop out, again, with about ten miles to go, darn it. I think my body is not used to the long days in the saddle and I am not sure I am eating enough.

"What an adventure!"
- Susan Muelken

Luckily, there is a tourist attraction ahead and we stop for a much-needed break. The Kootenai Falls Swinging Bridge crosses the Kootenai River and offers spectacular views of the river gorge and falls. We pull into the parking lot and stop our bike near a small wooden shack where a woman is selling cold sodas and snacks. The inside of the shack is "decorated" with pictures of bears, lots of bears.

There are not many other tourists around, so the bear lady starts showing us even more pictures of bears she keeps in a binder – and shows a lot, I think. We get the feeling that if we don't look at the pictures, she won't give us anything to eat or drink. We get a snack and Peter reluctantly walks down the trail to check out the bridge without me. I assure him I will be fine and just need time to sit, relax, and fill my tank. It is amazing what a coke and candy bar will do for you. I hope it will be enough to get me through the last ten miles.

The rest of the ride is slightly downhill and the wind has died down. We are riding along the Kootenai River and see lots of wildlife, including a pileated woodpecker, eagle, osprey, deer, huge ground squirrel, dead elk, and a flat, roadkill turtle. We get to Libby, Montana (pop. 2,628), by 5:00 p.m. and check into the Woodland RV Park. It is a nice campground with showers. We have to do laundry tonight, so after setting up camp and taking a shower, we walk into town to do laundry and eat dinner. The weatherman is calling for rain tonight. I hope we do not get soaked.

Chapter 4

Glacier National Park and the State of Montana

June 13-24, 2014
Total Miles 736/1,386 total

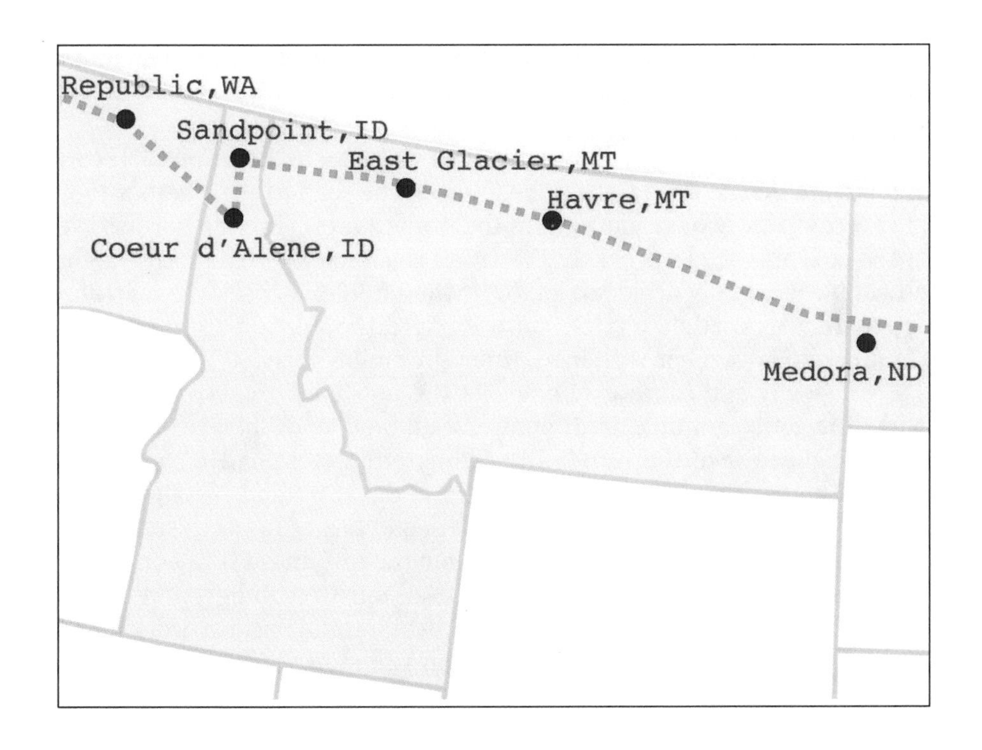

Day 13

June 13 - Libby to Eureka, Montana
75 miles (total miles – 725)
Cold and rainy, 50-60 degrees, rain for the first part of ride

Tracy

We are up at 6:30 a.m., make a cold breakfast, and are on the bike by 8:00 a.m. Our map has a warning for the section we are about to ride: "It is 70 miles between Libby and Eureka, and services are very limited, carry extra food and water." We heed the warning and make a quick stop in town for coffee, tea and donuts before we really get going.

We have discovered if we make a cold breakfast at the campground, we can get going much quicker in the morning. There is a thirty percent chance of rain today, so we want to get in as many miles as possible before it hits, if it hits.

Five miles out of Libby the rain starts. It isn't heavy, but it is cold. The air temperature is only 51 degrees. It does not seem too bad as long as we keep moving, with our tights and high-visibility yellow wind jackets. About fifteen miles from Libby, we come to the "fork in the road" and have to decide if we will travel on the east or west side of Lake Koocanusa. This is an important decision, which we made last night. Lake Koocanusa is over fifty miles long with just one crossing. We will travel on the east side because the west side has no services.

About ten miles down the road, we see a sign for a campground/resort and stop to decide if we want to head down the road to see whether they have a camp store or restaurant on the property. It is raining harder. We are soaked and need a break, but the road is in terrible shape and straight downhill. We finally decide to go for it when I double-check the map and see there are no other services until Rexford (population 105), which is supposed to have a bar with food, thirty-five miles away.

We slowly and cautiously navigate the pot-holed road, pass the RV park, the tent camping area, shower building, pool, playground, and finally right next to the lake is the campground store and restaurant – yeah. The parking lot is empty. We hope the store and restaurant are open. We park the bike, grab our supplies, and head toward the building.

Thankfully, the store is open. Although the restaurant is not open yet, the owner allows us to go in, spread out all our wet clothes, and brings us something warm to drink. When the restaurant opens, we order lunch and linger over our meal, hoping the rain will stop. Peter's socks are so wet from the rain coming off the front tire that he is trying to blot them dry with napkins. Good luck with that.

Peter

"What, you ride in the rain?" We get this a lot – usually as we are walking into some business soaking wet. "Yes, we bike in the rain." Actually, if we didn't bike in the rain, it would be really hard to make it across the country in any reasonable amount of time. Rain happens!

The trick to bicycling in the rain is to have a plan. If we get it right, it can actually be a lot of fun. But, if we get it wrong, it can be downright dangerous. We really don't mind riding in the rain all that much, except for being soaked, cold, and getting the bike really dirty. In fact, a light rain can feel pretty nice on a hot day.

We wear our normal bike clothes (shorts and jersey) when it rains on warm days. Our bodies create so much heat when we bike that we are usually covered in sweat anyhow. We don't get much wetter in a light rain, and the sweat gets washed away. All a raincoat would do is make us sweat even more. As the rain intensity increases, things get a bit more difficult. The first issue is our glasses get covered in rain and sometimes fog up. I often need to remove my glasses and hand them to Tracy so I can see. I wear glasses to protect my eyes from the sun, wind, debris, and to see clearly.

"So excited to follow your journey! Congrats on taking life by the horns (or the handlebars)!"
- Melissa and Jason

My eyesight has started to deteriorate with age; Tracy's, too. I am farsighted and have a minor astigmatism. Without glasses, I can see down the road but things, particularly signs, are a bit blurry. Up close, I cannot read the bicycle computer mounted on the handlebars without my glasses. The sooner I can read a sign; the sooner I can relay that information to Tracy. She cannot see the signs within about thirty degrees to our front because my helmeted head is in her way. I use the bicycle computer to determine our speed, but more importantly, the computer tells me how far we have traveled. Tracy's maps, which she can't read without her glasses, give her the distance from one turn to the next. If I cannot see the computer, I do not know how far we have gone.

In harder rain, it gets difficult for us to see and for motorists to see us. The rain stings our unprotected eyes and obscures our vision. It can even get hard for me to see the road surface ahead – think potholes. Bicycling 101 dictates that you never ride through a puddle because you can't tell how deep it is. I got flipped over my handlebars doing this once. Not cool! If I can't see the potholes, I can't avoid them.

We do not have fenders on the tandem. The rear rack, tent, and panniers protect Tracy from the road spray. The front tire, however, can kick up quite the rooster tail. The rain passes harmlessly under the tire at slower speeds. At higher speeds, the water clings to the tire and is thrown

Just another rainy day in Montana

backward toward my feet. If we are going straight, the road spray is deflected by the bike's downtube and my feet stay mostly dry. But if I turn the front wheel at all, the spray hoses my feet and my socks get soaked. I hate it when my socks get soaked!

At higher speeds, say twenty miles per hour or faster, water thrown off the front of the tire causes a rooster tail like the one formed behind a fast-moving speed boat. This rooster tail can hit me right in the chest with muddy water, trashing everything. Finally, if the rain gods are particularly angry and we have a strong headwind, the rooster tail will actually go higher and bend back farther, hitting me right in the face. Besides not being able to see, I usually get road grit in my mouth that I am often spitting out hours later. Fun, right?

Tracy usually fairs a bit better than I do in the rain because she is somewhat protected when she hunkers down behind me.

In cold rain (less than 70 degrees) things become more extreme. The first problem is my hands start to get cold. If they get cold enough, I lose dexterity and it becomes difficult to shift and brake. We carry glove liners for riding in colder temperatures, but they quickly get soaked in the rain and provide little warmth. As soon as I start to loose dexterity, it becomes unsafe to ride and we have to stop, find shelter, and warm up. As extreme as this may sound, there is an even bigger problem we need to guard against. Hypothermia!

According to the Mayo Clinic: "Hypothermia is a medical emergency that occurs when your body loses heat faster than it can produce heat, causing a dangerously low body temperature. Normal body temperature is around 98.6 F (37 C). Hypothermia occurs as your body temperature passes below 95 F (35 C).

When your body temperature drops, your heart, nervous system and other organs can't work normally. Left untreated, hypothermia can eventually lead to complete failure of your heart and respiratory system, and to death.

Hypothermia is most often caused by exposure to cold weather or immersion in a cold body of water. Primary treatments for hypothermia are methods to warm the body back to a normal temperature."

Signs and symptoms of mild hypothermia include shivering, dizziness, hunger, nausea, faster breathing, trouble speaking, slight confusion, lack of coordination, fatigue, increased heart rate. Moderate to severe hypothermia is indicated by shivering, although as hypothermia worsens, shivering stops and the victim may experience clumsiness or lack of coordination, slurred speech or mumbling, confusion and poor decision-making, such as trying to remove warm clothes, drowsiness or very low energy, lack of concern about one's condition, progressive loss of consciousness, weak pulse, slow, shallow breathing. Hypothermia can occur in temperatures as warm as 70 degrees.

Tracy and I have learned through experience that if we dress properly (bike shorts, tights, bike jersey, fleece jacket, wind jacket, gloves) and keep our breaks to a minimum so we don't cool off, we can usually ride for several hours at a time in 50-degree rain. It isn't fun, but we can do it. We have an acceptable margin of error assuming we dress appropriately and don't push our limits. In other words, if we have a problem, mechanical or otherwise, we can find or make shelter (set up the tent) and get warm before the situation becomes dangerous.

We have a huge safety advantage traveling as a team as opposed to a solo – each other. Tracy and I constantly monitor one another's physical and mental condition as we ride in ever more extreme conditions. "Are you good?" "I'm good." "You?" "I'm a little cold, but good for now." "How much water do you have left?" "I have two bottles left." "Are you drinking?" "Probably not enough, I'll drink some more now. Thanks." "Are you hungry?" "No." "When was the last time you had something to eat?" "I just finished a Cliff Bar." "What flavor? Ha."

After twenty-seven years of marriage, raising two children, and bicycling thousands of miles together, we know each other really well. If Tracy is struggling more than usual to read the map, I pay attention. Likewise, whenever I become a complete ass on the bike, I am either hungry, tired, cold, exhausted, or all of the above. It is time for a break.

Tracy

After lunch, we hop back on the bike with full stomachs and damp clothes. The rain has stopped, but it is still a cool and cloudy day. We are bicycling along Highway 37, which is located on the east side of Lake

Koocanusa. The views are amazing. The road is in great shape with a wide shoulder and very few motor vehicles. Bicycling on Highway 37 is like riding on a roller coaster. We have many climbs with long, rolling descents – fun. Although, this type of terrain tends to burn out our legs a bit.

We come around the bend at Holdup Gulch and see the longest, straightest, highest bridge I have ever seen crossing Lake Koocanusa. This is the only crossing of the lake in fifty miles. I can see why they have very few bridges crossing the lake; this one must have cost a fortune to build. We take a break at the bridge to eat a snack and snap some pictures.

We rolled into Eureka (population 1,037) and decide to stay at the Silverado Hotel after our long, wet day. I cannot wait for a nice, hot shower, and I head to the bathroom as soon as we get to the room. As I step into the shower, I slam my foot into the side of the bathtub and go down for the count. Crap! I think I broke the little toe on my left foot – great. Well, not much you can do for a broken toe, so I take my shower and limp out to Peter to tell him the news. We both laugh.

Day 14

June 14 - Eureka to Whitefish, Montana
60 miles (total miles - 785)
Cold and rainy

Tracy

We start the day at 9:00 a.m. with a steady rain (apparently, June is rainy season in Montana). No worries, we are dressed perfectly. We zip down our jackets on the uphills to stay cool and zip up on the downhills to stay warm.

The first part of our ride is on Old Highway – Tobacco Road, which is the original road connecting Eureka and Fortine (population 325), fourteen miles away. It is a great way for us to stay off Highway 93 for a while.

The views from Tobacco Road are great with a beautiful adjacent stream and cloud-covered mountains. As we bicycle around a corner, we come upon many cows walking down the road. It is not every day you get to share the road with a bunch of cows, and I reach up to turn on the GoPro camera. A few miles down the road, four cool old cars pass us, and again I turn on the camera for some prime video of the vintage Rolls Royce and Ford Mustangs.

Exiting Tobacco Road, we travel the rest of the ride on Highway 93. The road is fairly bicycle-friendly, but with the rain, wind, and fast-moving cars going by, it is not a very enjoyable part of our ride.

About twenty-five miles down the road, we see an extremely small diner, On The Fly Café. It only has two tables, but the patrons are friendly and the owner serves great food with an amazing sense of hospitality. We order giant cinnamon rolls, a latte for Peter, and tea for me. It is like being a guest in her home. We get many insights on the area from her and the patrons. Unfortunately, they cannot stop the rain.

Two miles down the road from the café, we take a right on Farm to Market Road – yeah. This is a quiet road with little traffic, although we do meet a touring bicyclist heading west. We stop to chat with the young man. He is literally shaking and tells us how terrible the road is going into Whitefish – our final destination. He explains the road is terrifying to bicycle; extremely narrow with lots of high-speed traffic, and the pavement is in poor shape. We wish each other luck and continue on our journeys. Peter and I agree it cannot be that bad and continue down the road. Unfortunately, six miles down the road, we take a right onto Highway 93 and are in for the ride of our lives.

> "Sorry the weather has been tough the last few days. It's hard to enjoy beautiful views in the rain, especially if you are wet and cold. Here's hoping for better weather!"
>
> ***- Barb and Tom***

Peter

The last four miles of Highway 93 into Whitefish are terrifying to bicycle – even with all of our experience. We haven't had much traffic all day, but now that we are closer to town the volume has increased dramatically. Everyone seems to have a big pickup truck and they drive really fast. The road only has two narrow lanes, and the edge of the asphalt surface is cracked and deteriorated, sometimes as much as three feet into the road. There is no shoulder. Deep ditches and steep walls edge the road.

I am forced to put the bicycle in the middle of our lane to find a ridable surface. With numerous short, steep hills and turns, it is almost impossible for overtaking motorists to see us until they are right on our rear wheel. There is nothing I can do to make us more visible and safer, and there are no other roads to Whitefish. Our best bet is to get off this piece of road as quickly as possible. Unfortunately, with a fully loaded tandem in these hills with rain-filled potholes, there isn't much we can do to go faster, no matter how scared we are. We feel like sitting ducks.

Tracy

We arrive in Whitefish (pop. 6,357), shaking slightly, at about 3:00 p.m. and decide on a hotel again to get out of the rain and warm up. The Stumptown Inn Super 8 isn't anything fancy, but after something warm to drink and a hot shower we are good to go. I am very careful getting in and out of the shower. Ha. We are hoping the rain will not be so bad tomorrow and we will be able to camp again.

We walk into town and hit the local Brewery, Great Northern Brewing Company. Dinner is down the block at the Buffalo Café. I have a hamburger and Peter has a buffalo burger. They are very good and definitely hit the spot after the long, cold ride. I am excited to get back to the hotel room to view the great videos from the day and put one up on my blog. Back at the hotel, I grab the GoPro camera to remove the SD card and discover the slot is empty – Oh, no. I forgot to put the card in the camera. It is still in the tablet. No video to watch.

Tracy's Blog

"Well, tomorrow is a special day and we want to wish all fathers a very happy Father's Day, especially our fathers (Gilbert Meisner and Paul Flucke) who we are not able to spend the day with. We love you both and will be thinking about you. We also want to wish Rod MacKenzie a special day and thanks for taking such good care of us during the first week of our trip!"

Peter

I don't tell Tracy, but I am really missing my girls tonight. Melissa is at graduate school in La Crosse, Wisconsin, and Alex is in Fiji taking part in a shark preservation program through Projects Abroad. I know they are both doing great, but they are a long way away. I'm sure I am more worried about them than they are about me. We should raise our children to leave home. Right?

Tomorrow we ride to Glacier National Park!

Day 15

June 15 - Whitefish to Essex, Montana
51 miles (total miles - 836)
Cold and rainy at the beginning of the day, stayed cloudy and cool, 50-60 degrees

Tracy

We wait to leave town until 9:00 a.m. because we are not planning to bicycle all that far and it is another rainy day. We also want to hit a bike shop to buy a couple of replacement water bottles and put a little more air in our bicycle tires.

Peter

Bike tires loose a little air naturally over time, a couple of pounds per square inch (psi) per day. If we let the tires get too low, it slows us down and they are more likely to flat if we hit a rock or a pothole, especially with the extra weight from all of our gear on the bike. We carry an emergency hand pump with us in case we have a flat, but the pump is very small and is only rated to 90 psi. We run our tires at 115 psi. It is a major workout for me just to pump up a tire to 90 psi. That pressure makes the bike rideable in an emergency, but it is way softer than we prefer. We avoid using the hand pump whenever possible. My kingdom for a floor pump.

Tracy

Little did we know that nothing is open on Sunday mornings in Whitefish. Oh well, off we go.

The first part of our ride is a bit rainy and cool, but on a nice, quiet road with little or no traffic. We have wonderful views of the Flathead River and mountains beyond. We make it to Columbia Falls in about an hour and meet an older local couple who are out for a Father's Day bike ride. Hey, us too. We talk with them for a while and then bike together to the city limits, where we continue on our own toward West Glacier. The ride to West Glacier has wonderful views of the snowcapped mountain peaks. We cross the Flathead River on a concrete bridge at a spot where rafting companies pick up their customers. We watch a boat come around the bend sideways – I am not sure that is the direction they want to be going.

The road becomes gravel on the far side of the bridge. Luckily, it is in pretty good shape and not too bad to ride. We come around a bend in the road and spot two touring cyclists taking a break. We stop and chat for quite a while. They are from Anchorage, Alaska – Pete and Deb. They are also biking to the East Coast. It is fun to meet them because we heard about them yesterday from someone at the hotel. (We often learn about riders ahead of us from westbound cyclists and other people we meet along the way. There is a kind of verbal telegraph among cyclists.) Deb and Pete tease us that we are known on route as "the tandem couple who just fly on the bike." They figured we would catch up with them soon.

> "Mike and Becky wish Pete a happy Father's Day. The downhill video was as exciting as the uphill video was exhausting. Proud of you both. We miss you."
>
> ***- Mike and Becky Nash***

We leave Deb and Pete and continue to West Glacier on our own, getting there about a half-hour later. The gravel only lasted for two and a half miles and it wasn't bad. West Glacier (pop. 227) is a small town located just outside Glacier National Park, separated by railroad tracks and the Amtrak station. We stop for lunch at a local café and have our first, and hopefully not our last, Huckleberry Ice Cream Float. One of our blog followers told us to make sure we get one, and boy is it delicious.

Peter wants a second one. I am hoping we can find them again. How have we missed these all of our lives?

As we eat, Deb and Pete stop in to check out the café and say hello. It felt good to know someone in a strange town. Could we be getting lonely?

Peter

Our plan since the inception of the trip has been to take the main Northern Tier route following the famous Going-to-the-Sun Road north from West Glacier through Glacier National Park into Canada. We even have our passports with us. Once in Canada, we will make a seventy-five-mile arc to the north, then east and re-enter the United States. The Going-to-the-Sun Road is an incredible feat of engineering. Its two lanes are literally etched into the side of the mountains as it rises from approximately 3,200 feet of elevation in West Glacier to 6,664 feet at Logan Pass and the Continental Divide. This will be the toughest climb we have faced so far. We are scared we might not make it, but are willing to give it a try.

There is a catch, though. Because of the character of the road and severity of the mountain winters, the road is closed and not plowed that time of year. It doesn't typically reopen, following annual snow removal heroics by maintenance crews, until the middle of June. As of several days ago, word was that there was only 100 yards of twenty-foot-deep snow left to be removed before the road would be reopened for the year.

If the road isn't open or we can't make the climb for some reason, we can always backtrack and take the alternate route through the U.S., which is much less steep and ninety miles shorter.

Tracy

Unfortunately, the Going-to-the-Sun Road is still CLOSED. Maintenance crews have yet to remove all the snow and figure it will not be cleared and open until June 21 – another week from now. So we must take the alternate route over Marias Pass (elevation 5,236 feet), which should still be beautiful, just not as big of a climb. We head out of West Glacier on Highway 2. It is a very narrow road with lots of traffic, especially near West Glacier. The road is busier than usual because the Going-to-the-Sun Road is still closed.

Peter

The road out of West Glacier is a paradox. The mountain air is fresh and clean, and the scenery spectacular. The two-lane road, on the other hand, is steep and narrow, with no shoulder and lots of traffic. It is almost impossible for overtaking vehicles to pass us without going into the oncoming lane – not a problem, unless there is an oncoming car. My

Peter does his best to take cover. Yet another reason to wear a helmet!

biggest fear is that someone will try and pass us, only to be met head on by a car coming the opposite direction. The passing vehicle would be forced to return to our lane to avoid the collision. With nowhere else to go, we will either be knocked off the road or squished into a cliff. There is an outside chance that a standard-sized car could pass us at the same time as a standard-sized car going in the opposite direction, but if one of those cars is a RV, and there are tons of them, we would never make it.

Some of the motorists following us hang back and wait for a wide spot in the road to pass. Unfortunately, most of them just try to squeeze past us. Why not? They won't get hurt if they sideswipe us! Seriously, this is a national park. Paradise. The rental RV drivers are the worst. They seem to have no idea how wide their vehicle is, or that their mirrors extend another foot or more to the side.

As we climb out of West Glacier, we are only able to go about eight miles per hour because of the steep grade, maybe six percent. Luckily, a kind soul is waiting patiently behind us in his RV and holding up traffic. This gives me plenty of room in which to operate. It is difficult to keep the bike going in a straight line at very slow speeds because of a lack of forward momentum. The bike tends to wobble from side to side as I fight to keep it balanced, and we take up a bit more room on the road than normal.

We enter a very narrow, blind curve like this. Hemmed in by a mountain on one side and a guardrail on the other, we are sitting ducks.

The road steepens slightly and the RV driver, for some reason, chooses this moment to pass us. As I try to shift into a lower gear, the bike throws the chain off the left side of the small front chain ring ("grannie gear") and it jams against the frame. We have no power and are at risk of doing some serious damage to the bike's drivetrain or even the frame if we keep pedaling.

"Stop! Stop!! STOP!!!" I yell to Tracy. Now, the last thing either of us want to do right now is stop, but we have no choice. We stop, dismount, and then run-push the bike forty or fifty yards uphill to a wide(er) spot in the road, where the traffic jam behind us can finally squeeze by. That was fun. Not!

We fix the chain, mount back up, wait for a big gap in traffic, and continue on our way.

Tracy

We make the final moderate climb of the day without incident. The weather has finally cleared and we are able to camp again.

We are staying at the Glacier Haven RV and Campground, six miles west of Essex (pop. 76) – out in the middle of nowhere. The campground is very well-kept and has the cleanest restroom and showers I have ever seen. We leave our bike at the campground and hoof it over to the registration building, which turns out to be a small store and café as well.

All of a sudden, our dinner plans change from canned tuna, noodles, canned mixed veggies and pudding, to shakes, burgers, and fries. The owners of the campground are very nice and register us without incident. Then they tell us this is their day off and that the café is closed. Bummer. Tuna and noodles it is. Our last hope is that they might sell us a couple of beers. Nope. They don't even have beer when they are open. Tea and coffee it is.

> "Congrats to Tracy and Peter Flucke on their cross-country trek. You can follow their progress and adventures at webikeetc.wordpress.com. Day 15 - 846 miles. Way to go you two!"
>
> ***- Mark Leland, via Facebook***

Back to our bike we go to set up the tent and make dinner. While we are waiting for our noodles to cook, the brother-in-law of one of the owners, who is visiting from Seattle, stops by our site. He brings two foldable lawn chairs and two cans of Olympia beer. He overheard us talking with the owners and had come to make our evening just a little more comfortable. We offer to pay him for the beers, but he won't take our money. He asks about our trip, we talk for a while, and then he wishes us a good night and a safe trip.

The couple from Alaska are staying here tonight also, and we have a chance to talk and get to know them a bit better. What a great evening.

It could be a cold night with the temperature predicted to drop to 40 degrees. Peter and I will have to snuggle to keep warm.

Day 16

June 16 - Essex to East Glacier, Montana
36 miles (total miles - 872)
Cold and wet when we started, but then it got a bit warmer and the rain stopped, 40-60 degrees

Tracy

It rained last night, but we were dry in the tent – still cold, though.

We leave the campground a little later since we are only bicycling thirty-six miles to East Glacier. The shorter ride has to do with the location of places to stop and the mountains. It was either go eighty miles with a mountain pass or shorter with a mountain pass. We decided on a shorter ride.

We begin the twenty-six-mile climb over Marias Pass and the Continental Divide (5,236 feet) a couple of miles down the road from the campground. We climb well today and arrive at the top two hours later. Not bad. We take a short break for a snack, take some pictures of a glacial waterfall, and then hop back on the bicycle to drop into East Glacier. The downhill is steady and gradual with amazing views of waterfalls and mountains in and around Glacier National Park. Just the mountain peaks are covered in snow. This must be the elevation where the Going-to-the-Sun Road is closed.

Tonight we are staying at Brownies Hostel and Bakery in East Glacier (pop. 363). A west bound cross-country bicyclist told us about Brownies and said it was a great place to stay, so we thought we would try it. East Glacier is small. There are only about twenty buildings in the whole town: the hostel; a two-pump gas station/car rental company with maybe three cars; two restaurants; a shop that sells nothing but spoons; a post office; and a few houses. I'm sure there is that proverbial "one horse" around here somewhere.

The hostel is an old two-story, wooden clapboard-sided building with a porch and a balcony. It looks like something right out of an old western, and word has it that it served as a brothel back in the day. The entire first floor is a bakery and small grocery store. There is a bicycling God! A stairway in the middle of the building leads to the second floor. Upstairs there is a common room with mismatched furniture that looks well-loved and very comfortable. Toward the back of the building is a long, narrow hallway where the bedrooms are located. There are men's and women's dormitories and several private rooms. We have a private room at the nominal cost of $40 per night. Everyone shares the men's and woman's restrooms and showers.

This is our first hostel. It is a great place to stay and we meet people from the United States and several other countries. Many are hiking the area, some bicycling, and several others are on their motorcycles.

After we are settled, we walk the three quarters of a mile down the two-lane road to Glacier Lodge, which we passed on our way in. It is cold and drizzling, but it is a short walk and with all our clothes on, we stay fairly warm and dry.

Peter

The lodge is situated in the southeast corner of Glacier National Park. It is a huge, beautiful, historic building built in 1913 for the Great Northern Railway. The sky-lit roof four stories above is supported by towering, 500- to 800-year-old, Douglas fir trees, thirty-six to forty-two inches in diameter. (The Doug fir is one of my favorite trees). At one end of the lobby is a giant fireplace that is kept burning constantly. The fireplace is so large we could easily walk right into it. It felt good to warm ourselves by the fire after our 40-degree walk from the hostel. There are two restaurants and 162 rustic rooms in the lodge.

Tracy

We wander around the lodge and run into the couple from Alaska who are staying there. We join them for a drink in the bar. Their plan is to spend the night at the lodge and get back on the road in the morning. The lodge is too expensive during the summer for most bicycle tourists to spend too many nights there.

We may take the day off the bike tomorrow and stay one more day in East Glacier. The weather is supposed to be terrible tomorrow – 40 degrees and hard rain. Yuck.

Peter

We walk back to the hostel and settle into the common room to take advantage of the Wi-Fi and get to know some of the other guests. Before I do anything else, I check the weather forecast for tomorrow and the next few days, as I do every night. "WINTER STORM WARNING for higher elevations." That doesn't sound good. What's "higher?" The forecast is for heavy rain the next two days in East Glacier and temperatures to drop into the lower thirties. Two feet of snow is predicted at 6,500 feet tonight, a mere 1,700 feet above us.

This isn't going to be rideable, at least not with any margin of safety. From our experience riding in 50-degree rain for the past several days, I know we just won't be able to stay warm enough, and safe, if we try to ride in what's expected. We decide to play it safe and see if we can get a room at the hostel for another night, just in case. I bop downstairs to the bakery and make a reservation for another night. No problem. We celebrate our deliverance from the inclement weather with something warm to drink and a Danish. I am good.

As we prepare for bed, it starts to rain like hell on the metal roof above our heads. We are glad to be inside, warm and dry.

Day 17

June 17 - East Glacier, Montana
0 miles (total miles - 872)
Rainy (pouring) and cold, 30-40 degrees

Peter

We are literally pinned down by the weather! Thank God we are not in a campground somewhere confined to our two-person tent. I love my wife but, honestly, maybe not that much. (Just kidding, sweetie.)

Yesterday, plan A was to eat lunch in East Glacier and then press on. After lunch, plan B was to spend the night at Brownies Hostel ($40 per night and over a bakery – mmmm). By this morning it has rained, hard, for twelve straight hours. The temperature is in the low forties and the forecast is for more of the same for the next twenty-four hours (winter storm warnings for higher elevations issued). Thus, plan C has become spending another night.

Now afternoon, it is still raining, even colder, and there is a reported four inches of snow in the pass we crossed just yesterday. At least we haven't gotten any snow here, yet. Plan D is now to stay here tomorrow night as well, and then head out the following day – come Hell or high water; maybe both.

We haven't left the hostel all day. We are getting to know the other guests well and loving life! No, really.

Tracy

We make good use of our day off the bike and run through the rain to do laundry at the laundromat next door. We meet a couple from Harpers Ferry, West Virginia, who have been in Glacier for about a week. They were able to explore the park before the weather became nasty and shared their experiences with us. They also told us to be sure to eat at least one meal at the lodge and to save room for dessert; their Huckleberry Bread Pudding is amazing.

Upon returning to the hostel, I ask the bakery staff for a box to pack up our beer glasses and other treasures, which need to be shipped home.

Tomorrow I hope we will be able to get to the post office. It will definitely not happen today – we got soaked just walking across the parking lot to the laundromat.

Day 18

June 18 - East Glacier, Montana
0 miles (total miles - 872)
Rainy (pouring) and cold, 30-40 degrees ... still

Tracy

We are spending a second day in East Glacier. It is just too cold and rainy to bike. We could ride if the temperature was warmer with rain or colder without any rain, but with the two together it is just not good to be out on the bicycle. We are concerned about being able to stay warm. Even trying to fix a simple flat tire could become dangerous quickly. I wonder how the Alaskan couple, Deb and Pete, are doing.

> "I'm ahead of you on the Northern Tier, in Circle tonight. A friend gave me your blog address. Amazing ride, isn't it? Be sure to wave when you blow by me. Safe riding."
>
> ***- John Wilson***

By late morning, we are getting really antsy. We were cooped up in the hostel all day yesterday. There is only so much reading, napping, and playing on the computer one can do. Not to mention that the internet is slow because all of the guests are trying to use it at once. It still beats being cold and wet. We are watching the radar and hoping the rain will let up so we can go for a walk and explore East Glacier later.

We finally decide to put on all of our clothes and go for it. If we get wet, we get wet. As Peter likes to say, "Underneath it all, we are all waterproof." The weather cooperates on our walk to the end of town, mostly. Just as we approach a small convenience store, the sky opens up again. We dash inside, glad to not be totally soaked. We grab a snack and a cup of something warm to drink, and watch the rain pour down on the gravel parking lot outside as we wait for the rain to let up. It doesn't. Ironically, our next stop is the post office next door, maybe forty yards away. We have our booty of beer glasses with us all packed up and ready to mail home. We have managed to keep them from breaking so far. I sure hope the United States Postal Service can do the same. We talk about making a dash for it, but it is raining so hard we will get soaked for sure. Finally, we just go.

The post office is small and a bit run down, but the older gentleman working the counter is very friendly and we get our package mailed without incident. We even dry out a bit.

The rain has mercifully let up some, so we head down the block to a small grocery store to get something for dinner. Wow, these prices are ridiculous. Almost $3.00 for a can of peas. We buy a few things so we can make dinner at the hostel, but we are seriously considering eating lunch at Glacier Lodge. We will walk right by the lodge anyhow; it cannot be much more expensive than buying supplies for lunch.

Lunch at Glacier Lodge is very relaxing, warm, and dry. I get the Huckleberry Bread Pudding for dessert and it is very good. The couple from Harpers Ferry who we talked to yesterday said we needed to try it. They were right – delicious.

Peter

Tracy loves bread pudding. Her grandmother, Goldie Wondrash, used to make it for her when she was a little girl. She always orders bread pudding when it is on the menu and then rates it. The lodge's Huckleberry Bread Pudding was a hit.

Tracy

The lodge is beautiful, and we get a great view of the mountains even with the rainy weather. It is amazing to see the amount of snow that has been added to the mountains since the storm started. We heard earlier that some additional roads have closed in the park due to the storm. Logan Pass is still not open and I am sure this storm will push the opening back even further.

Our plan now is to head out to Cut Bank (about forty-eight miles away) in the morning. If the weather is good and we are feeling good, we will head to Shelby, which is another twenty-two miles down the road. We need to get cruising and make up some miles due to our second day off the bike.

Peter is cleaning and checking over the bicycle to get ready to go tomorrow, and I am repacking our paniers. We are both excited to hit the road.

Day 19

June 19 - East Glacier to Shelby, Montana
73 miles (total miles - 945)
Cool, 40-60 degrees, light rain, overcast, tailwind

Tracy

After three days "stuck" in East Glacier due to the weather, we are finally able to get going again. We are up early and on the road by 7:00 a.m. The weather is cold, 40 degrees, with a light rain when we pull out.

Peter

We are using plastic bags in our shoes to cover our socks when we head out. The bags keep our feet dry, but more importantly, they keep the wind at bay and our feet from freezing – an old Wisconsin winter biking trick. We keep a stash of plastic bags on the bike just for times like this. Don't leave home without them.

Tracy

It feels good to be back on the bike and moving again. We head east on Highway 2 toward Browning, which is located on the Black Feet Indian Reservation, twelve miles down the road. We arrive in Browning about 8:00 a.m. and stop at a convenience store for a short break and a snack. I eye up the ice cream counter and see my favorite flavor – licorice. I have been searching for licorice ice cream since we started the trip and am very excited to see it. Unfortunately, it is too early in the morning and too cold for ice cream. Bummer.

We have our eye on Cut Bank, which is another thirty-four miles down the road. The weather is getting better, the temperature is going up, the rain is lighter, and the wind is pushing us along. The route is mainly downhill and we are cruising along. We get to Cut Bank very quickly at a massive average speed of nineteen miles per hour.

We stop for late breakfast at the Big Sky Café, which was recommended by a local I met at the gas station/convenience store we stopped at on the edge of town. We are talking with the waitress and she asks us where we are going and where we are from. An older couple at the table next to us is listening in and hears that we are from Green Bay. They (Kay and Nick) are also from Green Bay. In fact, Nick was a firefighter on the Green Bay Fire Department for thirty-three years. I tell him about working for the Village of Allouez and that I worked on the consolidation of the Allouez and Green Bay fire departments. He retired prior to the merger. Boy, it sure is a small world.

This is their first vacation in many years and they took Amtrak to Glacier National Park. Unfortunately, the train was held up for about thirteen hours due to the trains carrying fracking oil having priority on the rail lines. This is a big problem, especially in North Dakota where fracking is taking over the state. They finally got to Glacier National Park and could not enjoy the park due to the terrible weather. They decided to rent a car and head home. Not a real fun vacation.

The waitress tells us about a visit to the café from a bunch of Green Bay Packers football players last summer. She says about ten of them with their girlfriends and wives showed up for lunch on their way to Glacier National Park. She did not know who they were until a patron asked if she got their autographs. He then proceeded to tell her who they were. Just like home for us.

We are on the bike again and heading to Shelby (population 3,376). The ride is uneventful, but we do see several trains with numerous oil tanker cars. As we get closer to Shelby, we begin to see oil derricks everywhere and the roads begin to deteriorate. I am sure the roads are not able to hold up to the oil tanker truck traffic. We cruise into Shelby with a nice tailwind and only a bit of rain. We have many oil tanker trucks pass us as we bicycle to our hotel. Luck is with us and we get a room for the night; the hotel is almost full with employees who are working in the oil fields.

While doing laundry, I meet a young man from Paragon Geo Tech who is doing field testing to determine if oil is in the area. He says there definitely is and soon there will be more oil derricks near Shelby. The oil industry/fracking appears to be putting a lot of pressure on the area.

Tomorrow we head to Havre for our longest ride of the trip so far, 109 miles. The weather is supposed to be sunny, 70 degrees, with a 15-20 mph tailwind. Things are looking up.

Day 20

June 20 - Shelby to Havre, Montana
109 miles (total miles - 1,054)
Sunny and warm, 70 degrees, great tailwind of 20-plus mph

Peter

Apparently, today was payback for all the rain earlier in the week. It was sunny, warm, windy from behind, and full of firsts: first time over 1,000 miles on a bicycle tour; first time averaging 20.7 miles per hour for a day on a fully-loaded tandem; and first time over 100 miles in a single day on this trip. Wow!

This was a nice way to usher in (tomorrow) the first day of summer (longest day of the year) by hitting our two longest.

Tracy

The landscape has changed extensively – open prairie with rolling hills and small mountains in the distance. We are amazed by the number of trains we see and the number of oil tanker cars they are hauling as we travel across the country.

A mid-ride break is in order for lunch. We stop in Chester (pop. 847) for coffee and to eat our peanut butter and honey sandwiches, which we made at the free breakfast buffet at the hotel this morning.

Downtown Chester is small and there really is not much around. I see a woman heading into the library with her children, and I stop her to ask if there is a good coffee shop in town. She turns around and says, "Yes, in the library." Say what? So, Peter and I head into this cute little library, and sure enough, there is a coffee shop in the back. The librarian serves as the barista and she makes us both a great cup of coffee.

I ask her about the coffee shop and she says it has been open for about five years and they use the profits for library improvements and supplies. The coffee shop itself was built with the coffee profits, as were the new restrooms. Lighting and other amenities were updated as well. The coffee shop even delivers to local companies, schools, the hospital, etc. The librarian says they have a good business, being that they are the only coffee shop in town. What a great idea. I need a new book, and they have a book sale going on. I'm looking forward to starting my new book tonight.

We have started to see prairie dogs. There are hundreds of them running around in the grass and into their burrows near the road. They are very fast. We had one keep pace with us as we traveled down the road at thirty-five miles per hour. Unfortunately, several have not been successful trying to cross the road – poor prairie dogs. They are cute little guys, but I am sure they can be very destructive.

> "It's just crazy how many people you stumble across that you have some connection with!"
>
> ***- Barb Florack***

We get into Havre with lots of time to spare and hit the local brewery – Triple Dog Brewing Company. We actually get to the brewery early and have to wait about an hour for them to open. That is alright because it gives us a chance to relax and catch up on the local news. The brewmaster arrives promptly at 4:00 p.m. and invites us and another party in for a beer. We try the Dumpster Diver Stout and laugh at the name. It is very good.

Peter

Dumpster Diver Stout, how appropriate. Sitting in front of the brewery in our grungy biking clothes, in need of a shower, with all of our worldly positions hanging off our bicycle, it is easy to see how a passerby might think we are surviving on whatever we can scrounge. In truth, there is sometimes a very fine line between being a self-supported bicycle tourist and being homeless.

Tracy

We meet a nice young couple and the husband's father at the bar and chat with them for a long time. The couple is from Reno, Nevada, and the father from California. They are in town for the wife's twenty-year high school class reunion. She grew up in Havre. They give us some helpful tips, including how to pronounce "Havre" (as in "have-'er", not "Favre" as in Brett Favre, the former Green Bay Packers quarterback). They are very kind and buy us our beers. (Maybe we do look homeless.) We enjoy visiting with them and continue to be amazed at how kind everyone is. It is truly amazing. Score one more pint glass for our collection.

We are staying in a local campground this evening. It has showers, laundry and Wi-Fi - what else could we need? The campground host gives us a site close to the restrooms, laundry, and store. As we are setting up the tent, we see sprinkler heads and move the tent closer to the wooden fence to stay away from a potential soaking. Who knows when they will come on? We are the only tent campers and everyone that walks by us looks twice.

The campground is adjacent to Highway 2, so we are glad we have a site located at the back of the campground away from the road.

We climb in the tent after dinner to finish our blog and Facebook posts. I even have time to read a few pages of my new book. As we settle in, we notice the ground is shaking and we can hear a rumbling noise behind us. What is going on? The shaking and noise continue as we drift off for the night.

Peter

Looking forward to tomorrow. Same weather forecast!

Day 21

June 21 – Havre to Malta, Montana
93 miles (total miles - 1,147)
65-75 degrees, sunny with a nice tailwind to push us along

Tracy

I just have to know what was going on behind the fence next to our tent last night, so I stop in to the camp store to ask. The clerk explains that the only diesel locomotive repair facility for 300-plus miles is located behind the fence. Trains are repaired 24/7 and frequently idle while waiting for service. Now I know why we slept like babies last night – free massage and white noise.

Today we are riding to Malta. This will be an easy day of navigating for me because we will travel on Highway 2 the whole day. We hit road construction just east of Havre and have to travel on a gravel road for several miles. Luckily, the road is rideable, but it does slow us down.

The majority of the ride today is on the Fort Belknap Indian Reservation. Our travels through the reservations are done with caution due to the feedback we have received from locals and other cyclists. We are told to avoid staying overnight on the reservations and keep moving along.

The reservations have some beautiful areas, but you can surely tell how poor the Native Americans are and how much they are struggling. It is not uncommon for locals to see us and ask where we are going, and then warn us to be careful. We can tell it is hard for them to talk about it. They do not want to appear prejudiced, but at the same time, they do not want us to be naïve and get into trouble.

Peter

We are not paranoid, but we do elevate our level of awareness in hopes of avoiding any potentially bad situations. This is unfamiliar territory to us.

We were asked countless times as we prepared for the trip if we would be carrying a gun for protection. Frankly, this just isn't who we are. As a former law enforcement officer, I am highly trained in the use of firearms, but I am comfortable traveling without one. Assaults of bicyclists are very rare, so we felt our odds were good to begin with. The weight of a gun, like all of our equipment, was a consideration. "Do I really need this?" Also, with no way to carry a gun on my person, it would need to be stored in one of our panniers, making it difficult to reach in an emergency.

Theft of the gun was a concern as well. We wouldn't be without options, though. Because we are traveling together, we present a much less inviting target than a single traveler. We are both in good shape and able to run, or fight, if necessary. I wrestled in high school, hold a black belt in karate, and am a former Pressure Point Control Tactics Instructor. Tracy can be just plain nasty if really pushed.

Finally, and most importantly, we have a plan. We have a code word that I can use to tell Tracy to run or fight. As scary as this sounds, not having a plan is even worse. In over 16,000 miles of unsupported bicycle touring, I have never, not once, even considered using our code word. On the contrary, we have constantly been surprised by the kindness of the complete strangers we meet.

We are truly in Big Sky country now, and love it – the tailwind doesn't hurt. We often travel for five, ten, even twenty miles without seeing a human being or a man-made structure. The road is smooth, the terrain treeless and gently rolling. With my uninterrupted view, I am mesmerized by the patterns the wind makes in the seemingly endless wheat fields. There are virtually no crossroads to disturb the ebb and flow.

Judging time and distance out here is difficult for me without looking at the bike computer. We are not accustomed to the wide-open spaces. With not much else to do for hours on end, I start to pick a spot in the distance and guess how far away it is and how long it will take us to get there. At first, I am often off by miles. But with practice, I get pretty good at it. Once, I guessed an anomaly in the distance to be twenty miles away. I am only off by half a mile. The anomaly is a homestead with trees planted around the house. Civilization.

Tracy

We stop at the one and only convenience store in the little town of Dodson (pop. 124) for a snack. The store is very run down and most of the shelves are empty. The owner, an elderly man, tells us his business has been dying for the last several years. He explains there are no longer any small family farms in the area. All of the farms are now owned by corporations, 10,000 acres plus, and farmed by a couple of laborers using gigantic farming equipment. Also, the oil boom to the north has pulled workers away and ruined the area. He tells us that he no longer has the farmers coming in every morning for coffee and a snack, and the oil fracking has decreased the number of cross-country cyclists as well as the number of other travelers because of all the trucking and other negative things going on in the area. He has owned the business for many years and will probably end up having to close it soon.

We continue on to Malta and stay at a local campground, which is right – I mean right – on the railroad tracks. This area is known as the Hi-Line region because the Great Northern Railroad came through in the 1880s. Many of the towns along this route, including Malta, sprung up as supply points for area farmers. Highway 2 closely follows the railway. We have the pleasure of meeting two cross-country cyclists at the campground.

Kyle is a single twenty-something from Portland, Oregon, heading to Minneapolis, Minnesota. His arrival at the campground is definitely a wild one. Peter and I are just finishing dinner when Kyle rolls in. He flies into the campground with his hands in the air, yelling, "I just rode the farthest ever on my bicycle." We clap and congratulate him. He precedes to dig into his bicycle pack and pull out a fifth of liquor. He takes a slug from the bottle and offers it to us. Peter and I each take a pull and hand it back. Kyle tells us he rewards himself each day after completing his ride with a small drink and slugs down some more. I offer him some dinner, which he readily accepts and sits down to eat with us. During dinner, we learn more about Kyle and enjoy his great sense of humor and outlook on life.

As we are cleaning up from dinner and Kyle is getting his tent set up and organized for the night, Mark rolls in. Mark is about our age and from Fargo, North Dakota, where he works at a university. He has been bicycling across the country for several years along the Northern Tier Route and is completing the last section this summer. Mark is a seasoned bicyclist and makes a sedate arrival. After Mark gets his tent set up and has a shower, we all sit down to get to know each other better.

Because Mark is heading west, he is able to provide Kyle and us with lots of information on what we will encounter soon. He explains we need to be aware as we cross the reservation and to stay in Wolf Point at the RV park on the west side of town. He also tells us to stay on Highway 2 and not turn right onto Highway 1 as shown on the map, thirty miles west of Wolf Point. He says Highway 1 is isolated and not a good place to be.

Tomorrow morning, Mark will head west while Kyle, Peter, and I will be heading to Glasgow or Wolf Point. Kyle is for sure going to Wolf Point. Peter and I are debating on where we want to end. Wolf Point is a 124-mile ride and Glasgow is sixty-four miles. We will see what the weather and wind are like and make our decision tomorrow. The logistics concerning the Indian reservations are making it an even tougher decision.

When the trains come through, which they do all night, at times I think they are going to go right through our tent. There must be a state law that all campgrounds in Montana must be located between a highway and railroad tracks. No worries, we are getting lots of sleep. I guess fatigue can override anything.

As we are laying in our tent, Peter looks at me and says, "Do you smell that?" I smile and say, "Yes – marijuana?" We both laugh and figure it must be Kyle having a smoke before bed.

Day 22

June 22 - Malta to Wolf Point, Montana
124 miles (total miles - 1,271)
65-70 degrees, sunny and a nice tailwind

Tracy

I ask Kyle if he was smoking pot last night. He grins and says yes, it is his medical marijuana and he can legally smoke it. I am not sure he can legally smoke it in Montana, but whatever. Kyle is on the road before us. We hope we run into him again. He is planning to ride all the way to Wolf Point, so he wants to get an early start. Still not sure if we are going to stop in Glasgow or go all the way to Wolf Point, we are a bit less motivated to hit the road than Kyle.

We make it to Glasgow in good shape and stop for lunch. The weather looks good and we decide to do the extra sixty miles to Wolf Point. This will be our longest ride of the trip so far. Thank goodness for the tailwind. We take off after Kyle.

The route has lots of beautiful long, rolling hills with great views, but we pretty much just put our heads down and go for it. The tailwind is great and keeps us moving along. Although, the last fifteen miles to Wolf Point are a bit tough with the tailwind shifting to a crosswind.

All our riding from Glasgow is in the Fort Peck Indian Reservation. The only place to stay, according to our map, is Wolf Point. There is one

RV park on the west end of town and it allows camping. As we near Wolf Point, we look for the campground. All we see are fields until we come across a dilapidated old motel with a few fire rings and picnic tables in the front yard. Could that be the campground? Unsure, we continue east toward town.

> "I am reading your blog on a regular basis and enjoying it much. Your descriptions of Glacier National Park are bringing back many fond memories of our family trips."
> ***- Bob Fresen***

When we get to the outskirts of Wolf Point (pop. 2,621), we stop at a gas station for a snack and directions. We have several locals come up to us and ask where we were staying. They tell us to not stay in the city park as it is not safe. They say the best place to stay is at the RV park, back where we just came from. As we are leaving the gas station, we see Kyle cruise past. We give chase, catch Kyle and bike into town together. We all need groceries and dinner. We find the grocery store and decide to leave Peter with the bikes and our gear while Kyle and I shop.

Peter

We lean our bikes up against the front of the grocery store. I position myself in front of the bikes with my back to the store so I can see the parking lot and who is coming and going. Old habits die hard. From where I stand, I can see past the parking lot to the city park beyond. It is your typical small town, central-city park, but it is a mess. There are a large number of dirty and otherwise unkempt individuals, mostly men, loitering in the park. The majority are holding small brown paper bags seemingly wrapped around something such as a bottle or a can. Many of the park guests stagger when they walk. Hmm. There is no way in hell we are camping there tonight.

As I stand here in my best "Don't mess with me or my stuff!" posture, an old piece of shit boat of a four-door car pulls into the parking spot just in front of me. The car doesn't look particularly out of place. There is a big, thirty-something guy driving, a woman of about the same age in the passenger seat, and two young kids in the back seat. The guy gets out of the car. He is dressed in a dirty, sleeveless, t-shirt, messy baggy shorts, and mud-caked old tennis shoes which he is wearing like clogs. He slams the door and walks right toward me. Always feeling that a good offense is better than a good defense, I smile slightly, nod my head a bit acknowledging his presence and say, "Afternoon." He looks at me passively and nods slightly. He then walks to the right rear of his car, takes off one of his shoes and starts beating the crap out of the car's tire with his shoe.

I'm more than a bit concerned until I realize he isn't nuts; he is just knocking the mud off his shoes. Just breathe. With his shoes now mostly devoid of mud, my new friend walks to the front passenger door, lets the woman out, and hands her some money. She disappears into the store. Crazy guy looks up at me and starts walking in my direction again. "Where are you from and where are you going?" he asks. We strike up a conversation and he is a really nice guy. He lives on the reservation with his family and works for the Bureau of Indian Affairs. Interesting.

"What do you do for BIA?" I ask. He looks at me, considering. I offer that I am a pedestrian and bicycle safety consultant. "How did you get into that?" he asks. I look at him, considering. "I used to be a cop and a bike cop," I say. He smiles and says, I'm a narc (narcotics officer)."

"How's business?"

"Way too good," he says.

I ask him where the best place is to camp in the area. "Not in the park," he says.

"You think?" I say, smiling.

He agrees with the locals we met that the RV campground on the west side of town is the only place to stay. He tells me the owner of the campground is a great guy and a former Native American bail bondsman. "He will make sure nothing bad happens to you out there." According to my new friend, you have to look for trouble in Wolf Point, but in other parts of the reservation, trouble finds you. Good to know. The woman returns from shopping. The man and I say goodbye in the standard cop way, "Be safe, Brother."

Tracy and Kyle return from shopping and Tracy asks me, "How'd it go?" "I'll tell you later," I say and smile. We work our way back to what was in fact the "campground" with Kyle.

Today's mileage ties our longest tandem ride EVER. Too pooped to pop, Tracy refuses to do a lap around the campground parking lot to break the record! Wimp.

The campground is sketchy at best. The only building on the property is a dilapidated old motel that serves as the campground office, home to the campground owner and one other family.

Tracy

The campground is indeed very sketchy. There are men's and woman's showers, and I seriously consider not taking one after walking into the restroom/shower facility. They are filthy, but so am I. I really can't stand climbing into bed in this condition. Therefore, I decide to grin and bear it and take a shower. At least the water is warm. Peter also decides to take a shower; Kyle could not do it and stays stinky.

The shower facilities are located right next door to the family living in the motel. After eyeing each other up, we strike up a conversation. The teenage boys are very interested in our trip and have many questions for us. One of the boys says he would love to do what we are doing and get away from the reservation, but he doesn't have a bicycle. I tell Peter later I would love to send him a bicycle.

Another couple arrives at the campground later by car. They are from Somerset, Wisconsin. They are driving to Seattle, and then the husband is going to be biking back to Somerset. They are nice to talk to and we are able to give them lots of advice about the route. Too funny, again, it is a small world. Mr. Johnson was a fifth grade science teacher for our youngest daughter's college roommate, Natalie. He of course knows Natalie and her family.

Our stay at the campground is uneventful. Tomorrow morning we will head south, off the reservation. It is great to be riding with Kyle. He is a nice young man and adds a bit of comic relief and smiles to our trip.

Day 23

June 23 - Wolf Point to Glendive, Montana
108 miles (total miles - 1,379)
Cloudy and warm, 70-78 degrees, cross and slight tailwind

Tracy

We all start early in the morning, 8:00 a.m., for the long ride to Glendive. We are now leaving Highway 2 and heading south on Highway 13 toward the town of Circle. There are no services from Wolf Point to Circle, fifty-four miles away. Adventure Cycling changed their route a few years ago after the oil fracking boom began in Williston, North Dakota. This was due to the heavy oil truck traffic on Highway 2 and bicyclists saying they did not feel safe on the route due to the narrow road and increased traffic.

The fifty-three miles to Circle are tough. It is windy and the route is mainly uphill. We are pooped when we get to Circle and relax over a long lunch with Kyle.

Peter

We have been playing leapfrog with Kyle as we ride most of the morning. We are slightly faster than he is on the flats and much faster on the downhills. He usually smokes us on the uphills. Regardless of who is in front or the topography at the moment, when the other stops for a break, they are invariably passed in short order. It is rather comical and we make a game out of it and the miles fly by. On one long climb, Kyle hits it hard and passes us early, only to run out of gas at the top and stop for a break. Knowing we have him, Tracy and I pedal hard. As we streak by

Kyle, we laugh and simultaneously flip him the bird. He laughs.

To say we are pooped when we reach Circle is an understatement. We are flat out of gas (or carbohydrates as it may be). We are okay as we dismount and park our bikes at a restaurant for lunch. We even make it into our booth in good shape, but then our bodies shut down. After the effort of riding 124 miles yesterday, the excitement of Wolf Point, the hills and wind this morning, our tanks are on "E." Even after eating, relaxing and downing four cups of coffee, I really have to push myself to get back on the bike. This is rare.

Tracy

We hop on our bikes again and began the last fifty-five miles to Glendive. We are told by the locals that we will have a twenty-mile uphill climb to the Continental Divide, and then it will be downhill for the last thirty-plus miles to Glendive. We can do this.

Peter

This is a tantalizing climb. Shortly after leaving Circle, the view ahead opens up and I can see a gap in the mountains far in the distance. I presume this is the Continental Divide. We pedal toward the gap for the next hour and a half. Sometimes I wonder if we are really making any forward progress. Eventually, we make it to the Divide and are looking forward to the downward run. We should be good from here.

Tracy

We begin to head downhill and I ask Peter how fast we are going. "Twenty-five," he replies. Sweet. Then I feel the back end of the bike start to wobble a bit. Strange. All of a sudden, "BANG!"

Shit! Our back tire has blown out.

Peter

My first indication that we are in trouble is the "BANG!" I never feel the wobble – I'm probably too far forward on the bike. The bang is like a flash-bang grenade. I am stunned for a moment. Tracy screams, "Peter, Peter, Peter!" followed by, "We're okay, we're okay, we're okay."

I yell, "What? What? What?" as I put a death grip on the handle bars and fight the urge to slam on the brakes, knowing this will cause us to crash for sure. Because you steer a bike with the front wheel, a rear tire blowout is survivable. I force myself to relax. The back end of the bike is squirrely, but even with all of the extra weight on the bike, I still have control. I gently apply both breaks and, gingerly, start to steer us to the side of the road.

No back brake! Really? We're good. All I need is the front break; it will just take a little longer to stop. Safely stopped at the side of the road, I turn to my left and look back at Tracy. We both smile slightly and shake our heads. "Glad that worked out," I say.

Tracy

We inspect the bike and discover that the blowout destroyed the tire and the tube. No worries, we have all the supplies we need to fix everything. Peter begins to fix the flat after we take off all the bike bags and remove the tire.

He gets the new tire and tube on the rim and is using a CO_2 (compressed air) cartridge to fill the tube. The first cartridge leaks, blowing CO_2 everywhere, and does not fill the tire. The second one jams on the valve stem and Peter rips the inner tube at the stem getting it off. No worries, we still have two more inner tubes, but we are out of CO_2. So tube number two goes on and now Peter has to use the emergency hand pump to fill the tube. This is very difficult and it is impossible to get to the full tire pressure of 115 psi.

Peter

At this point, I am really pissed – mostly because I am afraid I will not be able to fix the tire. I am the team mechanic, for better or worse, and I feel a great deal of responsibility to keep us rolling. I finally recognize that I am yelling at Tracy because I am angry/scared, and I need not to do that. I tell Tracy to walk back up the road forty yards and, "Do anything. Just leave me alone!" (I'm sorry honey. I love you.)

Tracy

I walk back up the road, knowing Peter needs some space, and try to figure out what I can do to improve our situation. Just then, along comes a minivan with North Carolina license plates going our direction. As it passes I see that it has a bicycle rack with a bicycle on the back. I think, "Maybe they have a floor pump." I wave my arms frantically. The van slows, pulls a U-turn in the middle of the road, and comes to a stop on the shoulder across the road from us. I cross the road to talk to the driver. I explain our situation and ask if they have a floor pump.

The van contains a family: mom, Mandy; dad, Russ; and their teenage twin daughters, Mary Bowen and Anna Teer.

While Peter pumps up the tire with Russ, Mandy tells me they are from North Carolina and Russ is biking across part of the country from east to west. He is doing the same trip we are, but in stages over several years. Mandy and the girls are sagging for him. Russ actually bicycled to Wolf Point today, but after Mandy and the girls checked out the area, they decided to drive back to Glendive for the night. Mandy says she just

Peter works on fixing our blown tire shortly after crossing the Continental Divide. Luckily, it was a nice day and we were about to experience yet another random act of kindness.

was not comfortable in Wolf Point and felt they would be safer staying another night in Glendive. I am glad they made that decision, otherwise we would not have crossed paths.

We put everything back on the bike and are ready to hit the road again when Russ asks if we want them to take any of our gear to town. We hand them our tent. Russ also offers to reserve a hotel room for us. Yes, please. Before leaving, Russ hands Peter a couple of CO2 cartridges – he has a box of them under the rear van seat – and gives Peter his cell phone number. They turn around, wave, and are gone. We are alone again.

This amazing family is our "random act of kindness" for today.

Peter

I check the bike over one more time before we pull out, only to discover that the rear brake doesn't work. Upon further inspection, I discover that when the rear tire exploded, it went with such force that it dislodged one of the brake shoes. I didn't know that could even happen. The brake shoe is hanging by a cotter pin – useless, unless I can get it back in place. I have every tool I need to fix the bike, except the pair of pliers I need to pull and replace the cotter pin. Screw it. We still have the front brake and the rear (auxiliary) brake. I can make that work. We will just get the brake fixed in Glendive tomorrow.

Tracy

We continue on our ride, all downhill thirty-five miles to Glendive. It is an easy ride with a nice tailwind, although we are paranoid that the tire will blow again. We even stop once just to check that everything is really okay.

The phone, which is mounted on the bike's top tube just in front of me, rings and I answer it. It is Russ. He has reserved a room for us on his credit card at the Holiday Inn Express in Glendive. Great. Now all we have to do is get there.

We make it to Glendive, but not until about 6:00 p.m. (We left Wolf Point at 8:00 a.m.) We are tired, hungry, and oh so grateful. It has been a really long day on the bike.

We give Russ a call when we get settled in and cleaned up. He invites us to go to dinner with them, so of course we do. Our choices for dinner are a family restaurant or a brewery. That's an easy choice, especially after the day we just had.

During dinner, Mandy tells us that they ran into Kyle at a grocery store in town. Again, what a small world. Kyle was worried about us and waited for us at several places along the route. They told him we were fine and just had a back tire blow out. He was relieved.

We have a great dinner and enjoy getting to know them better. They are truly caring people. This family is one to model. They provided us with help and companionship when we most needed it. They even pay for dinner.

We return to the hotel for a good night's sleep, anticipating a much-needed day off the bike the next day. We are pooped and eventually realize why. We have been on the bicycle for five straight days and averaged over 100 miles per day – 507 miles total.

Day 24

June 24 - Glendive, Montana
7 miles (total miles – 1,386)
Beautiful, 65-75 degrees, sunny and windy

Tracy

After a leisurely breakfast at the hotel, we head out to run errands. Grocery shopping is first on our list, and while heading to the store, we bicycle past the laundromat and see a familiar bicycle parked outside. We can see Kyle inside doing his laundry and go in to say hello. We are excited to see each other, and after hugs we tell him our story about yesterday and he tells us his.

He camped at the state park last night where he hung out with a couple from Wisconsin who are also bicycling across the country. We think it is Karen and Alan from Madison, who are friends of a friend of ours. We hope we will meet up with them one of these days.

Kyle asks if he can use the shower at our hotel before he takes off for Medora, sixty miles down the road. Absolutely, and I tell him he definitely needs a shower. He agrees. I give him another hug and the room key. We continue on to complete our errands. I will miss Kyle and hope we will run into him again.

We spend the day in Glendive completing some necessary tasks including grocery shopping, laundry, lunch, and a coffee break. We also need to stop at Sb's Bicycle Repair for some supplies and to fix our back brake. After searching for about a half hour, we finally figure out that the shop is out of business. We hope Dakota Cyclery in Medora is still there.

We spend the rest of the day relaxing and getting ready to take off in the morning.

Chapter 5

North Dakota - A Windy State

June 25-30, 2014
Total Miles 538/1,924 total

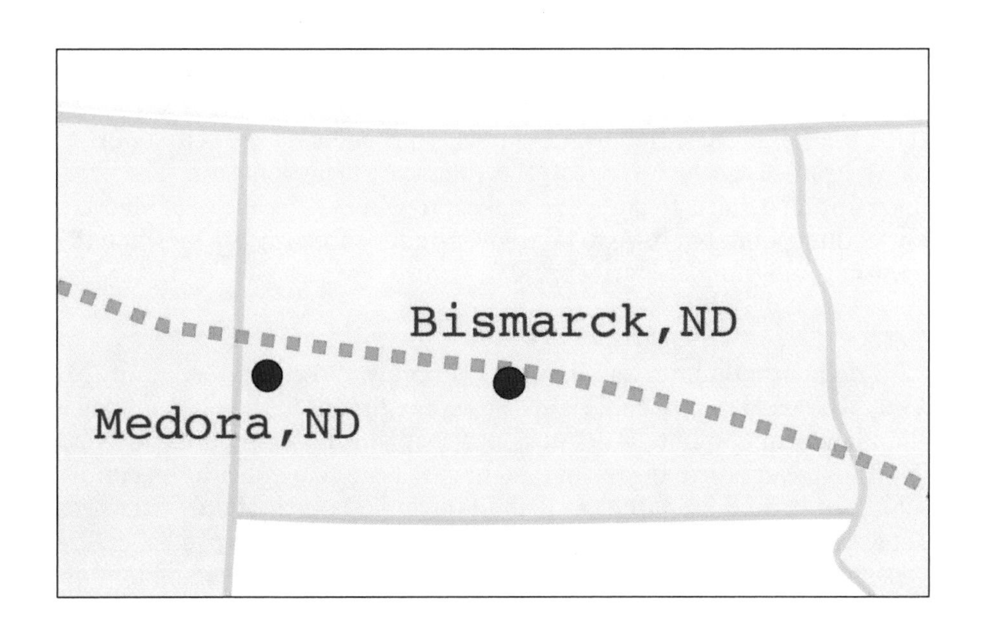

Day 25

June 25 – Glendive, Montana, to Medora, North Dakota
65 miles (total miles – 1,451)
60 degrees, cloudy, rain, storms and nasty headwind of 18-20 mph

Tracy

We leave Glendive early because we want to get to Dakota Cyclery in Medora, North Dakota, (sixty-five miles away) for repairs and supplies before they close. The route immediately puts us on Interstate 94 East. This is the first interstate bicycling we have done on this trip, and yes, it is legal to bicycle on the interstate in Montana. We are battling a nasty quartering/headwind (over twenty miles per hour) which limits our speed to between eight and ten miles per hour. We have to stop every forty-five to sixty minutes to rest.

Riding on the interstate is not as scary as it sounds. Although it is intimidating bicycling down the first freeway on-ramp. There actually is a nice big shoulder for us to ride on and the drivers are very good about changing lanes when they come upon us. The truck drivers are especially good. Ninety-eight percent of the time they move over if they can. The other good thing about being on the interstate is the sight lines are really good and drivers can see us from a very long way back. The first forty miles of our ride this morning is on Interstate 94 and battling the headwinds.

Upon entering North Dakota – yay! – our route moves to Old Highway 10. It is a great road to ride, quiet with little or no traffic. It is located in the Little Missouri National Grasslands. The headwind starts to diminish as we head east, which is great, but then the storm comes in. The skies open up and it starts to pour. We make it to within three miles of Medora, our ending point, but have to take cover under a freeway bridge when the lightning and thunder start. Crack!

Peter

I do not do thunder and lightning! Frankly, it terrifies me. Funny for a guy who used to be a cop, right? Being caught out in the open during a thunderstorm is my single greatest fear. I will do almost anything to avoid it. I have never been a big fan of loud noises. I can remember hiding under a blanket behind my father as a child during a Fourth of July fireworks show because I was scared of the noise. When our girls played soccer, I was always the first one into the car when bad weather threatened.

Then there is the park ranger thing. Apparently, park rangers are among the professionals most likely to be struck by lightning. We were always on the lookout. When I was a ranger, I spent countless hours warning boaters about approaching thunderstorms and imploring them to stay off the water until the danger had passed. Shortly after I left the profession, one of my partners called to tell me that two fishermen had taken a direct hit and had been killed while out in their boat. Rational or not, out in the open in a thunderstorm, I go right into fight or flight mode. Just get me out of here. I am fine if I am in a safe place or even in our tent if I have done everything possible to be safe. I can actually go to sleep.

We are safe from the lightning under the bridge, but we are soaked and the temperature has dropped significantly. To avoid hypothermia, we strip off the wet clothes from our upper bodies and replace them with dry clothes from our panniers. We have stopped the rapid heat loss from our bodies, but we are still cold. We snuggle under the bridge out in the middle of nowhere and things really aren't all that bad.

As we stand here snuggling under the bridge, an elderly couple pulls up next to us in their car and asks if we would like I ride into town. I immediately say, "No, but thank you." I thought our plan was to do the entire trip under our own power. Silly me. After the car pulls away, Tracy tells me she would have been okay with accepting a ride. Sorry about that, sweetie. (Not really.)

Eventually, the rain lets up. We peek out from under the bridge from time to time to see if the storm has passed. We can't really tell, because the sky is still covered in low, grey clouds, and hills to the west block our view of any approaching weather. After about forty-five minutes under the bridge, we decide it is safe to go despite continuing light rain.

We pull out from under the bridge and climb back up onto the interstate, thinking the worst is over. We make it about a mile and a half down the road toward Medora then, all of a sudden, flash, bang, the thunderstorm is back. Wide eyed, I quickly look around for anywhere to take cover. There is none. "Go! Go! Go!" I scream to Tracy. Despite having already ridden sixty-three miles and half frozen under a bridge, I slam my feet down onto the pedals for all I am worth trying to outrun the storm. We make it to Medora (pop. 112) just as the storm abates. I am a wreck.

We get to Dakota Cyclery just before they close. It is a pretty nice shop given the size of the town. There are three people working when we arrive: the owner, who is a woman in her upper forties; the mechanic, the owner's son; and a teenage boy who seems to be learning the ropes. Mountain biking appears to be more of their thing than road biking, which is understandable given where we are.

Our first order of business is to get the rear brake pad put back into place. The owner tells us her son will do that after he is done with another repair. We also need to replace the lightweight spare tire which is on the back wheel with a more durable tire and replace the two water bottles I left in a bar days ago. (It still pisses me off I did that.) The owner says she can help us with these items.

Unfortunately, the shop doesn't have a 700 x 28 mm, 115 psi, replacement touring tire. The closest thing they have is a 700 x 32, 90 psi, tire. That will work. I'm not real excited about putting the new tire on the back of the bike though. I'm concerned that with all the weight on the back, we might have a problem with flats. I decide to have them move the front tire to the back and put the new tire on the front. From experience, I know we can get approximately 1,500 miles out of a rear tire and more than twice that out of a front. The front tire should have plenty of life left in it.

My hands have been getting pretty sore lately from all the road vibration and horsing the loaded tandem around, even with my padded bicycling gloves. I change hand positions frequently, but it just isn't doing the trick anymore. My hope is that having the larger, softer tire on the front of the bike will give me some relief. If my hands get much worse, we will have to start riding fewer miles or take some additional days off so my hands can recover.

While we wait for the mechanic, the shop kid starts replacing and rotating tires. I have learned over the years that not all bicycle shops, mechanics and helpers are created equally. Consequently, I keep an eye on the kid as he works. The removal of the tires goes fine. When he installs the front tire on the rear rim, he has to ask me how many psi to put into the tire. It is admittedly a bit hard to read the "Inflate to 115 psi" printed on the sidewall. As he starts working on the front tire, I get distracted talking to the mechanic who is now fixing the back brake. When I return my attention to the kid, I ask him how much pressure he put in the front tire. He says, "115 psi, just like the back." "Holy crap!" Not cool! That tire is only rated for 90 psi. He could have blown it right off the rim. I walk over and immediately let 25 psi out of the tire. I am so glad I asked. Unlike a rear blowout, a front blowout almost always results in a crash.

The mechanic replaces the brake pad and adjusts the brakes. We grab two large water bottles, settle our bill, and are on our way. Relief.

Tracy

Medora is a cute little "Wild West" tourist town located right next to Theodore Roosevelt National Park. It is small, but offers a lot to visitors, including direct access to the park and the Maah Daah Hey Trail, a 144-mile mountain bike trail that connects the south and north units of the national park. It is just beautiful here with Badlands-type rock formations surrounding us.

Peter

We had planned to camp tonight, but with being soaked and needing to make repairs to the bike, we decide to check into a hotel. The only room we can find is $189 plus tax - ouch!

Peter wipes down the bike while keeping the hotel room neat and clean.

I ask the middle-aged desk clerk if she has a secure room where we can store our bicycle for the night. She says, "We have a bike rack outside." Tracy looks at me out of the corner of her eye, grins, and waits for me to explode. It has been a really long day and I haven't eaten lately. I say, "Could we just put it in our room?" She says, "No. We do not allow bicycles in the hotel." (Really. Every other hotel we have been in does – better hotels than this one.)

I lean into the desk in my muddy, smelly biking clothes and say, "I'm sorry, maybe you don't understand. We are bicycling across the country on a $6,000 tandem bicycle. It is our only means of transportation and I want to make damn sure it is here when we are ready to leave in the morning."

She looks around, smiles sheepishly and says, "Well, if you have a bike that is that expensive, I am sure you will take care of our room."

"We will. Thank you."

Tomorrow we hope to check out the park and more of the surrounding area, specifically Painted Canyon, which we have heard is worth a stop.

Still living the dream — at Teddy Roosevelt National Park.

Day 26

June 26 - Medora to Glen Ullin, North Dakota
90 miles (total miles – 1,541)
80 degrees, partly cloudy, headwind 8-10 mph

Tracy

We are still trashed from yesterday, but are loving the clean sheets on the king-sized bed in our really expensive hotel room. We linger a bit and finally hit the road about 8:00 a.m.

Peter

I do my daily pre-ride safety check on the bike while Tracy finishes packing. Tracy calls me the "safety guy." I think it's a compliment. As I check the newly repaired back brake, I discover that the knucklehead mechanic who worked on it yesterday didn't tighten the brake shoes. I could twist them by hand. The net result of this minor oversight could have been another blown rear tire. The brake pads would have likely twisted with normal use causing them to rub on the tire. Bang! Wow, am I pissed. I readjust and tighten the rear brake shoes and forty-five minutes later we are, finally, on the road.

Tracy

We were planning to check out Theodore Roosevelt National Park and Painted Canyon Visitor Center, but due to the late start we settle for a bird's eye view from Interstate 94 as we ride by. It truly is beautiful and I take some video of the view. We continue east on Old Highway 10 through Dickinson all the way to Glen Ullin. Old Highway 10 is a Scenic Byway and the sign has a buffalo on it, so we assume we will see some buffalo. We don't see any buffalo, although the view and road are very nice. A huge piece of the road has just been repaved.

The road is hilly and there is a moderate headwind, which is making the ride a bit of a slog. But by the time we get to Hebron (seventy-seven miles in) we still feel good, so we decide to continue on to Glen Ullin and a ninety-mile day.

We get into Glen Ullin (pop. 807) at about 6:30 p.m. and find our campground. We again meet up with Pete and Deb from Alaska. We have not seen them since East Glacier. We share our adventures over a six-pack of Leinenkugel's Summer Shandy, brewed in our home state of Wisconsin. It sure tastes good after a long, hot day.

Deb and Pete tell us about leaving East Glacier in the rainstorm. They did not get as far as the next town, Browning (twelve miles away) before needing to take cover. They were cold and soaked. The only shelter they could find was an abandoned silo with a small office next to it. They took temporary cover in the silo, but knew they needed to find a cleaner place to spend the night. Luckily, Deb must have been a thief in a former life and was able to jimmy the lock on the office door with a credit card. Impressive. That is where they spent the night. Not ideal, but much better than the silo. Now I really think Peter was smart to insist we stay in East Glacier to sit out the storm.

Unfortunately, the campground does not have any showers or laundry, so we go to bed stinky. Yuck. We experience our first thunderstorm while camping during the evening. Everything comes through the storm okay, with only a few minor drips in the tent.

Day 27

June 27 - Glen Ullin to Bismarck, North Dakota
63 miles (total miles – 1,604)
Warm and partly cloudy, 70-80 degrees, slight headwind, 5-8 mph

Peter

Last night we truly tested the sea worthiness of our ship, or our tent as it may be. The word in the campground was severe T-storms after 1:00 a.m. The word was right. The storm hit with a vengeance. Wind, rain, thunder, lightning, we got it all. We didn't sleep much, but through it all, we stayed warm and dry – albeit somewhat ripe for the lack of a shower.

We are on the move early. Packing up when everything is wet isn't fun. Hopefully we will be able to dry things out tonight. We are excited to get going because we have a date with a couple from Warm Showers in Bismarck (sixty-three miles away). Warm Showers is an online community where people offer to host touring cyclists. They have offered us a warm shower, clean bed and dinner. Yes, please!

Tracy

After the storm last night, we decide to eat breakfast at the convenience store in town since there isn't anywhere dry to sit here at the campground.

We get on the road by 10:00 a.m. and ride the first twelve miles on Interstate 94. We could ride on Hwy 139, but rumor has it that road is in poor shape and gravel in many places. Deb and Pete decide to ride Hwy 139 (they have wider tires on their bicycles) and we head off to Interstate 94. The ride isn't too bad except for the hills and a headwind again. We are getting used to it. We have our second (rear) flat about twelve miles out. This time, a metal wire went through the tire and about a half inch into the tube. Peter finds the wire, removes it, and puts in a new tube.

This tire change was much less eventful than our first one, except for the compressed air adapter shooting into the middle of the freeway. Crap, now I have to run into the freeway to retrieve it. I wait for a big gap, dash out, and grab it.

We get off the interstate in New Salem and run into Deb and Pete. They said Hwy 139 was not too bad. We tell them about our half-hour delay to fix our rear tire. They figured something happened, because otherwise we would have been way ahead of them.

We begin traveling on the newly paved Scenic Byway (139). Very nice.

We get into Bismarck (pop. 61,272) and our first stop is the Laughing Sun Brewing Company. We are really looking forward to a good beer. It has been awhile since we have been able to hit a microbrewery. They have good beer and we meet three young men from Rice Lake, Minnesota, who are biking from Rice Lake to Spokane, Washington. They are fun to talk with (kindred spirits) and are having a great trip so far, as only three young men can.

> The Warm Showers Community is a free worldwide hospitality exchange for touring cyclists. Check out their website at https://www.warmshowers.org/

This evening we will have our first Warm Showers stay in Bismarck. Our hosts are Joyce and Ron Gerhardt. I am a bit nervous about our stay. Before we left on our trip, I completed the necessary paperwork and got us registered on the site. I told Peter I was not so sure I wanted to stay at some stranger's house, but it was probably good to have as a backup.

I checked the Warm Showers website three days ago, reviewed the hosts' personal page and reviews, and then sent messages to a couple of different hosts in the Bismarck area. The prospective host then checks our personal page and sends us a message letting us know if they are able to host. Both of the hosts responded that they could put us up for the night. We decided to stay with Ron and Joyce.

They are especially gracious hosts and provide us with a bed, shower, laundry, dinner, breakfast, and anything else we need. Kyle, the young man we have been biking with, is also here tonight. It is fun to hang with him again. We have been having a great visit and will miss Kyle when he takes off south tomorrow to meet up with his friends.

Ron and Joyce have been Warm Showers hosts for many years. They really know what a cyclist needs, being cross-country cyclists themselves. They take a picture when we arrive and ask that we write in their guestbook before we leave. Dinner is amazing and definitely fills us up. After dinner, Ron and Joyce have to leave to watch their daughter play softball, but before they go, they show us how to use the washer and dryer and tell us to make ourselves at home. When they get back, it is banana splits for everyone – yummy.

Day 28

June 28 – Bismarck, North Dakota
0 miles (total miles – 1,604)

Peter

It is raining like hell outside when I wake up. This worries me, because we have only arranged to stay with Ron and Joyce for one night and I really don't have a plan B. Maybe the rain will clear out later. I dress quietly in my street clothes and head to the kitchen. Joyce told us last night that she would put the coffee pot on a timer. I can smell coffee as I enter the mostly dark kitchen. I find the coffee pot and pour myself a cup. Looking out the window I discover it is raining so hard that the visibility is almost zero. It is not safe to ride in this, even with our florescent jackets and lights.

As I stand there looking out the window, I hear Ron somewhere behind me say, "I bet you would like to stay another day." I turn to face him. After letting me stew for just the right amount of time, Ron smiles, laughs quietly, and tells me we are welcome to stay as long as we need to. He reassures me this is not a problem at all. He says they have had Warm Showers guests stay as long as five extra days due to weather or mechanical problems.

I tell him we will stay for a while and then make a break for it when the rain lets up. It never does. I assure him we will leave promptly tomorrow morning. He couldn't care less.

Tracy

Kyle decided to take off in the rain, and after hugs and good wishes, we bid him farewell. We watch him leave and he is totally soaked by the end of the driveway. We head back inside to spend the day catching up and getting to know our hosts better. About three hours later, Ron's phone rings. It is Kyle. He is soaked and has a mechanical problem. Ron and Peter jump in Ron's truck and head the thirty miles down the road to rescue him. They fix Kyle's tire and he decides to continue.

Ron and Joyce continue to be extremely gracious hosts. They have plans with family this afternoon, but leave us with the run of the house. After they leave, we discover a note on the kitchen island and a set of keys. They have left us the keys to their second car. We are welcome to use it to run errands. Really? Who does this? What amazing people.

Later in the day we have a chance to meet their son, Tom, daughter-in-law, Brenna, and their grandson, when they come over for dinner. We enjoy meeting them, and the conversation about North Dakota and the

Our wonderful Warm Showers hosts, Ron and Joyce Gerhardt. Friends forever!

oil fracking was interesting. Dinner is delicious and definitely fills us up for our anticipated long ride tomorrow. Special thanks to our first Warm Showers hosts, Ron and Joyce. What a great experience for our first Warm Showers stay. Now I cannot wait for the next one.

Peter

Ron and Joyce serve us banana splits for dessert, again! We are now officially Warm Showers fans for life. Ron is a huge Green Bay Packers football fan, so we are hoping to someday host them in Green Bay and return at least some of their kindness. What a world!

(We finally did it. We invited Ron and Joyce to come to Green Bay and stay with us in the fall of 2015 and go to a Green Bay Packers game. Unfortunately, their schedule wouldn't allow them to make the trip. Everything finally worked out, though, in 2016. They made the two-day drive to Green Bay in early November and stayed with us.

We took them on a tour of Green Bay and even got them a double-top-secret tour of a neighbor's "basement," which is really a Packers museum featuring original lockers, signed footballs, helmets, you name it. Our neighbor is one of the official scorekeepers for the Packers and helps run the scoreboard for home games – a job he inherited through marriage. I see Randy leave his house three hours before every home game to get set up. His knowledge of the Packers is amazing. Ron and Randy hit it off immediately. Ron and Joyce saw the Packers play the Baltimore Colts that Sunday. It would have been a perfect weekend if the Packers could have managed a win. After the game, I received a text message from Ron's son, Tom, thanking us for helping Ron check an item off his bucket list. It was truly our pleasure.)

Day 29

June 29 - Bismarck to Little Yellowstone Park
(near Enderlin, North Dakota)
157 miles (total miles – 1,761)
Sunny and warm, 70 degrees
Extremely strong west wind 20-30 mph, great tailwind

Tracy

We get going early because we are thinking that with the predicted strong tailwind we can really put the miles in today. Little did we know that today would be epic! We start the ride by going off route a bit at the recommendation of our host, Ron.

Peter

The official Adventure Cycling Association route has us going south out of Bismarck, then east, then back north, before finally heading east to finish the day. This route will have us battling a nasty crosswind right out of the gate. At least the wind will be pushing us into the road when we head south with a west wind. When we turn north, however, the wind will be trying to push us off the road. We will almost certainly crash if I can't stop the front wheel from leaving the pavement.

Ron, being intimately familiar with bicycling the area, has suggested we go east out of Bismarck on Interstate 94 for approximately sixty miles before dropping south on Highway 30 for eighteen miles, and then getting back on route and heading east on Highway 46. This way we will only have one section of crosswind and it won't be trying to push us off the road. Ron says Highway 46 is the longest, straightest, and flattest uninterrupted section of road in the United States. Sweet!

Tracy

Ron's reroute is a great idea and allows us to make good time early on. With the tailwind and us heading due east out of Bismarck, we are able to travel between twenty-eight to thirty-five miles per hour along Interstate 94. We are flying!

We stop for a break at a rest stop on 94. As we are relaxing and enjoying a snack at a picnic table, a man comes up to us and asks if it is legal for us to bicycle on the interstate. We explain that it is in Montana and North Dakota, because frequently there is no other option. He then asks how fast we were going. He is amazed by our speed and how long it took him to catch up with us. He wishes us luck and continues on his way.

Peter

The eighteen miles we go south on Highway 30 are tough. The crosswind is so strong that there are one- to two-foot waves with whitecaps on the famous North Dakota Prairie potholes. Prairie potholes, or sloughs, are water-holding depressions of glacial origin. Most of North Dakota's wetlands are prairie potholes, which provide nesting and feeding habitat for migratory waterfowl and wading birds.

We are forced to lean into the wind, toward the edge of the road, to stay upright. I am constantly steering and counter steering to adjust for wind gusts. This constant back and forth is exhausting for me because of the fifteen pounds of weight in the panniers on the front wheel. Our progress is slow and we are forced to take breaks every six miles or so.

Tracy

We finally make it through the southbound section and are very happy to begin traveling east again. Just as we turn the corner, we see a couple of bicyclists on the side of the road and stop to say hello. To our surprise, they are Alan and Karen from Madison, Wisconsin, and we know them. Actually, we know of them. They are neighbors of a good friend of ours and one of Peter's bicycling education mentors from Madison, Arthur Ross. Arthur had told us they were also traveling the northern tier route and we have been hearing about them from other cyclists, but had yet to meet up with them. We talk a bit, then continue east on our own. With this wind, we are way faster than they are on their single bikes. We meet up again in the next town for lunch. After lunch we head out on our own again.

Peter

We have near-perfect biking conditions. The road is straight and flat with almost no traffic or stop signs. The temperature is moderate and the tailwind is insane. We are moving along at thirty to forty miles per hour now, almost without pedaling. It feels like we are being pushed along by the jet stream itself.

From time to time, I look down at the bike chain and Tracy asks what

> "Just pulled into a gas station in Sterling, ND, on a fully loaded touring bicycle wearing bicycling clothes and a helmet. Bought coffee, a Coke and donuts, and took them to the counter to check out. The clerk says, 'Any gas or diesel with that?' Really?"
>
> ***- Peter, on Facebook***

I am doing. I tell her I think the chain has fallen off. But, nope, it is right there where it should be. That's strange. There is no resistance on the pedals when we start pedaling again after coasting for a while, just like when the chain falls off. I finally realize, after much consideration, that we are simply out of gears. We are going so fast that when we pedal at our normal cadence of ninety revolutions per minute, there just isn't any resistance. This isn't uncommon on a steep descent, but I have never experienced it on a flat road with the tandem loaded. The riding is easy, but we almost get blown over every time we stop for a break, so we just keep riding.

By the time we call it quits for the day at Little Yellowstone Park (near Enderlin pop. 886), we have traveled a personal tandem record 157 miles. We spent eight and a half hours on the bike and averaged 19.9 miles per hour. We briefly consider riding another seventy-five miles to Fargo, but decide not to tempt fate. Epic!

Tracy

We spend the night camping with Karen and Alan at Little Yellowstone Park, which is located on the Sheyenne River. It is a beautiful campground in the middle of nowhere. Karen and Alan also had a great day of riding and put in 124 miles. I think it was their PR (personal record). Unfortunately, the campground does not have showers, so we wash off as much as possible in the river. Brrr. After the long ride, I think we will all sleep like logs.

Day 30

June 30 – Little Yellowstone Park to Fargo, North Dakota
75 miles (total miles 1,836)
70 degrees, sunny and windy
Great tailwind 20-30 mph from the west

Tracy

We bike with a great tailwind again today toward Fargo. Most of the ride is east bound, with only a smaller section going north. Yea! The ride is uneventful except for the fact that our legs are tired from our massive miles yesterday.

Peter

"The ride is uneventful," Tracy says. Really? This is proof once again that even though we are on the same bike, there can be a much different view and feel from the front than the rear. We only traveled north bound for six miles today, but that six miles contained one of the hairiest riding experiences I have ever had.

> "May the wind be always at your back!"
>
> ***- Barb Erb***

We had been traveling east bound on Highway 46 at between twenty-five and thirty-five miles per hour for quite some time when we turned north onto Highway 15. The road was good and there was very little traffic, but the crosswind kept trying to blow us off the road. It wasn't uncommon for us to catch a gust of wind from our left that would move us to the right three feet or more before I could straighten us out again. I was forced to ride almost in the middle of the travel lane to make sure I had room to maneuver so we wouldn't get blown off the road. There was no shoulder, just a white fog line.

I heard a truck approaching from behind us about three miles into this north bound run. With no oncoming traffic and taking the truck's wind blast into consideration, I only moved us slightly to the right to give the truck a little more room to pass. I was anticipating that the truck would block the crosswind as it passed, so I prepared to reduce our lean into the wind to avoid oversteering left into the side of the truck. That worked perfectly, and it was actually kind of nice to have the truck running next to us and blocking the wind for a few seconds.

Then it hit! As the truck pulled past us, we were smacked by a tremendous gust of wind that spilled off the back of the truck and knocked us hard to the right a good five feet, right to the edge of the road. By the time I could react, we were balanced on the four-inch fog line with nothing but ditch to our right. I twisted the handlebars as hard as I could to the left and hoped that the bike would respond. I could literally feel the bike frame bending beneath us as it tried to react to the severe input. Finally, the bike straightened up and I was able to steer "normally" back into the crosswind.

I was truly shaken and pulled us to the edge of the road and stopped for a couple of minutes to regain my composure. When I had my wits back, I told Tracy just how close we had come to crashing. I really don't think she fully appreciated how close we came. I had Tracy check behind us regularly for trucks for the last two miles of this northbound stretch. I fully planned to pull to the edge of the road, stop, and wait for it to pass if she saw one – live to fight another day. No more trucks came before we turned east onto Highway 16 toward Fargo.

The rest of the ride to Fargo was "uneventful," but now we have trees and the landscape is starting to look a lot more like home.

Tracy

We find a great bicycle trail at the western edge of Fargo (pop. 105,549) and follow it right into the city. The trail is very well-maintained and has some nice amenities to dress it up: benches, landscaping, flowerbeds, etc. It runs along the Red River, which is very high and in flood stage due to recent storms that have hit the area. We find our hotel, clean up, and walk the bike a couple of blocks to the downtown area to hit the bicycle shop, which is in an old train depot. Cool. We need air for our tires and want to explore the area. It really is a nice downtown with lots of restaurants, coffee shops, and small stores. We have fun exploring.

Our new friends from Madison, Karen and Alan, are also in town, so we go out to dinner with them. We have a great meal, lively conversation, and became even closer. It was a very nice evening.

Tomorrow we will be into Minnesota, land of Peter's birth. Our map gives us two choices from Fargo: head north and take the on-road Heartland Alternate to Bemidji and Walker, Minnesota, or take the Trails Alternate. Normally, trails are not a good idea for us due to our narrow tires, but all the trails are paved in Minnesota, so we decide to head south and east on the Trail Alternate.

Day 31

July 1 – Fargo, North Dakota, to Fergus Falls, Minnesota
88 miles (total miles – 1,924)
Cold – 50 degrees and rainy, slight tailwind

Tracy

Today we get up and going early because we know the weather will not be ideal, and it isn't. It is a day of getting soaked, drying off, and getting soaked again.

We stop in Fargo to eat breakfast and park our bike in front of the restaurant as usual. We eat and are getting ready to go when a young lady walks into the restaurant and asks us about our bike and our trip. She is a nurse from the local hospital and has just gotten off her shift. She is very interested in our trip and wishes us luck. She says that someday she would like to do the same thing. I hope she does.

It is nice to finally get into Minnesota, although it happens with no fanfare. No Welcome to Minnesota sign or anything. The roads are fairly quiet and have good shoulders to travel upon. If it wasn't for the rain, this would be a nice ride. Unfortunately, the weather just makes it tough. Also, Peter seems to be coming down with a cold and does not feel well. It is an even longer day for him.

Once we get to the outskirts of Fergus Falls, Minnesota (pop. 13,138), we are able to follow a bike path into the city. We are happy to be done for the day because we are cold and wet. It is nice to be back in beautiful Minnesota, despite the weather.

> "Our first day in Minnesota seemed to be about right for the Midwest this summer -- rainy and cold. The high for the day was 58 degrees and there was a cross-tailwind blowing at 12-17 mph. Then there was the rain. In a nutshell, we went through the full wash/dry cycle at least five times throughout the day. I am getting a bit tired of washing and lubing the bike and drying out gear, but otherwise, all is well."
>
> ***- Peter, on Facebook***

Chapter 6

Minnesota - Great Trails and Family

July 2-3, 2014
Total Miles 234/2,158 total

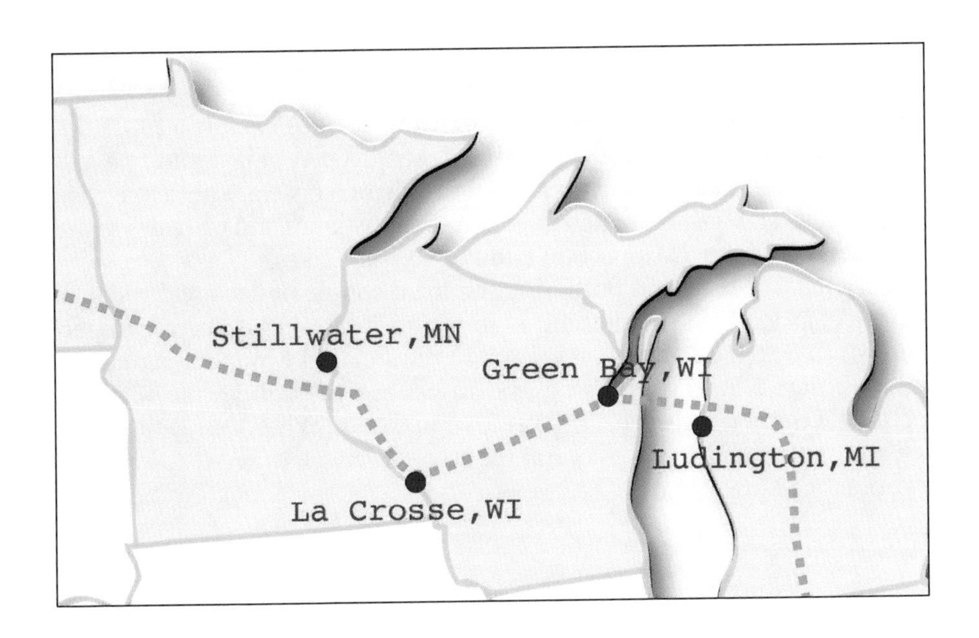

Day 32

July 2 - Fergus Falls to Bowles, Minnesota
112 miles (total miles - 2,036)
Beautiful, sunny and 70 degrees, slight tailwind

Peter

We hit the road early this morning to give ourselves the option of biking 112 miles to Bowles. This will allow us, by my calculations, to attempt biking 120 miles tomorrow to Stillwater, Minnesota, where we plan to meet our daughter, Melissa, and her boyfriend, Dillon, for the evening. They will drive over from La Crosse, Wisconsin. We really miss them.

> "Our first delay came when our quick breakfast at a small town cafe took 1.5 hours. I guess they had to kill the cow to make the hash."
> ***- Peter, on Facebook***

Tracy

Peter seems to be feeling better today. I think a good night's sleep is all he needed.

Today we will bicycle the Trails Alternate route, which has us on recreational trails all day. Our experience has been that Minnesota trails are typically paved and in good condition. We sure hope they are. We are looking forward to being off the public roads for the day and are hoping to make good time.

We start out on the Central Lakes Trail, which begins in Fergus Falls and runs approximately fifty-seven miles via Alexandria to Osaki, Minnesota. The trail is wide, fourteen feet, fifty-five miles long, paved, and well-maintained. It is a great trail to ride on so we are able to cruise right along. The trail is located adjacent to many lakes and provides some unbelievable views. (Minnesota, Land of 10,000 Lakes)

My left eye has been bothering me for a couple of days and today it is worse. It feels like something is in it and it is really sensitive to sun and wind. Not good when you are out in the sun and wind for six to eight hours a day. I have been using eye drops, but they do not seem to be helping. I think it is time to seek professional help. When we reach Osaki, we stop at the chamber of commerce so I can check to see if there is an eye doctor in town.

Peter

I am feeling like a very bad husband. I knew Tracy had a sore eye because she had mentioned it yesterday. We had even discussed what it felt like and had decided she probably had gotten a piece of gravel in it during the incessant rain. I looked at her eye, but didn't see anything. I was hoping she hadn't scratched her cornea, because I have heard that can be very painful. Her eye didn't look bad at the time and she wasn't complaining about it much.

For better or worse, Tracy has a very high threshold of pain and I have no idea just how much pain she is in. I really had no clue why she wanted to stop at the chamber of commerce other than to find out what was going on in town. When Tracy asked the receptionist if there was an eye doctor in town, I was shocked. "Why do you need an eye doctor?" I asked. "Is it really that bad?" Me, clueless.

Tracy

There isn't an eye doctor in town, but there is one sixteen miles down the trail in Sauk Center (about an hour's ride). Peter and I jump back on the bike and head to Sauk Center so I can get my eye checked. Thank goodness we are traveling on a trail today, because navigation is easy and I do not have to worry about reading the map. I ride to Sauk Center with my head down and my eye closed due to the pain.

We find an eye doctor at a clinic called Eyes on Main and the doctor is able to see me right away.

Peter

A middle-aged man walks into the lobby of the eye clinic while Tracy and I are waiting for her to be seen by the doctor. I just figure he is here for an appointment. But, instead of going to the receptionist's desk, the man walks right up to us and asks if that is our bike out front. I say that

The beginning of our ride on the Minnesota trails

it is and explain that we are bicycling across the country on the Northern Tier Bicycle Route. Tracy is having an eye issue and she is going to get it checked out. He welcomes us to town and asks if we have heard of the Lake Wobegon Trail and if we will be taking it out of town. We have, and we will be taking it to Bowlus right after Tracy's appointment, we hope.

He is very excited by this and explains that he is the head of the friends group for the trail. I tell him how much we have enjoyed the trails so far today and what great shape they are in. He is clearly pleased by this. The man says that we will love Bowlus and that we must stop at Jordie's Trailside Café for a meal and to say hi to Jordie.

Tracy

The doctor says I am experiencing a corneal erosion. According to the American Academy of Ophthalmology, "Corneal erosion affects the cornea, the clear dome covering the front of the eye. The cornea is composed of five layers. The outermost layer is the epithelium. When the epithelium does not stay attached correctly to the corneal tissue below, including the layer called the Bowman's layer or the basement membrane, this can cause a condition called corneal erosion."

Symptoms include: feeling of something in the eye; light sensitivity; blurred vision; watery eyes (particularly on awakening); dryness. The doctor really does not know why it happened, but gives me some drops to moisturize my eye and says that if it does not get better in five to seven days to get it checked again, because it can become infected and that would not be good. Unfortunately, the eye drops I was using actually were making it worse. They were to "get the red out" and were actually drying my eye out even more. Good thing we stopped.

"Our second delay was in Sauk Center, where Tracy spent 1.5 hours having a very painful corneal erosion (eye) checked. She got some eye drops and will be fine, but it was a long day for her."

- Peter, on Facebook

So now our navigator can't read a map and has trouble checking behind to see if any cars are coming. Not good. The eye feels like there is something in it and hurts and burns. It also looks great, red and swollen. At least I know what the problem is now.

***

Peter and I jump back on the bike and head for Bowles. We are now riding on the Lake Woebegone Trail. It is another great paved trail and at least fourteen feet wide. It is well-maintained and goes through many small towns that are definitely embracing the trail and have many amenities: restaurants, stores, public areas, etc., to take advantage of.

We leave the Lake Woebegone Trail at Albany and take the Lake Woebegone Spur to the Soo Line Trail, finally arriving in Bowles (pop. 290) just before 8:00 p.m. We head straight to Jordie's Trailside Café. The Café closes at 8:00 p.m. and we are hoping they are still open and serving dinner. There is literally no other food in town. Fortunately, they are open. There is one other couple in the restaurant and they are just finishing their meal, but the waitress seems happy to see us and takes our order. We made it.

We notice that the Café is decorated with all kinds of neat bike stuff as we start to unwind from our very long day. We feel very much at home here.

After a very good meal, we ask about camping. The waitress tells us we need to speak with Jordie and calls her over to our table. Jordie is a very nice woman and explains the camping options to us. We can stay in the city park across the road for $10 or in her pavilion for free. We decide to pitch our tent in her pavilion and are glad we do.

The pavilion is in the middle of a beautiful garden decorated with all manner of bicycle art, pictures, and sculptures. Jordie, her daughter, and mother developed and maintain the garden. Jordie is planning to add restrooms, a shower, washer and dryer in the pavilion, which will be great. For now, we need to use the restrooms in the park. Unfortunately, there are no showers.

Jordie gets it and is really providing a great place for cyclists in the area to stay. What a wonderful end to a very long day. Thank you, Jordie.

Day 33

July 3 - Bowles, Minnesota, to Osceola, Wisconsin
122 miles (total miles - 2,158)
Beautiful, 70-80 degrees, sunny and slight tailwind or no wind

Tracy

We got in to Bowles late last night and did not have a chance to explore the city. Therefore, this morning we took a quick tour. For a small city, they have a lot to offer including a restaurant, grocery store, and even a hair salon. The Bowlus Community Center, located adjacent to the Soo Line Trail, is a beautiful building with restroom facilities for trail users and rental availability for special events. Camping is allowed in the park. The community definitely welcomes trail users and the economic impact of the visitors is apparent in the community.

Peter

The ride yesterday to Bowles was beautiful and the trails were great, but the day was long and hard, especially with Tracy's eye issues.

Today may be a tough one for Tracy. Her eye is still very sore when she wakes up and the sun and wind make it worse. She probably won't see much on the ride because she really just has to keep her head down and look at the ground. Poor kid. I ask her if she still wants to try and ride the 120 miles to Stillwater. She does. My wife is a stud. It will definitely be a long day on the bike, but we both want to get as close to Stillwater as we can so Melissa and Dillon can come and meet us for the night. We are so excited to see them!

We push hard, but by 1:00 p.m. we know we won't make Stillwater today. We are just too tired. I had miscalculated. Apparently, Stillwater is a 140-mile ride from Bowles, not 120 miles. Wishful thinking, I guess. Change of plans – Osceola is about twenty miles closer (only 122 miles), so we call the kids and tell them to meet us there instead. An extra twenty miles at the end of the day is no big deal for them, by car. Ha.

Tracy

Peter is feeling really strong on the bike today, so he pushes hard and is able to get us as far as Osceola. The winds are really light, which helps a lot and allows us to cruise right along. The route is mainly through rolling farmland. Peter tells me it looks a lot like Wisconsin. I don't see much of it.

Peter

We roll into Osceola about 5:00 p.m., find the kids and grab a hotel room. After cleaning up, we head out to dinner. We have a fun night, but Tracy crashes early with an ice pack on her eye. Oh well, we will see the kids again in a couple of days in La Crosse, Wisconsin, and can catch up more then. It was so nice to be with family again.

Chapter 7

Wisconsin - Friends and Family

July 4-14, 2014
Total Miles 462/2,620 total

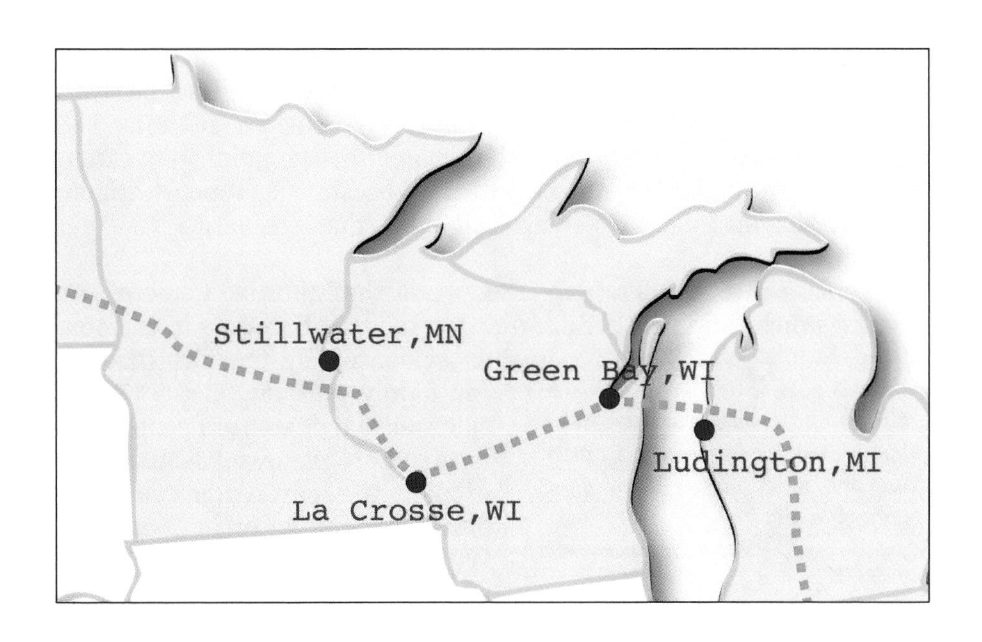

Day 34

July 4 – Osceola to Prescott, Wisconsin
53 miles (total miles 2,211)
70 degrees, sunny with a headwind

Tracy

We celebrate the holiday today by sleeping in until 9:00 a.m. Upon waking, Melissa takes one look at my eye and says, "Your eye looks terrible." It actually does feel better, but it's still sensitive to light. After showers and some bad hotel coffee and tea, we head out to breakfast with Dillon and Melissa. It is so nice to have the company. We give the kids big hugs after breakfast and finally pull out of Osceola about noon. A little late, but what the heck. It was nice to sleep late and take our time this morning. We may be getting a bit burned out after thirty-four days on the road and 2,211 miles on the bike. We are most definitely looking forward to taking a day off when we reach La Crosse in a couple of days.

> **Tracy's Blog**
> "Happy Fourth of July, everyone. We hope you have a nice day with friends and family."

Peter

We were hoping for an easy day today, but it is not to be. This part of the state is beautiful, but the wind is in our face and the hills along the St. Croix River are significant. There are countless streams feeding the river, many of which have cut deep ravines in the often-steep river banks. The road rises and falls sharply through this area. At one point we go from screaming downhill at 42 mph only to crawl back up at 5 mph – with me shifting like a madman to keep up – all in less than 100 yards. Now that was a hill.

We stop in Stillwater (pop. 18,225) on the Minnesota side of the river for lunch. Apparently Stillwater has the best fireworks in the area as evidenced by the fact that we can hardly walk the bike down the sidewalk in the throng of people that have gathered in town. There are lots of smiles to be seen. After a delicious lunch, we fight our way out of town. We are traveling on Chestnut Street and the map tells us to head south on Second Street. We turn right and are looking straight up a massive hill. We manage a few pedal strokes, but then have to bail off the bicycle and push in up the hill. This is the first time we have had to push the bicycle on this trip, and interestingly it occurs in Minnesota rather than the Cascade

> "The only easy day when you are bicycle touring is the day you quit, and we are having way too much fun and meeting too many cool people to quit."
> ***- Peter, on Facebook***

Mountains. Not too bad. With all the tourists in town, we had many people watching and encouraging us on the climb.

Tracy

We follow Highway 21, Stagecoach Trail, toward the small town of Afton and take a quick right into town after crossing Trout Creek. As we take our turn, I see a large group of people having what must be a Fourth of July party. A man comes out to the road and asks us to stop, so we do. He introduces himself and asks us where we came from and where we are going. He tells us he enjoys seeing all the cross-country cyclists that come by, invites us to his party, and tells us we can even pitch our tent and stay the night if we want. We thank him for his gracious invitation, but explain we need to put in a few more miles to get to La Crosse by the next day. What a nice man.

Pushing the bike up a hill for the first time on the trip in Stillwater, Minnesota

Peter

Our new friend from Afton tells us the ride to Prescott is going to be hilly. Boy, is he right. The twelve-mile ride is a tough one, with us crawling up many hills and screaming down the backside.

Tracy

As we are coasting down the first hill, I notice the chain bouncing and slapping me in the leg. Weird. It should not do that. I do not say anything to Peter right away because I want to wait and see if the same thing happens on the next hill. It did. I tell Peter and we stop to check it out. He is not sure what is going on, so we continue on our way. By the end of the day, my lower leg is covered with grease and dirt.

Peter

Our plan today was to go to a campground between Prescott and Red

Wing. However, we are out of gas and having some mechanical problems, so by the time we reach Prescott (pop. 3,746), after riding just fifty-three miles, we grab a motel room (definitely not a chain), get some dinner, watch the local fireworks, and call it a night.

Day 35

July 5 – Prescott to Fountain City, Wisconsin
84 miles (total miles 2,295)
Warm, 70-80 degrees, partly cloudy with a moderate headwind

Tracy

We leave the St. Croix River at Prescott and follow the Mississippi River south toward La Crosse on the Wisconsin side via Highway 35, The Great River Road. The Great River Road is a wonderful ride. The road has a wide shoulder, is not too busy, and the views of the Mississippi River and the towering bluffs are breathtaking. The ride is easy with only a few climbs early in the day.

The Adventure Cycling Association Northern Tier Route crosses back into Minnesota at Red Wing, but we decide to continue south on the Wisconsin side on Highway 35 instead.

Peter

We decide to go off route for two reasons: 1) We have ridden the Minnesota side of the river in the past, and 2) With Tracy's eye not 100 percent, we think navigation will be easier on Highway 35. This was a good choice all around.

Tracy

There are many small towns along Highway 35 to explore. It is nice to see the historic buildings, have people to watch, and services so close at hand. This is a far cry from some of the other parts of the country we have traveled thus far. We pass through the towns of Diamond Bluff, Hager City, Bay City, Oakridge, Warrentown, Maiden Rock, Stockholm, Lakeport, Pepin, Nelson, and then stop in Alma.

We have lunch in Alma and visit one of the massive Mississippi River Lock and Dams. While there, Peter starts talking to a couple of young men and their mother. They are from the area and we are looking for information about a new campground near Fountain City. It just so happens that Sleepy Hollow Campground, near Merrick State Park, is owned by the young men's uncle, and the mother has a campground brochure that she gives to us. Now we know where we will be spending the night. We head to the local coffee shop and have a drink and a treat, and then take off for the nineteen-mile ride to the campground.

Peter

The ride to the campground is uneventful, except for the bike's rear chain slapping Tracy's leg (hmm), one wrong turn, and the last 1.8 miles.

The chain slap is confounding me. There shouldn't be enough slack in the chain for it to hit Tracy's leg. It seems like the rear derailleur arm just isn't taking up the slack like it should. I check the spring tension, but it feels normal. The slap only happens when we coast. What the heck? Well, at least it's rideable. We may have to get it checked by a real bike mechanic when we get to La Crosse.

Highway 35 is a major state highway, well-marked and very easy to follow for the most part. Tracy's eye is still bothering her, so knowing the highway will take us right into Fountain City, we are not paying any attention to the map. Our general direction of travel is southeast. That should be good enough to get us there. I have become navigationally complacent and am simply following the highway straight ahead. There are few traffic lights or stop signs to contend with.

In the little town of Nelson, really just a crossroads, we come to a stop sign at a T intersection and a road coming in from our left. We stop, check for traffic, and pull straight through. The road looks the same. As we continue on, we enter a marsh. Interesting. We have been high and dry all day on the Wisconsin side of the river.

"Tray (a family pet name for Tracy), are we supposed to cross a marsh?" I ask. "I don't know," she says. "I'm not watching the map." "Okay." We continue on. The marsh seems to be getting larger. We pass a highway sign, "26."

"Where's Highway 35?" I think to myself. "Tracy, do you think we are on 35?" I ask. "I don't know," she says.

I think to myself that maybe the two highways run together here and we just haven't seen the sign for 35. We continue riding.

We have traveled about three miles since leaving Nelson. I checked our mileage when we entered the marsh and I got suspicious about our route. If we are off route, this little mistake will have cost us about six miles by the time we get back to Nelson, from here. Then I see it, the "Welcome to Minnesota" sign. Nuts!

We stop and pull out the map. Sure enough, Highway 26 heads south and crosses the Mississippi River back into Minnesota. Not our plan. We eat a snack, drink some water, and head back to Nelson. When we get back to Nelson, we figure out what happened. At the stop sign, Highway 35 takes a ninety-degree turn to the left while the road straight ahead becomes Highway 26. This is the first time the road has done this all day. My bad, I missed the sign. Lesson learned.

Highway 35 near where our campground should be runs along the edge of the river to our right and is almost at river level. This means there is no room for a campground on the river side of the road so the campground must be up in the bluffs somewhere to our left. But where? The bluffs are almost vertical as we get to the nineteen-mile mark (really the twenty-five-mile mark after I add in our six-mile navigational error). Finally, we spot a campground sign on the bluff side of the road at the entrance to tiny two-lane Waumandee Creek Road. I can't imagine where this road is going to go but straight up.

I turn onto the road and it immediately doubles back the way we just came. Really? Fortunately, it is relatively flat, for about 100 yards. Then we see another campground sign which tells us to turn right, straight up the bluff, onto Lower Eagle Valley Road. In our lowest gear (30 x 34), we climb as hard as we can at between 4-5 mph. The road's incline decreased a bit after about a quarter mile, but then it pitches up again. It does this three or four more times. Just when we think we are going to have to dismount and push the bike, the bluff splits and we are delivered to the entrance of a spectacular hidden valley with the campground on our left. No cars, no trains, bliss. This was a serious gut-buster, but we made it. We are invincible. Not.

Tracy

The campground is very nice, but very new and it looks like they are still working out some of the kinks. The gentleman (Rod) who owns and runs it is a retired farmer and has decided to turn some of his land into a family campground. The property has been in his family for four generations. He asks how we found the campground and we tell him about the chance meeting with his nephews in Alma. I am checking out the camp store for supplies while we are visiting and ask if he sells beer. He explains he does not have a license to sell beer, so we pick up a few supplies for dinner and head to our campsite. Before we leave, he tells us our site does not have a picnic table and invites us to come back to the office later and use the picnic shelter and table out front to make dinner.

We head to the showers, which are great, but Peter and I agree they probably will not hold up to the abuse they will get from the campers. The hardware in the shower building appears to be residential quality and is already failing. After our shower, we head back to the office to do laundry and make dinner.

We are in for a surprise when we enter the office. Rod called his wife at home when we were gone and asked her to bring over a couple of beers for us. We sit and talk with them for a long time about his new business. He explains that he has always wanted to run a campground and decided now was the time. He also tells us about the difficulties he had with his neighbors when he was going through the zoning process. Several neighbors did not want the campground and fought it. The town had no problem with the campground and gave him the approval to go ahead. He explains that he lost sleep over whether he should do it or not because he did not want to upset his neighbors. In the end, he decided to go ahead because it has always been his dream. Even in a small town, change can be difficult. We can see eagles riding the air currents down in the valley as we talk.

Peter

Today was a much better day than yesterday despite the ailing bike, getting a little lost, and that final climb.

Day 36

July 6 – Fountain City to La Crosse, Wisconsin
48 miles (total miles 2,343)
Warm, 80-85 degrees and sunny

Tracy

Today we are up early and get on the road by 7:00 a.m. We stop at the Kwik Trip convenience store in Fountain City for breakfast #1. Our plan is to bike eighteen miles to Trempealeau and meet Melissa and Dillon for breakfast #2 at the historic Trempealeau Hotel. Doubling up on breakfast has become common for us as we are finding we need the additional calories. We have been to the Trempealeau Hotel several times over the years. It is a great place for breakfast and right on the Mississippi River.

Our plan for the day and the ride are going well until we get into Trempealeau and discover that the hotel is no longer serving breakfast. Now what? Luckily, a local man is up and about and tells us to head south on Highway 35 and we will find the Mrs. Sippy's River Town Bistro on the edge of Trempealeau. The restaurant is owned and operated by the former chef from the hotel. We call the kids and tell them to meet us there instead.

This isn't the historic Trempealeau Hotel, but the food is very good and it is a nice place to relax and catch up. After breakfast, we give Melissa and Dillon most of our gear and beat feet for La Crosse (pop. 51,320), hoping to avoid more rain. We are only twenty miles away.

Peter

We have stripped our gear down to just the essentials for the short ride into La Crosse. The bike feels funny with so little weight on it, but it does make it a little easier to manage the ailing drivetrain. We adjust quickly and head for Onalaska, where we will ride the local bike trails to the University of Wisconsin-La Crosse, just a few blocks from Melissa and

Dillon's apartment. Tracy received her undergraduate degree (Recreation Administration) from UW-La Crosse, so she always enjoys being back on campus.

When we reach the outskirts of town, we discover that the trail we plan to take to Melissa's apartment is closed due to flooding. We have been getting a lot of rain. Neither of us is exactly sure how to get to Melissa's on-road from here. Time to Google Map it. Navigating the last few miles is a challenge, especially because the bike is getting worse and we really need a day off. We finally make it after Tracy learns a few new words from me. Sorry, honey.

We receive a very warm welcome from Melissa and our two cats (Mio and Grayson). All we have to do now is figure out how to get the tandem up to Melissa's apartment on the fourth floor. We are hoping it will fit in the elevator, and it does just barely. We have to lift the front tire up into the upper back right corner and put the back tire in the bottom front left corner. Perfect. I hope no one wants to get in with me. We will be off the bike tomorrow for some much-needed R&R and bike repairs.

Day 37

July 7 – La Crosse, Wisconsin
0 miles (total miles 2,343)
Warm, 80-85 degrees and sunny

Tracy

Today is a rest day and we are thoroughly enjoying our time off the bike. We have not had a day off for the past eight days and have traveled 742 miles, an average of almost ninety-three miles per day. No wonder we have been so tired (and a bit grumpy). We need a day off.

Melissa and Dillon's apartment is very small, one bedroom with a living/dining room and tiny kitchen. We are sleeping on the floor in the living/dining room. Tight for four people and two cats, but no one seems to mind and we enjoy our time together. We sleep in late and plan to spend the day hanging with Melissa and Dillon, doing laundry, playing with the kittens, getting the bike fixed, and other miscellaneous tasks.

Peter

Getting the bike's drivetrain repaired today is a priority. We pretty much are stuck here until we can get it fixed. Tempting. Luckily, Smith's Bike Shop is only a few blocks from Melissa's apartment and they open at 9:00 a.m. After breakfast, we limp the bike to the shop and wheel it up to the service desk, where we are met by mechanic Scot McCollum, who

I know. Small world. Scot has been involved with bicycling and bicycle advocacy in Wisconsin and Minnesota longer than I have. We are in good hands, if he has time to work on the bike. This is the busy time of the year in the bike business.

I describe the issues we are having with the bike and also tell him we are hoping to leave town tomorrow morning. He has another repair he is working on, but agrees to look at our bike as soon as he is done. We leave the bike with Scot and cross our fingers that it is nothing major and he can get it fixed yet today.

Scot calls me midafternoon to report both bike chains (the one that connects Tracy's pedals to my pedals and the one that goes to the rear cassette) are severely stretched and the cogs are worn. Not too bad. He thinks this is our problem and suggests we replace them all. I agree. This type of wear and tear is completely reasonable given the number of miles we have ridden and conditions we have been riding in, although I am not quite sure why this would make the chain slap Tracy's leg. Whatever. The bike's rear tire is worn, so I ask Scot to replace that as well. Scot says he will have the bike fixed by the end of the day. Hallelujah.

We walk back to the bike shop about 5:00 p.m. Not only does Scot have the bike done, but he has pulled the entire drivetrain and cleaned it in their industrial washer. "Can't put a new chain and cogs on a dirty bike," Scot says. Thank you, sir. The ride back to the apartment is silky smooth.

Tracy

We take Melissa out for dinner and then to the Pearl Street Brewery, where we score another pint glass. Dillon is working, so he can't join us. The day has been fun and relaxing. Tomorrow (Tuesday) we leave for Necedah and should be back home in Green Bay by Thursday. We will leave for Manitowoc on Monday to continue our trip to the east. We are looking forward to seeing neighbors and friends when we are home.

Peter's Blog

Tomorrow we start our push to Green Bay and home (Ashwaubenon) for a few days. If you are in northeastern Wisconsin and want to ride with us or just stop in to say hi, here is our tentative itinerary:

Tues. July 8, La Crosse - Necedah
Wed. July 9, Necedah - Custer
Thurs. July 10, Custer - Green Bay
Fri. July 11, open house, 1-5:00 pm, Angela's cupcakes for all, BYOB and something to pass
Sat. July 12, Green Bay
Sun. July 13, Green Bay
Mon. July 14, Green Bay - Manitowoc (S.S. Badger to Ludington, MI) with Tracy's parents

Day 38

July 8 – La Crosse to Necedah, Wisconsin
77 miles (total miles 2,420)
Nice, 70-75 degrees, partly cloudy with a good tailwind

Tracy

Today we leave La Crosse about 8:00 a.m. after breakfast and visiting with Melissa and Dillon. It was great to spend a couple of days with them and squeeze our kittens. Everyone is doing well and we all enjoyed our visit. Thanks for putting us up, Melissa and Dillon.

Sparta, Wisconsin
"Bicycling Capital of America"

Peter

It was hard to leave Melissa, Dillon, and our two cats this morning after a great rest day. Leaving their very tiny apartment did ease the pain some, though.

Tracy

The first thirty miles of our ride is on the La Crosse River State Trail. The crushed-limestone trail is well-packed and in good shape except for the trees that have been blown down across it in recent storms. We are forced to dismount and go around, or climb over, at least four downed trees. Luckily, we don't have to unload the bike. The ride is not too difficult, despite the unpaved trail and the trees.

We make it to Sparta, "Bicycling Capital of America," and stop for a second breakfast at Ginny's Cupboard, a favorite restaurant of ours. We reminisce that the last time we biked to Ginny's we were so wet from a rainstorm that Peter kept stealing napkins to blot the water out of his socks. It didn't help. Ha. The warm pecan rolls, coffee, and tea are delicious as always and are enough to get us to our next stop.

The next forty miles are on county roads and Highway 21. The county roads are great with little or no traffic, but Highway 21 is a bit of a challenge with lots of traffic, a rather small shoulder, and very narrow, shoulder-less bridges. Fortunately, we do not have to travel on the highway for too long and the motorists are good about going wide around us. We get into our home for the night, the St. Joseph Inn and Campground near Necedah (pop. 914), at about 3:00 p.m. Easy day.

We were planning to camp tonight, but there is a chance of rain and they have a small cabin available for a whole $8 more. We take it. The young man who checks us in says the cabin is pretty rustic (although it does have electricity, heat and air conditioning), and we will need to use the showers and restrooms across the road. We just laugh and tell him it will be fine and are excited to get it. This is our first cabin stay of the trip and it is very nice and comfortable. No need to set up the tent or pack it up wet in the morning from the rain which arrives at about midnight. I guess it is all about what you are used to.

> "Tracy, hope all is going OK with your eye. Take it easy and I will pray all will be OK. I feel so bad for you."
>
> ***- Judy Schroeder***

We have another pleasant surprise this evening when Chuck and Cleva Bickford show up for a visit just after we finish our showers. Chuck and Cleva are the parents of the wife of Peter's best friend from high school. Got that? They live in New Lisbon, which is only about twelve miles down the road. They have been following Peter's Facebook posts and knew we would be close to them. Cleva sent us a message last night to see if we could get together. We said definitely.

They offer to show us the sites and then take us out to dinner. Of course, we are thrilled to go. We have a nice evening and it is great to catch up with them. We haven't seen them in several years. Dinner is delicious (thanks for treating, Chuck) and the dinner company is even better.

My eye is much better. The eye drops have worked and the eye is pretty much 100 percent. I plan to go to our eye doctor when we get to Green Bay just to have him make sure all is well. Peter is very happy I can read the maps again and navigate.

Day 39

July 9 – Necedah to Amherst, Wisconsin
72 miles (total miles 2,492)
Beautiful, 70-75 degrees, sunny with a headwind

Tracy

We get up early and enjoy breakfast in our little cabin. It is nice to have a space to cook and a table to eat at. We are on the road by 8:00 a.m.

It feels good to be back in Wisconsin and have all the great county roads to bicycle on. I don't think we have had a car pass us for hours and the area is so beautiful, lots of farms and rolling hills.

The fifty-plus mile ride to Plover is good, but tough. The route we are taking east of the Wisconsin River does not have any towns to stop in to grab something to eat or drink, and we both bonk due to not eating enough. We are forced to take more breaks than normal to let our calorie-deprived bodies catch up with our effort. We truly should know better by now, but we just tried to keep going on Cliff Bars and PowerBars. Not quite enough. We also have been dealing with a tough (10-15 mph) headwind for the last thirty miles, which hasn't helped.

Peter

I don't think one day off the bike in La Crosse was enough for us to fully recover. Duh!

Tracy

We definitely need lunch by the time we reach Plover around 1:00 p.m. Luckily, there is a Chinese buffet in the strip mall, which has lots of food to fill us up. Pretty sure we eat our money's worth. We head next door to O'so Brewing Company after lunch and have a couple of beers. The beer is good, the brewery is fun, and of course, Peter has to buy another beer glass.

Peter

All of this is true, but Tracy left out the best part: the nap. Our plan for the day was to bike to Plover, check out O'so Brewing Company, bike to Amherst to check out Central Waters Brewery, and then head to our Warm Showers stay just a few miles away. Two breweries in one day, what could be better? What we didn't realize at the time was how hard the ride would be and that the O'so Brewery tap house didn't open until 3:00 p.m. Even after we replenished our calorie deficit (stuffed ourselves) at the Chinese buffet and bought more sunscreen, we still had a half hour to kill before the brewery opened. What to do? That's easy, take a nap.

The tap house bartender woke us up at 3:00 p.m. sharp. Yup, we were

The picnic table outside O'so Brewing Company's Tap House in Plover, Wisconsin, was just the ticket for a quick nap while we waited for the establishment to open for the day.

both out cold on the picnic table near the front door. Embarrassing? Who's to say? We sampled some great beer and bought a commemorative pint glass, as has become our custom. We are building up quite a collection.

We found out that Central Waters is closed on Wednesdays, bummer, so we point our bike to just south of Amherst and our second Warm Showers home stay. We reached out to Kris and Cathey about hosting us via email while we were in La Crosse. They responded right away that they would be happy to host us. We were going to be their first Warm Showers guests. They told us they wouldn't be home until 5:00 p.m., but we were welcome to arrive anytime in the afternoon. They said we could relax on their back deck and they would leave a cooler for us with drinks and snacks. Sounded good to us.

Kris and Cathey live in a beautiful home in the woods that overlooks a trout stream. They are not home from work when we arrive around 4:30 p.m., but the cooler full of all our favorite beverages and snacks is waiting for us on the deck as promised. (This is a trick we have adopted when we are hosts.)

Tracy

Kris and Cathey are very gracious and welcome us to their home with a pizza dinner on the deck. Kris is a veterinarian and has riding across the country on his bucket list. They moved from the city to this property recently and love the solitude. The only downside of the move was that their new king-sized bed wouldn't fit in the new master bedroom, so they had to put it in the very nicely finished basement, where we will be sleeping. Bummer for them, but great for their guests.

Day 40

July 10 – Amherst to Green Bay, Wisconsin
75 miles (total miles 2,567)
80-85 degrees, warm and sunny

Tracy

We are excited to get on the road this morning because we are going home for a few days. Only seventy-five miles to go. Unreal.

Our day starts with homemade scones, fresh fruit, coffee, and tea. What a great way to start a bicycle ride. The scones are so good we ask for the recipe. Many thanks to Kris and Cathey for making us feel so welcome.

Peter

Since we are off route again today, we are on our own for navigation. Between the awesome Wisconsin State Bicycle Maps, the Google Maps bicycle function, and our years of experience bicycling this part of the country, we are flying home like homing pigeons.

Tracy

Our route takes us again on several county roads and we enjoy the beautiful scenery and quiet setting. The route goes through Weyauwega, where we stop to visit with the city administrator and a colleague of mine, Patrick Wetzel. It is great to see Patrick and we have a nice visit. He has been enjoying his job and has lots of exciting things going on or in the works.

I noticed the chain hitting my leg again while bicycling to Weyauwega. Strange. We just put new chains and cogs on the bicycle in La Crosse.

Dried Cherry Scones

Ingredients

2 cups flower
4 teaspoons baking powder
½ teaspoon salt
¼ cup butter
¼ cup sugar
½ cup dried cranberries
½ to ¾ cup milk

Glaze

1½ cups powdered sugar
3-4 tablespoons milk
1 teaspoon vanilla extract or orange extract (optional)

1. Sift flower, salt and baking powder in a bowl. Cut in butter with fingers (or food processor or pastry blender) until mixture appears crumb-like.
2. Add sugar and cranberries.
3. Mix in milk a little at a time to make soft dough. Too much milk will make it too wet.
4. Pat dough into an 8-10 inch circle on a pre-heated baking stone or cookie sheet. Use large knife to cut circle into 8 wedges, but leave them touching on the pan.

Bake for 10-12 minutes in a 450-degree oven until toothpick inserted in thickest part comes out clean.

For glaze, mix ingredients together, adding milk until desired consistency. Drizzle over warm scones.

Evidently that wasn't the problem, or just part of it. I began to pay more attention to when the chain is slapping my leg. It appears to happen when we are coasting. I tell Peter that if we keep pedaling or if he shifts into the larger chain ring up front so the chain is tauter, the chain does not hit my leg. This works for a while, but then it becomes apparent we need to get the bicycle to a bike shop when we get back to Green Bay.

Peter

I am starting to think that the bike's free hub, on the rear wheel, is not completely disengaging when we try to coast. This is forcing the chain to go slack on the top between the rear hub and Tracy's pedals. The bike is quickly becoming a fixed gear tandem, where the pedals and rear wheel are tied directly together. We need to continue pedaling, at least softly, at all times to keep the chain from slapping violently. We can't coast, which is exhausting. Thank goodness we are almost home. I am really hoping that our mechanic, Jeff Wentworth at JB Cycle & Sport, can fix this. If he can't, we will have to replace the hub, which means completely rebuilding the rear wheel. We probably have enough time at home for Jeff to do this, but it will be expensive even if we can find the parts. This is a fourteen-year-old road touring tandem after all. Fingers crossed.

Tracy

From Weyauwega, we head to New London on County Road X, a beautiful road located adjacent to the Wolf River. There are a number of houseboats tied up to the river banks, which add to the river life vibe.

We stop for lunch in New London and Peter calls Jeff at the bike shop to let him know what is going on with the bicycle and that we will be bringing the tandem in for repairs. After lunch, we cruise right along – no coasting. I think we are both excited to get home.

About twenty miles from home, a couple of reporters and a cameraman from WLUK Fox 11 in Green Bay show up to take video of the rest of our ride into town. They are getting footage for a story they plan to do on our trip. It is difficult for us to look normal on the bike with the chain acting up, but we fake it for the cameras. When we arrive home (Green Bay pop. 104,779, Ashwaubenon pop. 17,777) at about 5:00 p.m., they interview us to complete the story. It is fun to have them along for the end of today's ride. (Here is the link to the story: http://fox11online.com/news/local/ashwaubenon-couple-rides-tandem-bike-across-country.)

Peter

It is both strange and wonderful to be home. I'm sure we are suffering from a combination of fatigue and culture shock. Having said that, after a couple days of rest, bike repairs, catching up with friends and paying bills, we agree that we will be ready to leave for Manitowoc, the S.S. Badger car ferry, Michigan, and the rest of our adventure. Tracy's parents will be joining us for the trip across Lake Michigan on the S.S. Badger.

Days 41, 42, 43

July 11-13 – Green Bay, Wisconsin
0 miles (total miles 2,567)

Tracy

We arrived home on Thursday evening, July 10, and will stay in Green Bay through the morning of Monday, July 14. It is nice to be home and sleep in our own bed. We drive the tandem to the bike shop on Friday morning as soon as it opens. We are anxious to hear what Jeff has to say once he gets the bike apart.

Peter

Wow, it is weird to drive our minivan after not driving for over a month. The car keeps wanting to hug the right curb. Maybe it is me. Ha.

Tracy

We have an open house on Friday night at our home, and several friends stop in to visit and hear all about our adventures. It is great to see everyone, but several of them do mention how thin we look.

We weigh ourselves this evening and discover we have each lost more than five pounds. We were ripped when we started the trip forty days ago, so five pounds is a lot for us. If we continue to lose weight like this, it could affect both our strength and our health. It is time for us to start upping our calorie intake.

Over the weekend we have a chance to visit with more friends, do laundry, pay bills, restock for the rest of the trip, eat up and, most importantly, relax. I also get my eye checked by my eye doctor. Everything is fine. The moisturizing drops should keep me going for the rest of the trip. Peter will start using them as well. Every two hours is the recommendation. Got it, sunscreen and eye drops. What next?

> ***Tracy's Blog***
>
> "Hope to see you tomorrow, Friday, July 12, at our house anytime between 4:00 p.m. and 9:00 p.m. BYOB and a treat to share. We need the calories!"

Peter

Jeff calls and reports the bike is good to go. The Hadley rear hub we have is very well-made, he says. It was just all gunked up on the inside from years of use (more than 25,000 miles). All it needed was a good cleaning. The hub should outlast the rest of the bike. Yes! We pick up the bike late Saturday and add a new pair of bike shorts and gloves each to our tab. Ours are trashed after over 2,600 miles of hard riding.

The friction, sun, and sweat are hard on our clothes, but drying them is even worse. We hang-dry them at home, but we usually have to machine-dry them on the road so we don't have to wear or pack them away damp. They get funky really quickly when wet. Jeff and Matt Bergeon, an employee at the bicycle shop, present us with a head light, tail light, and tire repair boot. They say we can have everything for free, but we have to promise to use the lights every day from now on. We agree and thank them for the gifts.

Tracy with her parents, Gilbert and Dorothy Meisner, prior to boarding the S.S. Badger ferry in Manitowoc, Wisconsin

Tracy

Although we enjoyed being home, we are both ready to get back on the road again come Monday morning. We are excited to take the S.S. Badger ferry across the great inland sea (Lake Michigan) to Ludington, Michigan, and visit my parents. It should be fun.

Day 44

July 14 – Green Bay, Wisconsin, to Ludington, Michigan
53 miles (total miles – 2,620)
Partly cloudy, 65-70 degrees, tailwind

Tracy

We get up early to head to the S.S. Badger car ferry in Manitowoc (about forty miles), where we will cross Lake Michigan with my parents to Ludington, Michigan. We are on the road by 7:00 a.m. We are excited to be on our bike again and don't want to miss the boat.

The ride to Manitowoc includes about twenty miles on the Fox River State Recreational Trail. This is the most heavily used trail in the state, but this morning it is deserted. The trail is in great shape and well-maintained (paved south to Greenleaf, then gravel). Thanks to Brown County Parks. (Peter was involved in the development of the trail, which was built in 2000.)

We have ridden on the trail so many times we can almost do it with Peter's eyes closed. Once we leave the trail, we travel east, up and over the Niagara Escarpment, on county roads that roll us through the countryside with little or no traffic. It is an easy ride because we are so familiar with the area and enjoy the route. Our legs feel pretty good, but it will take us a few days to get back in the groove.

Tracy

We arrive in Manitowoc at 11:30 a.m. and meet my parents at Warren's, a local restaurant. My parents grew up in Manitowoc (dad) and nearby Two Rivers (mom). We used to eat at Warren's when I was young and the place still looks the same. The food is good and fills us up before the four-hour ferry ride to Ludington.

We roll our bike on board the ferry for a 2:00 p.m. (CT) departure. The ride is fun and relaxing, and we have a great chance to catch up with my parents. We arrive in Ludington (pop. 8,078) at 7:00 p.m. (ET). We have made it to the Eastern Time zone and our seventh state. Only seven more states to go.

Mom and Dad's car cost $66 to make the crossing, while our tandem was only $6. Traveling by bicycle definitely has its advantages.

From the ferry, we "race" Dad and Mom the four miles to our hotel where we check in, clean up, and then walk next door to the Big Boy restaurant for dinner. Peter and I both grew up eating at Big Boy, but all of the restaurants in Wisconsin have now closed. This is a favorite stop for us. We are hungry (always) and glad to get a good, filling meal.

S.S. Badger Car Ferry

The S.S. Badger is the largest car ferry ever to sail Lake Michigan at 410 feet. She has provided a safe, fun, and reliable shortcut across the huge inland sea for more than 60 years. The S.S. Badger is a national treasure, offering a cruise experience that links us to an earlier time when a sea voyage was the ultimate travel and vacation adventure.

As the only coal-fired steamship in operation in the United States, the S.S. Badger operates on domestic fuel, and the company has an extraordinary commitment to maintaining a unique propulsion system that has been designated as a national mechanical engineering landmark. The S.S. Badger offers an authentic steamship experience unmatched anywhere else.

Text from the S.S. Badger's website

Chapter 8

Michigan - A Challenge To Travel Through

July 15-18, 2014
Total Miles 301/2,921 total

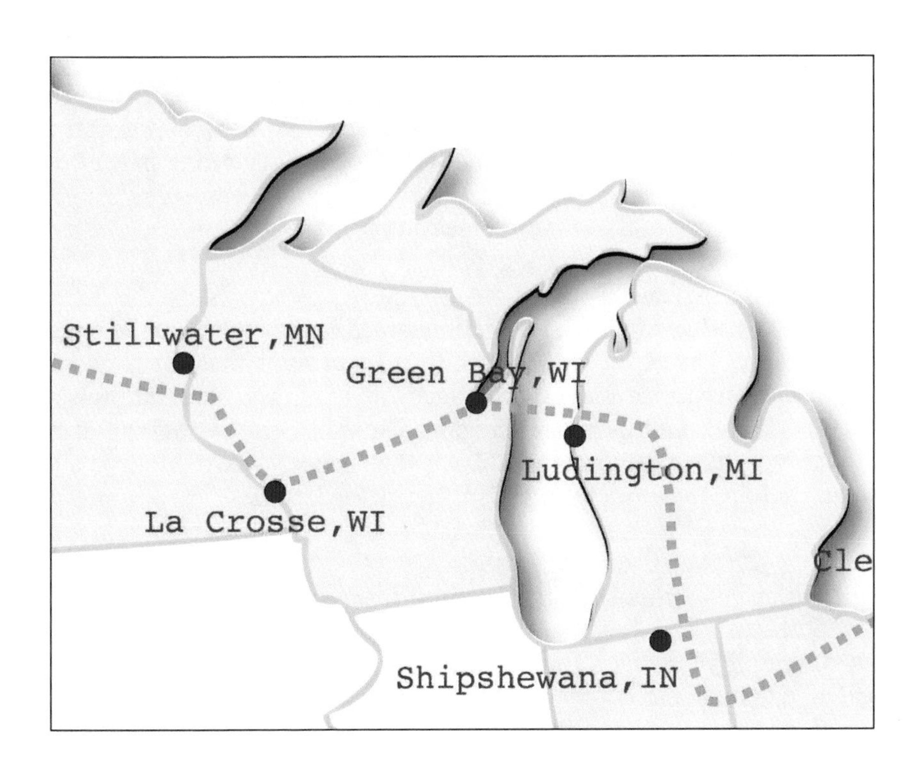

Day 45

July 15 – Ludington to Reed City, Michigan
70 miles (total miles 2,690)
Cool, 55-65 degrees, overcast, threatening rain all day
Nice tailwind, it feels like a fall day

Peter

It is back into our tights and jackets today as the temperature isn't predicted to rise above the mid-sixties and there is a forty percent chance of rain.

Tracy

We have breakfast with my parents and then they head north to Upper Michigan. We are heading east and then south, but strangely, our route takes us north first. This is due to the number of unpaved roads in Michigan and our need to follow the paved ones. Michigan is not at all like Wisconsin when it comes to paved roads. In Wisconsin, almost all roads are paved thanks to our farm-to-market heritage. In Michigan not so much. We thought navigating in Michigan was going to be difficult, but it is really just a matter of following the pavement.

We finally start heading east, then south, after traveling north for the first fifteen miles. The northwest wind helps push us along as we start to travel toward Indiana, our next state. Much of the beginning part of the route is familiar because we biked across Michigan (east to Bay City) a couple of years ago and took the same route.

Peter

The Adventure Cycling Association route we are following is called the Northern Lakes Bicycle Route. It runs around the north end of Lake Michigan, utilizing the S.S. Badger Car Ferry between Manitowoc, Wisconsin, and Ludington, Michigan. The route moves inland from Ludington, forty-one miles to Wolf Lake, then heads south to Monroeville, Indiana, where we will rejoin the Northern Tier Route.

Tracy

We stop for a break at a gas station in Freesoil (pop. 144), a small town northeast of Ludington. The gas station is the same one we stopped at a couple of years ago. The last time we were here we met two older local men and talked with them for quite a while. They were very pleasant and interesting. While visiting with the gas station attendant today, I see a sign that says "Old Farts Club" and ask her about it. She says two older local men meet there each morning and a friend of theirs made them the sign as a joke. I ask if they could be the same men we met a couple of years ago, and it sounds like they are. We ask her to say hello to them for us (who knows if they will remember us, but we sure remember them) and continue on our way.

Our route next takes us south and east along some very quiet roads with forests and grasslands. There is not much farming in the area. The land seems to be mostly used for grazing and woodlands. Peter speculates that the soil may just be too poor to support farming.

We decide to go off route about four miles to Reed City (pop. 2,425) to stay at their municipal campground for the night. It sounds nice and has showers.

Peter

Our only real hiccup today is a "Road Closed" sign and a set of road construction barricades. We are using Google Maps to navigate to Reed City because we are off of the Adventure Cycling map and are struggling a bit because of poor connectivity here in the middle of nowhere. Now this.

From the barricades, we can see more barricades and construction equipment about one quarter mile down the road to the east. We have learned over the years that "Road Closed" doesn't always mean "Road Closed." I don't take breaking the law lightly, but with so few paved roads out here, any detour could be significant and it is getting late. We are feeling kind of screwed. Maybe we can sneak through.

While I hold the bike, Tracy slides past the first set of barricades and walks toward the next. I watch her anxiously. She approaches the second set of barricades, slides past, stops, and looks straight down. A few seconds later she turns around and starts walking back toward me, slowly shaking her head from side to side. Not good news. When Tracy returns, she tells me there is a bridge out and no way to get through, even if we unload the bike and carry it. Now what?

I pull out my phone, hoping I can get a signal. One bar. After waiting several minutes, I am able to get Google Maps up and running. Slowly. Any paved-road detour will cost us ten to twenty miles, that's a long way at this time of the day. There is one other possibility.

Using Google Earth (slowly), I spot what appears to be a path running north-south through the woods just past the construction. We may be able to use that. With no good alternatives, we decide to give the path a try, if we can find it.

We mount up and backtrack west about a mile to the nearest paved road that heads north. We turn right and start looking for another road that will hopefully take us east to the path. After about another mile we find what we are looking for. The road to the east is only one lane wide, but it is paved. Down the road we go, trying to remember where we are in case we need to backtrack. It would be easy to get lost out here. I'm not sure we aren't already lost, but I don't tell Tracy.

The heavily wooded road twists right (to the south, I think) and then straightens out again. East? After about a half mile, the pavement ends. Is this a driveway? No sign of our path yet. How much farther do we go? The path should be about a mile and a half from the road we turned on. Maybe as much as a mile left to go. The gravel looks rideable. We ride on. Bears?

Finally, we find it. Our path turns out to be a combination ATV/vehicle trail. Hmm, must be a Michigan thing. The trail is only about eight feet wide and heavily overgrown, which we can handle. The trail surface is the bad part. It is all loose sand/gravel and heavily rutted. There is no way we can ride it, and I'm not sure we can even push the bike through it. Decision time: ten to twenty miles on road or one, maybe two, miles off-road? The trail heads due south, according to the shadows and the moss on the trees. We decide to go for it.

With me in the front and Tracy in the back, we start pushing the bike. This is miserable. The sand/gravel is so loose that the bike's wheels are sinking in, and the front wheel constantly wants to plow to the side, making it hard for me to keep the bike upright. There is no way one of us could make the bike move. We stop to rest after about a quarter mile.

"What do you think?" I say to Tracy. "I don't know," she says.

We keep pushing. I do my best to keep us out of the deep sand, but I'm not having much luck. We are both dripping sweat and the bugs are getting bad.

"Wait!" I say. "Did you hear that?"

"That sounded like a car on pavement," she says.

Could it be? We push a bit faster. Sure enough, after another hundred yards of slogging, we are delivered from this bug-infested gravel pit right to the road we had started from, but this time we are on the opposite side of the missing bridge. We did it! I knew it all along. It looks like all of that time in the woods in forestry school paid off. It is way better to be lucky than good.

Tracy

We arrive at Rambadt Memorial Park Campground at around 5:00 p.m. and make it under the open-air pavilion roof just as the sky opens up. The campground host is gone, so we bundle up, make dinner under the shelter, and wait for the host to return so we can pay our camping fee and get the key to the showers. We really need a shower.

Peter

Dinner is good, but we are cold and stinky and really want to take a shower, get our tent set up and go to bed. The ground is wet from the rain, so we are hoping the campground host will let us set up our tent in the

Peter pushes the bike out of the bug-infested "gravel pit" road that saved us many miles of riding due to a missing bridge.

Tracy's turn to pose with the bike on a picturesque suspension bridge near Reed City, Michigan.

pavilion. There is only one other camper in sight and he is way down at the other end of the campground.

After dinner, I walk over to inspect the locked shower doors. Even though I don't have a key yet, I discover that with just the right motivation, the women's shower door, miraculously, is not locked. The men's shower door proves to be a bit more secure, so Tracy and I take turns guarding the showroom door and taking a shower. Just as we finish our showers, the camp host returns and we gratefully pay our $20 fee for the evening.

The temperature is predicted to drop into the upper forties tonight, and the campground host allows us to pitch our tent in the pavilion where we will be warm and dry.

Day 46

July 16 – Reed City to Trufant, Michigan
83 miles (total miles 2,773)
Cold, low 60s, cloudy and slight tailwind

Peter

I spent a restless night camped way too close to Highway 10 near Reed City.

Tracy

Today we wake up to a cold day at our campsite at Rampart Memorial Park. Luckily, with our tent pitched under an open-air pavilion, we were at least able to avoid the heavy morning dew and a soaked tent. We have our typical camp breakfast (instant oatmeal, coffee and tea), then put on our tights and jackets to keep us warm on the bicycle.

We are off route about four miles and are looking at the map to figure out the best way to get back on route when a gentleman who maintains the flowers at the park comes over to say hello. He has lived in the area all his life and is able to give us directions to get back on route, including street names, not the typical, "Just turn by the big oak tree on Mr. Smith's farm. You know."

The route for the day is through some very beautiful areas of Michigan, but definitely not direct. There are lots of hills and quick turns which require a fair amount of energy and concentration. It appears Adventure Cycling has decided to run us a bit in circles in Michigan. This could be due to the lack of paved roads, but it still seems extreme to us. In addition, we are traveling in areas that have little or no services, which makes it hard to find supplies and somewhere to stay. Oh well, we will continue to make do.

We stop for a snack about thirty miles into the ride in Big Prairie Township after traveling past the Hardy Dam. Hardy Dam, or Hardy

Hydroelectric Plant, is an earth-filled embankment dam and power plant complex on the Muskegon River built in 1929. At the time of its completion, it was the largest earthen dam in North America east of the Mississippi River. Its impoundment forms a lake with over fifty miles of shoreline.

We are taking a break on a bench by a convenience store when two gentlemen come up and ask about our trip and where we are going for the night. They are salesmen for Artic Ice. We tell them our story and say we are looking for a place to spend the night. We are thinking about staying at the Lincoln Pine Resort about fifty miles away. They are familiar with the resort, say it is very nice, with showers and a laundry, and give us directions.

Peter

Tracy bonks about thirty miles later. She is having trouble concentrating and reading the map. I hope she is not sick, but I am pretty sure she just needs some real food. We limp into the city of Coral (pop. 1,261) to find something to eat.

Tracy

Because of the limited services, we are not able to find a restaurant for lunch until nearly 2:30 p.m., too late in the day. We are hungry and I am a bit bonked because I have not had a good lunch to keep me going. We find we can only go so far without a good meal. The snacks, power bars, Gatorade, etc., just do not do it.

We finally get to Coral, which is supposed to have a restaurant. When we get there, the restaurant is busy with the staff cooking and getting the baking done for tomorrow, but they are closed today. Out of desperation, I stick my head in the door anyway to double-check, and they say they are closed. We are standing outside deciding if we want bar food on one end of town or convenience store food on the other when the restaurant owner walks outside and tells us she would be happy to feed us, even though she is closed. We are overjoyed and head back into the restaurant, where she makes us a delicious wrap and gives us some fresh-baked cookies.

The Coral Bakery and Bread Company opened just six weeks ago. Jacquie Fase, the owner, already has quite a business. We are hopeful she will be successful. This is a retirement job for Jacquie and her husband. She is currently the transportation coordinator for the local school district and has held a very stressful job for twenty-some years. She is very much looking forward to retiring from the school district next year for a lot of the same reasons municipal employees are leaving the public sector everywhere: the jobs have just gotten tough. Random act of kindness #1 for the day.

Peter

Refueled, we take off for the last twenty miles to the resort. Tracy bonks again fifteen miles later. We slow down and limp into the resort.

Tracy

We get to the Lincoln Pines Resort at about 5:00 p.m. and stop at the office to check in. The young woman in the office greets us with, "You must be the bicyclists who are biking across the country." We ask her how she knows and she says, "The two salesmen from Artic Ice stopped in and told me to expect you." She then proceeds to give us a campsite, for free. We are sure the salesmen either paid for the campsite or suggested she give it to us for free. We never find out. Random act of kindness #2. The campground is beautiful and well-kept. We enjoy our visit.

Peter

After warm showers, dinner and laundry, the day is looking much better, especially to Tracy. We even find a penny at the campsite.

Tracy

I have really been struggling emotionally. This makes it difficult for me to navigate because I have so many other thoughts going round and round in my head. Peter does not know this, but I am lonely and frequently find myself in tears as we travel down the road. I miss my family, friends, kittens, and home. Our relationship has also become difficult. It is especially tough when I make a mistake when navigating. I know Peter will go off on me, so I am afraid to ask him to stop to check the map. Peter thinks my problems are from a lack of food, which I am sure is not helping. However, the trip is really starting to take its toll on me emotionally and I am not sure I want to or can continue. Only time will tell.

Day 47

July 17 – Trufant to Hastings, Michigan
56 miles (total miles 2,829)
Warmer, 65-70 degrees, sunny with a slight headwind

Tracy

We get up at about 7:30 a.m., have breakfast and pack up as best we can. There wasn't any rain last night, but the high humidity left our tent's tarp and ground sheet soaked from condensation. We air-dry the tent as best we can, but have to pack it up mostly wet. We finally take off, albeit a bit waterlogged. We stop at the park office to thank the park attendant for the free camping.

We are not sure where we are going to end our day because today's route bypasses Grand Rapids to the east and there is nothing in the way of basic services, hotels or even camping. We plan to just start riding and then later in the morning make a decision on where to end. Our first townships are Harvard and Grattan. Both are small with little or no services. We continue on to Smyrna, which has no services at all. So, on to Saranac, where we finally find a nice restaurant.

> "Let's hear it for not one, but 2 acts of kindness. I'm going to try doing more and hope everyone reading Peter and Tracy's blog will do the same."
>
> **- *Ruth Flucke***

Two gentlemen walk into the restaurant after we are seated. As they sit down next to us, the waitress yells across the bar, "Do you want the usual?" I lean over and tease them, "You must be regulars." We strike up a lively conversation while we all eat lunch. They are very interested in our trip and helpful to us in deciding where to end our ride for the day. With their input, we decide on Hastings, Michigan (pop. 7,350), twenty-five miles down the road.

Peter

On the tandem, only one person is allowed to have a bad day at a time. Today is my day to struggle. Fortunately, Tracy is feeling better. My legs are heavy and sore, and I have a headache. The great weather and scenery are mostly lost on me. We decide to detour slightly to the city of Hastings and their new Holiday Inn Express. The hotel will allow me to rest, we can dry out the tent, do laundry, and hopefully watch the Tour de France on TV. That will make me feel better.

I'm looking forward to a good night's sleep, free hot hotel breakfast, and getting back on the bike in the morning.

Tracy

Peter is not feeling so good and does not have a lot of power in his legs, so a shorter day and a hotel for the night are definitely the way to go.

The end of our ride is on the Nash Highway, which makes both of us smile because it reminds us of our former neighbors, Mike and Becky Nash. We really miss them, although we are sure they are enjoying their new life in Door County, Wisconsin.

We have a nice dinner in Hastings, do our laundry, and enjoy watching the Tour de France on TV (We have only been able to watch the Tour two times so far. Bummer.)

Day 48

July 18 – Hastings, Michigan, to Shipshewana, Indiana
92 miles (total miles 2,921)
60-70 degrees, sunny with a slight headwind

Peter

It is hard to leave the comforts of the Holiday Inn Express and the Tour de France (first day in the Alps) on TV this morning, but leave we do.

Tracy

We get up, have breakfast at the hotel, and head out by 8:00 a.m. for a long day on the bike. We have decided to bicycle ninety-two miles to Shipshewana, Indiana, because there are not many, or any, places to stay along the route. We head four miles down County Road 179 to get back on route from Hastings.

Peter

The route today is hilly with lots of navigational twists and turns. We are both kept very busy with all of the bobbing and weaving. I am feeling better, but still not 100 percent. I'm hoping part of my issue is a lack of calories, so I have gone to a see-food diet. If I see it, I eat it! Convenience store chocolate-covered mini donuts, at 370 calories per package, are my favorite.

Tracy

The ride is very nice, despite all the hills, twists, and turns. Our route travels adjacent to several lakes and natural areas. One spot on the map near Yorkville looks like it will be particularly beautiful because the road appears to run right along Gull Lake. I am disappointed when we get there, because we can't see the lake past all the huge houses situated around it. I wonder if there is even public access to the lake. It would be a shame if there isn't.

From Gull Lake we travel on to Galesburg for lunch at a nice local restaurant. We stop at the only bicycle shop in town, Billy's, after lunch. The owner, an older man named Billy, has owned the shop for thirty-two years and has many wonderful stories about professional and amateur cyclists he has worked with. We borrow his floor pump and top off our tires.

Peter

This is an old-school bike shop and a real pleasure to explore. The shop is more of a museum than a bicycle shop. It does not have the supplies you would normally find, so replacing our bicycle computer (it has been working on and off) with a new one is not an option. Oh well, we will just have to make do with what we have.

Making due without a bicycle computer may not seem like a big deal, since the bike works just fine without it, but it is. We use the computer to help us navigate, and navigation is becoming more and more difficult for us as we fatigue from our journey. Tracy has turn-by-turn directions for our route when she is using our Adventure Cycling Association maps to navigate. After we make a turn, she will tell me how far it is to our next turn, which way we will be turning, and the name of the road we will be turning on. The turn can be miles or just feet ahead. I look at the odometer on the computer, calculate what the approximate mileage reading will be when we reach our next turn, try to memorize that distance, and then call it out to Tracy in case I forget. Through trial and lots of error, we have found this to be a good system for us. Without a functioning odometer, I have no way of knowing exactly how far we have traveled. Fortunately, there is a workaround. I can estimate distance the old-school way.

I have gotten pretty good at estimating the speed at which we are traveling. I am usually within one mile per hour, maybe two. I also have memorized how many minutes it takes us to go a mile at various speeds (e.g. 20 mph = 3-minute mile; 15 mph = 4-minute mile; 12 mph = 5-minute mile; 10 mph = 6-minute mile).

With this information, I can estimate how long it will take us to get to our next turn. I usually calculate a time range so I know when to start looking for the turn or if I have missed it. The clock on the computer is still working, so now when Tracy gives me a distance, I quickly estimate our speed, convert that to minutes per mile, and multiply that by the distance (e.g. two miles at 12 mph = 10 minutes).

There is a lot of concentrating involved with this method, and I often have to ask Tracy to stop talking while I make my calculations. I am proud that I have this skill, but it sure will be nice when we have a working computer again.

Tracy

We continue our ride, traveling through the little towns of Scotts and Centerville. Down the road eighteen miles we enter Indiana. Yay, another state.

Peter

One of the unexpected benefits of today's route is all of the porta potties. They are everywhere. Since they are always at the roadside edges of fields (mostly corn), all we can figure is that they are there for the farm workers. Must be another Michigan thing. Regardless, it sure beats trying to inconspicuously duck into the woods wearing a high-visibility biking jersey. Ha!

Tracy

Before leaving on our adventure, I went to lunch with my best childhood friend. Katie is a debutant, and even had a coming out party when she was sixteen. Katie and her friends' biggest concern for me on our trip was where I would go to the bathroom. I laughed and told her, "Wherever I can find something to hide behind." She was aghast. So, when we saw our first porta pottie in a field in Michigan, Peter took a photo of me standing next to it and sent it to her.

We are only about five miles into Indiana when we pull into Shipshewana Campground and Amish Log Cabins in Shipshewana for the night. I decide we should stay in a cabin when the campground manager tells us that for $30 more, we can get an Amish Camp Cabin with beds for four, heat, air conditioning and lights. Luxury. It is easy to choose the cabin. The cabin is beautifully built by local Amish craftsmen and even has a porch swing. We are the only ones in the camp cabins area and have the restrooms and showers all to ourselves.

Peter takes a load off on the porch swing of our Amish Camp Cabin a few miles into northern Indiana.

Chapter 9

Indiana and Amish Country

July 19-20, 2014
Total Miles 179/3,100 total

Day 49

July 19 - Shipshewana to Monroeville, Indiana
88 miles (total miles 3,009)
Mid 70s, sunny, winds calm, beautiful day

Peter

Last night was a tough one. Tracy and I fought before we went to bed. This isn't the first time we have had words, but prior to this they have almost always happened on the road in the heat of the day. The wear and tear of the trip is starting to affect us, both physically and emotionally. Even the simplest tasks are becoming difficult.

I am still losing weight and I am getting weaker. I just don't have the same power I had earlier in the ride. My hands are sore from the pounding of the road, braking, and controlling the weight of the front panniers. I switch hand positions often, but it doesn't help much anymore. I cringe and get testy when the road surface is poor. As I struggle to keep going, I am leaning on Tracy more to make up for my deficiencies.

My main jobs on the front of the bike are to keep us from crashing or getting hit by another vehicle. I am almost 100 percent responsible for our safety and there is nothing I take more seriously. Unfortunately, this is becoming more difficult for me to do as I become more fatigued from the physical and mental stresses of our adventure. To maintain the high level of awareness I feel I need to keep us safe on the bike, I have started to push other distractions out of my mind.

> "Together you guys are an unstoppable machine. The pilot and navigator may each waver, but the engine will push on."
> ***- Kyle Fordham***

I ask Tracy to check behind us for traffic more often when we are negotiating traffic, and I am asking her for directions more often because I can't stand the thought of making a wrong turn and getting lost. I have become very "precise" with Tracy because I don't want to risk miscommunicating with her, missing a turn, or a car. I am in full "cop mode," born of years of carrying a gun, responding to emergencies, and operating on too little sleep. To me, everything has become an emergency. "Clear left." Clear Right." "Gun!" I only want the information from her I need to get the job done and be safe. I know this is withering for her, but I can't help myself. I am that worn down.

Tracy is suffering, too. Although I cannot see her face while we ride, I can tell she is in decline. At her best, Tracy is really good at checking for traffic next to and behind us so I can focus on what is in front of us. Often, I will hear "clear back" from her, even before I am aware I am thinking about changing lanes. Her anticipation is that good. Now, however, she doesn't check for traffic when she normally would, and when she does, she often talks too quietly for me to be sure of what she said. She is exhausted, too. If I mix up "clear" and "car," it could be disastrous. To make sure we get it right, I ask her to give me the information I need in a certain way, "car right," not "There's a blue minivan over there." I just can't filter and process that much imprecise information quickly enough anymore. What's really scary for me is when she mixes up "right" and "left." When this happens, I often look away from an approaching car instead of toward it. This cannot happen. We will die! When she gets it wrong I try to explain what I need in a different way and why. When she gets it wrong again, I get irate.

The hardest part of all this is that we are dealing with the stresses of the trip differently. Instead of making each other stronger, we are tearing each other down. I am acting unilaterally and like everything is an emergency. Tracy just needs my patience and a hug. I am truly afraid for our safety, the success of our trip, and even our marriage. I have been badgering Tracy with "Do you want to keep doing this?" and all she will say is, "I don't know." "Then what do you want to do?" "I don't know."

Tracy

Yesterday was tough, not the ride as much as the way Peter and I are interacting. I am not sure I want to continue. The stress is too high and I am afraid this will be the undoing of our relationship.

Bicycling across the country is not an easy task. The long days on the bicycle, sleeping somewhere different every night, nutritional challenges, and constant change are taking a toll on me. Navigating has become harder, I am constantly looking at the map and double/triple checking our next turn, I just cannot remember from one minute to the next. Then add my fear of getting a direction wrong and experiencing Peter's wrath. Is it even worth it?

We have not been talking much on the bicycle except for me to provide directions to Peter. The directions have to be very precise, "Car Back" or "Clear." When I provide a direction in a slightly different manner, all hell breaks loose. My self-esteem is taking a hit and I am starting to feel like a complete idiot. I do not think I can continue like this.

When I see something cool, want to point out something to Peter, or just talk, it does not happen. I feel like I am traveling alone on the bicycle and have no one to share the ride with. I feel very lonely.

This morning, after a sleepless night, I struggle to get out of bed and get ready to go. I did a lot of thinking last night and have decided to continue on the ride, hoping things will get better. The funny thing is I really like being on the bicycle and the thrills it brings, but will this be enough to keep me going? We will see.

Peter

In retrospect, after more than twenty-five years and 35,000 miles of unsupported bicycle touring with Tracy, including two more cross country trips (Mississippi River via Canada in 2015 and Historic Route 66 in 2016), I'm not at all surprised I was acting like this and that things were breaking down the way they were. I am a middle-aged man, a first-born child, educated in the sciences, I have a black belt in karate, and am an ex-EMT and ex-cop. These, and myriad other things, affect how I deal with normal everyday life, stressful situations, and emergencies.

I am a control freak – a little less so now thanks to my free-spirited youngest daughter, Alex, and bicycle touring. The weather doesn't care what I want. Now, add to this the fact I was probably malnourished, the extremes of our adventure, and certainly fatigued from so many miles, so many days on the road, and so little time apart from Tracy, and there you have it. I am both a recovering cop and control freak.

Day in, day out, on and off the bike, Tracy and I are great partners. We love, respect, and trust each other. We have built a wonderful life together and have raised two incredible children. From this base we succeed and thrive. In an emergency, I will bet on myself every time to keep myself and those around me safe and sound. But it is the stressful situations, especially over time, where I have failed as a teammate. I jump far too quickly into "emergency mode," which invariably breaks down Tracy and our team. I am still working on this one.

(Working with Lee Hyrkas, a sport nutritionist at Bellin Health in Green Bay, before our 2016 trip made a huge difference in both our physical and mental wellbeing. Thank you, Lee.)

I am up first today, as usual, and start the day with an incredible view of a mist-covered farm field from the porch of our cabin.

Tracy

We finally have breakfast and take off to experience Indiana. The weather is beautiful and so is the ride. We are bicycling through northern Indiana and what is predominately Amish country. We thoroughly enjoy bicycling through the area with almost no motorized vehicles. It is us, other bicyclists, mainly Amish, wagons drawn by massive draft horses, up to four of them, and many Amish buggies. We have never seen so many buggies. I think because it is Saturday, many Amish families are heading to town or visiting. It is nice traveling down roads with very few or no cars. It is much quieter and calmer due to the lack of motor vehicles.

> "We all dream of doing things in our lives that would be a great experience. Most of us never find time, but you are living the dream."
>
> ***- Mike Beno***

Peter and I like it and need it. The Amish people are very friendly and I think our tandem bicycle is intriguing to them. As we bicycle past their homes, buggies, or bicycles, there are frequent waves and hellos.

This area of Indiana is truly beautiful and the Amish farms definitely add to the beauty with their well-maintained homes, gardens and yards.

Peter

The only minor issues I have in Amish country are navigating the tandem along the strangely rutted roads and avoiding the massive amounts of horse manure. It is a good way to practice my bicycle handling skills.

It is not uncommon on older rural roads for there to be ruts in the travel lanes where car wheels go. One on each side of the center of a lane. This wear pattern usually allows us to comfortably bicycle on the right side of the right rut where the pavement is, usually, better and we are, mostly, out of traffic. On these particular roads, however, the ruts are narrow, very deep, and in the middle and far right-hand edge of the lane. If we ride in the middle of the ruts, the bottom of our low-riding front panniers actually scrapes the edge of the ruts from time to time. Probably best to avoid this.

I am forced to ride a narrow, flat ridge of pavement where the right car tire rut normally would be. This lane positioning feels really strange, but it isn't an issue with virtually no motor vehicle traffic. Then I figured it out. These ruts weren't made by car tires; they were made by Amish buggy wheels. The buggy drivers always seem to stay as far to the right side of the lane as possible, even running on the gravel shoulder if they can. This is what has caused the strange road wear pattern. It must have taken a lot of buggies over a lot of years to do this to the road. I wonder how many bicycles it would take.

There are oversized shoulders on some sections of the roads, kind of like a bicycle lane on steroids. These appear to be buggy lanes. We believe the buggy lanes were added to the road to try and reduce the damage the buggies do to the roadway. They are great places to bicycle.

Tracy

All too soon, we are out of Amish country. We wish we had spent more time and explored some of the towns in the area. We do stop in LaGrange (a town located on the edge of the Amish area) for lunch. Peter is still struggling to take in enough calories (and in America, just imagine). Two eggs, potatoes, hash, toast, a blueberry pancake and coffee, lots of coffee, put a dent in his hunger.

There are some buggies and Amish people in town, but I am sure nothing like you see in Shipshewana. According to a brochure I picked up, Shipshewana has a lot of cool shops and restaurants that would have been fun to check out. The town is located more in the center of the Amish community and appears to be the place tourists and locals frequent. We will have to come back someday to better explore the area.

After lunch, we stop at a small grocery store to stock up for dinner and then push on for Monroeville (pop. 1,300), sixty miles away. The ride is tough with lots of little hills that wear out our legs. We are definitely ready to be done by the time we get in.

Our plan for lodging is to stay at the Monroeville Community Center in the city park. According to our map, there is "bicyclist only" camping, indoors there. We are not sure if we have a place to stay, though. I left two messages for the facility contact, but we did not get a call back. I don't even know if there is a hotel or campground in town. I don't think so. We will figure it out.

We should not have worried. When we pull into the city park where the community center is located, an older man is walking down the sidewalk toward us. He waves, and says, "Welcome to Monroeville, Tracy and Peter." What a wonderful welcome.

Warren is a volunteer who takes care of the community center. He brings us inside and goes through everything with us. The building has a full kitchen, private bathroom with shower, washer, dryer, tables, chairs, cots for sleeping, and an entertainment cart with a TV, games, videos, etc. The community center is FREE for touring cyclists to use. To say the least, this is a welcome surprise. We are the only guests that evening, so we have the whole place to ourselves.

Warren gives us the key to the community center and tells us to leave it in the "Bicyclists room" when we head out in the morning. He then suggests we check out the local ice cream shop, Whippy Dip. Of course, we take his advice and head to Whippy Dip for some delicious ice cream after dinner.

On a side note, the Monroeville Community Center received the June Curry Trail Angel Award from Adventure Cycling in 2005. The Trail Angel Award is named in honor of June Curry, the famous Cookie Lady of Afton, Virginia. June assisted cyclists on the TransAmerica Trail from 1976 until her death in 2012. More than 10,000 touring cyclists enjoyed her hospitality at her home in Virginia. For thirty-nine years now, Monroeville has provided complimentary lodging and services to traveling bicyclists.

The award is truly deserved and they continue to welcome cyclists into their community and provide them with everything they need at no cost. We are very lucky to be able to take advantage of their hospitality. Another act of kindness, but this time from an entire community!

Day 50

July 20 - Monroeville, Indiana, to Bowling Green, Ohio
91 miles (total miles 3,100)
80-85 degrees, foggy in the morning, clear and sunny, calm winds to a very slight headwind

Tracy

After cleaning up (leave it better than you found it) and signing the community center's guest book, we leave a donation and the key, and head to the Blueberry Pancake House in Monroeville for breakfast. The blueberry pancakes are huge and to die for. Yum. What a great way to start the day.

We bike out of town into the fog. Pretty thick for a while. Thank goodness Jeff and Matt from JB Cycle gave us that set of lights when we were in Green Bay. We have them on in flashing mode, white to the front and red to the rear, so hopefully anyone else on the road will be able to see us. Traffic is light. Five miles down the road, we enter Ohio and our first Ohio city, Payne.

The majority of our ride today is on the Ohio Byway, which goes past many fields and along several different rivers, including the Maumee River. The byway is a great ride, low traffic volume, flat, beautiful views, and evenly spaced towns to visit. We even encounter our first Towpath along our route. It is an alternate route, which we decide not to take. The map directions said, "Walk your bike on this unimproved towpath trail for 2.5 miles." Pushing our fully loaded tandem for two and a half miles is just not going to happen. Been there, done that.

Tracy and a sign for the Ohio Byway

In Napoleon, we stop for lunch at Subway, the first time on this trip. Subway is Peter's favorite and he has been craving a Subway sub. The young women working the counter are very excited about our trip and ask many questions. We give them our business card so they can find our blog and Facebook posts through our website (www.webike.org). They immediately pull the sites up and are looking at the posts. Thank goodness, we are the only customers in the place.

We meet a touring cyclist taking a break at a gas station just before Bowling Green. His name is Julio and he is from Columbia, South America. He started in New York and is headed to San Francisco. He is a bit down because his knee has been hurting him all day and he is worried about it. We talk for a while, and just before we take off in our separate directions, he gives us a hug and tells us he is feeling better and not so down. He thanks us for cheering him up. We hope his knee holds up and he enjoys and completes his trip.

Too funny. Earlier in the day we saw another touring cyclist going west. We waved and stopped to chat, per tradition. He yells, "Keep going!" in a very British accent and waves us along. We laugh and decide he is either sick of Americans who always want to talk or in witness protection and did not want us to get a good look at him.

We are hungry and need to find a hotel when we arrive in Bowling Green (pop. 30,043) at about 5:00 p.m. We find a Starbucks, our first in a while, and decide to stop and figure things out. We must stand out like a sore thumb in front of Starbucks in our biking clothes with the fully loaded tandem, because people keep coming up to us wanting to talk about our trip. We are happy to oblige. We hang around outside the coffee shop for a half hour talking with people before we can even get inside.

The first person to approach us is a young man, a traveling musician from Nashville, Tennessee. He is very intrigued with our trip and we talk for a long time. He has just been in Traverse City, Michigan, playing at a wedding and is driving home. We exchange business cards so we can check out his music and he can follow our progress. Nice young man and obviously very talented.

Next, a father and his two boys (sixteen and seventeen), who are on a motorcycle trip, stop to chat. They were waiting in line to talk with us. Funny. The youngest boy is driving a car with all their supplies. Dad and the older boy are riding the motorcycles. They are from Detroit and are heading back home after a three-day adventure. They are having a great time and it seems like they are truly enjoying their time together. They have many questions and are fun to talk with. The younger boy will have his motorcycle license by next year and will join the other two on their "bikes."

Finally, a young couple from Ohio come up and ask about our trip. They are marathon runners and are interested in comparing the workload for a cross-country bicycle trip to running a marathon. Peter loves this conversation. He has run several marathons, including Boston,

A late-afternoon stop at Starbucks in Bowling Green, Ohio

and running was a big part of our training for this trip. They are getting married in six weeks. Maybe the musician from Nashville can play for their wedding. We finally make it inside. The bike is quite a conversation starter.

Peter

We check into the Best Western Falcon Plaza hotel for tonight and tomorrow night. We have ridden every day since we left home seven days ago (533 miles) and need a break. Our power output has been dropping off and we continue to be grumpy, although today was a pretty good day. I am surprised it has taken so long for us to get to this point. It was bound to happen.

After we returned home from the trip, I was telling Tom Huber, a good friend and the former Wisconsin State Bicycle and Pedestrian coordinator, that we really started to break down as a team at about mile 3,000. Tom, who is married and has also bicycled across the country, laughed and said, "Three thousand miles? My wife and I wouldn't have made it 100." I laughed. Thanks for the perspective, Tom.

We order in pizza and are catching up on the Tour de France. Tomorrow we will sleep in, explore Bowling Green, and take a nap, or two. Our next big city will be Cleveland.

Chapter 10

Ohio and the Ohio Byway

July 21-26, 2014
Total Miles 313/3,413 total

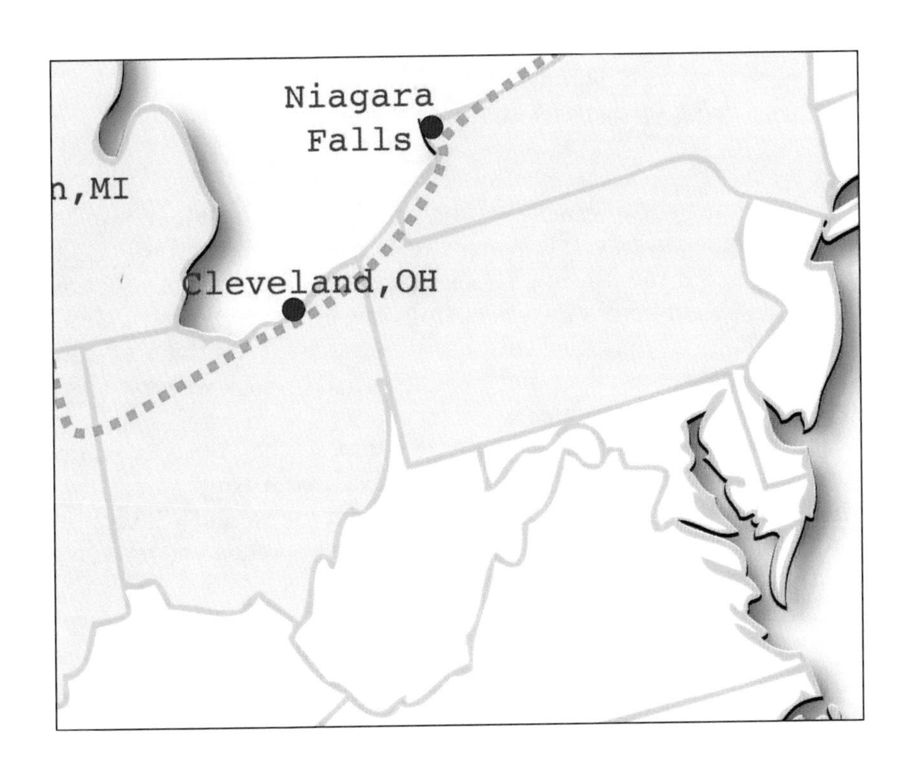

Day 51

July 21 - Bowling Green, Ohio
0 miles (total miles 3,100)
Warm day, 80-plus degrees and sunny

Tracy

Today is a day off the bike and we are hanging out, doing laundry, topping off the bike tires, and exploring Bowling Green. We are having a nice day off and have even had time for a nap.

One more act of kindness to relate. We were at the laundromat earlier and the attendant came up to me and asked if we were hiking or biking. I told her about our trip. She then said, "I see your small laundry soap bottle is empty. Can I fill it back up for you, and is there anything else you need?" It was so simple for her, but huge for us. We were planning to purchase more laundry soap later today, but probably would have had to throw most of it out because we carry so little with us. Thank you, Bowling Green.

Day 52

July 22 - Bowling Green to Vermilion, Ohio
84 miles (total miles 3,184)
Hot, 94 degrees, sunny with a slight tailwind

Tracy

We get going early because we know it is going to be hot and we have quite a few miles to travel. Bowling Green is a nice city and we take the time to check out the Bowling Green State University campus (home of the Falcons), right across the street from our hotel. Very pretty. Getting out of Bowling Green is uneventful as we are only a few miles off route. Today's route takes us along many country roads, which will probably be quiet and with very few vehicles.

One thing we have found odd in Ohio is that the gas station/ convenience stores do not have public restrooms. A couple times when we have stopped, we have been told to go down the street to Subway and use their bathrooms. Thank goodness for Subway. When you have to go, you have to go.

About forty-five miles into our ride, we come into the town of Clyde (pop. 6,325). We have been traveling on the North Coast Inland Trail for the past eight and a half miles from Fremont. We ask a couple in town for a suggestion on a good place to eat. They send us to the local coffee shop for a nice lunch with a bit of Clyde history included. Evidently, there is a man in town who normally hangs out by the trail and buys cross-country cyclists lunch or breakfast at the local coffee shop in exchange for stories about their trip. Unfortunately, he is not in town when we come through. It would have been a pleasure to meet him, and free lunch is always nice.

Our map shows the trail ending in Clyde, but they recently extended it approximately four miles east out of town. We check with a gentleman in the coffee shop, show him our map, and review the map addendum with him. (Typically, our maps come with an addendum, which provides updates to the map. "The North Coast Inland Trail now extends eastward through Clyde to S. Ridge Road/TR 175.") He tells us to take the trail and we will end at the same end point as our directions. He says the trail ends at South Ridge Street and our map addendum tells us the same thing.

We thank him for his help and head for the trail. We get to the end of the trail and discover we are probably another two miles beyond where we should be. Out comes the GPS to try and get us back on track. After a couple of false starts, we finally get back on route and are not so lost.

Peter

Road construction is a fact of life, but damn, it can get annoying sometimes. Apparently, Erie County has picked this summer to replace all of the culverts running under twelve-mile-long Strecker Road (County Road 15) between Clyde and Avery. Lucky us. We have seen this before. In order to replace the old culvert (a necessary evil), road workers use a backhoe to dig a trench across the road the width of the culvert (roughly four feet), dig up the old culvert, replace it with a new culvert and backfill the trench with gravel. Unfortunately, they can't repave the road right away because the gravel needs to be compacted and settle first. These gravel road patches are usually drivable with a car, but they can vary widely in terms of their bikeability, especially with a fully loaded tandem. At best, we can bike over them cautiously. At worst, we must stop and walk the bike across. A real pain, and slow.

The bad news on this particular construction project is there is a culvert approximately every mile along the road. The good news is they seem to be bikeable. Whoever patched these things did a really good job. I slow way down for the first five or six patches, but they are all smooth and match up almost perfectly with the asphalt road edge. Often motor vehicle traffic causes depressions in the gravel patches through compaction and by kicking gravel up onto the road, but not here. By the eighth, ninth, and tenth patches, I don't even bother to slow down. Then the eleventh patch appears in the distance.

From far away, the eleventh patch looks just like the previous ten. I call out "Gravel" to Tracy, just as I have done with every patch before, to warn her that there will be a little bump, but I don't slow down. Bam. The bike's lighter front wheel drops into a six-inch depression in the patch.

Bam, Bam, BAM! The front wheel bumps out of the ditch, then the much heavier back wheel drops in, and then violently bounces out. I almost lose my grip on the handlebars. "Stop, stop, stop," Tracy yells out. "Are you okay?" I yell back. "One of the big bags is loose," she says. "Stop!" "I'm trying." I gingerly pull the bike to the side of the road and stop. "That was fun," I say.

Tracy jumps off the bike and grabs the large rear pannier to her right to stabilize it. It is still attached to the bike rack, but by only one hook.

The panniers are designed to attach to the bike's rear rack by two fixed hooks on the top and one adjustable hook on the bottom. When we load the bike in the morning, I hold the bike while Tracy hefts the twenty-some-odd-pound bag up and hooks it over the rack's outside rail. Once it is seated properly, she secures the bottom hook via a synch strap which holds everything fast, and then secures the strap's end with a Velcro closure. We always double-check that all four bags are secure before we pull out in the morning and we routinely check them throughout the day. If a bag were to fall completely off the bike, the bag or the contents could be damaged, we could crash from the sudden weight shift, or from the bag or a strap getting caught in one of the bike's moving parts (wheel, chain, derailleur, pedals). We have only had a bag come loose once or twice before, and never have we lost one completely.

Tracy removes the loose pannier and checks it over while I do the same with the rear end of the bike. Surprisingly, everything seems fine. The bag is undamaged, the bike's brakes work, and both wheels are still running true, straight. Amazing. I thought the bike would be trashed for sure. These forty-spoke wheels are truly bombproof. We reload the bike, double- and triple-check the bags, and are on our way again.

Tracy

We finally get to Huron (pop. 7,149), which is a city located on Lake Erie. This is the second Great Lake we will pass on our trip. Lake Ontario will be next. We are now riding on Highway 6 adjacent to Lake Erie. Our views of the lake are amazing. The day is so clear you can see forever.

Peter

Although it did get hot today, the roads were flat and in good condition, mostly. The wind was behind us and there were towns frequently where we could get something to eat and drink, and hang out in the air conditioning for a while. It was a good day on the bike overall.

Tracy

Our overnight is at the Firefly Resort and Campground between Huron and Vermilion, where we arrive around 5:00 p.m. It is located right on Lake Erie and has a great beach. We are hot and tired after our long ride. We change into our swimsuits and take a very refreshing swim in the lake. The water is not too cold (especially by Great Lakes standards) and feels wonderful. We bob with our heads just above the water letting our bodies cool. After the swim, we relax in the multicolored Adirondack chairs overlooking the beach and just watch the water for a while. Eventually, we get our tent set up and make dinner. We end the night at the campground's Tiki bar enjoying the air conditioning, visiting with other campers, and having a couple of cold beers. Nice way to end the day.

Day 53

July 23 - Vermilion to Cleveland, Ohio
45 miles (total miles 3,229)
Cool and rainy, 70 degrees, moderate headwind

Peter

We only have forty-five miles to bike to Cleveland today, but we were awake way earlier than expected and it is raining. It will be interesting to see how the day goes. We have learned over the past weeks that the days that start out the worst often end the best.

We were in our tent with the lights out by 10:00 p.m. last night. There were still some campers up and sitting around their campfires, but no one was obnoxiously loud. It didn't take long for us to fall sound asleep.

I awoke sometime later to a loud radio playing. Tracy seemed to still be sleeping. I tried to ignore the radio. Damn campers. Unable to fall back to sleep, I check the time on my phone. It's 1:00 a.m. Seriously?

Tracy

At about 2:00 a.m. I heard a loud radio go on, one of our neighbors, and continue to play for several hours. Peter seemed to sleep right through it. An unexpected thunderstorm hits at 3:30 a.m.

Peter

The storm was bad, but what was worse was the loud radio continued to play, only now it was just static. Probably because of the storm. I was pissed. This ride has become hard enough not to have to do it with no sleep and in the rain. Could be I need a bit more sleep.

After stewing for a while longer, I finally climbed out of the tent, wearing nothing but a pair of shorts. The grass was cool and wet on my bare feet. I followed the sound of the offending radio to a camper maybe fifty yards away. I approached the camper cautiously, figuring that whoever let the radio screech so long must certainly be really drunk. I have dealt with enough drunks in my time not to want to step into that. The noise was coming from an external speaker on the camper. There was no one up. I looked for the radio on the outside of the camper. Nothing. It must be inside. Reluctant to wake the sleeping bear in the camper, I returned to the tent.

“You awake?” I said quietly to Tracy.

“Yeah.”

“What the hell is up with that radio?” I said. I told her about my little trip to the camper and asked her what she thought we should do.

“I don’t know,” she said.

“Can you sleep with this noise?” I said.

“I can try,” she said.

Finally, I couldn’t $#@&!% stand it anymore! I climbed back out of the tent, stormed over to the camper, and gently knocked on the camper door. No answer. I knocked again, a bit louder. Nothing. I slinked back to the tent. The sun will be up in a couple of hours anyway. A short time later, the radio went silent.

Tracy

We start our day with a lack of sleep and wet. At least the rain has stopped.

While we are making breakfast and packing up, a man comes over from the loud-radio camper and sheepishly asks if we heard his radio last night. We say we did, trying not to look too pissed. The man apologizes and tells us how sorry he is. He says the radio is old and he did not even realize it was playing. (Really?) We can tell he feels bad.

Peter

Despite only a thirty percent chance of rain and with nothing showing on the radar, it starts to rain again. I do my regular pre-ride safety check on the bike and notice that when I give the rear wheel a spin, it is a bit out of true and there is a rhythmic tink, tink, tink sound. Oh, oh. That sounds like a broken spoke. That would be a first on this bike. Yup, there it is, a broken spoke, on the drum brake side of the hub. It must have happened when I bounced the bike through the gravel road patch yesterday. Funny, I didn’t notice the broken spoke when I checked the bike back then.

The bike is rideable, but I need to remove the broken spoke so it won’t catch on anything and do more damage. I also need to get rid of the tink, tink, tink noise. That will drive me nuts, especially with as little sleep as I have had. I unscrew the threaded end of the spoke from the spoke nipple at the rim. Unfortunately, the hooked end of the spoke that goes through the hub is behind the drum brake and I can’t get it loose. It will have to stay there until a mechanic, hopefully in Cleveland, can remove the drum brake and replace the spoke. No worries. The wheel should be good for another forty-five miles. I tape the broken spoke to a good one to keep it from flopping around. Good to go.

Tracy

Off we finally go at about 10:30 a.m. The day is gloomy and it is raining very lightly. It is kind of like being in a car wash when you are going through the spot free rinse, light but steady rain.

We bicycle on Highway 6 and then Lake Road toward Cleveland. Lake Road is a beautiful street with huge trees and amazing, big homes located along the Lake Erie shoreline. It is twenty-five miles of big, beautiful homes. Unreal. It reminds us of North Lake Drive near Milwaukee, Wisconsin, but much longer. Too bad the weather is so miserable and gloomy, because I think we are missing a whole bunch of great views. Oh well, we will just have to come back someday.

We enter Cleveland through Edgewater Park, an urban park with paths that drop us right into the city. It is still raining. The bicycle lanes and routes are clearly marked and easy to follow into Cleveland. They have really done a nice job with their bicycle and pedestrian accommodations here.

We are staying at the Cleveland Hostel, located on the edge of a revitalized area of downtown. Soaked, we arrive at about 3:30 p.m. The hostel is bare bones, but very nice. We have a private room and bath, access to a shared kitchen, living space, and rooftop patio with views of the

Our shelter for the night in Cleveland, Ohio

Cleveland skyline that are to die for, all for only $75 per night. Oh, wait, we get an $8.50 per night discount because we are bicycling. Seems only fair after the day we have had, and we aren't using a parking space. Other hotel rooms we checked in town were in the $180-$220 per-night range. Peter's favorite thing about the hostel, though, is it is located within walking distance of no less than three microbreweries. I think we will be shipping glasses home again.

Peter

After a shower, we take the bike to a nearby shop to have the spoke fixed. Unfortunately, the drum brake on the tandem must be removed to fix the spoke and the shop doesn't have the necessary tool. We will go looking for a different shop tomorrow. We go grocery shopping and then make dinner in the hostel. Finally, normal food. When we are done with dinner, we meet up with Jacob VanSickle, executive director of Bike Cleveland, and several other bicycle types at Market Garden Brewery, just down the street. Bike Cleveland is one of our clients. It is great to talk bikes with such dedicated professionals and advocates.

Back at the hostel, Tracy and I go up to the rooftop patio to enjoy the view and reflect on the day. Not bad overall.

Day 54

July 24 – Cleveland Ohio
18 miles (total miles 3,247)
Beautiful, sunny, 70 degrees and moderate wind

Peter

The number one thing on my mind when I wake up is getting the broken spoke fixed on the tandem's rear wheel. We struck out with the bicycle shop we stopped at last night, but with more than a dozen shops in town, surely someone will be able to help us. I am reluctant to leave Cleveland with a broken bike. How long will the wheel hold up with all the weight we are carrying, and where will we get it fixed if not here?

With no other options at the time, I researched "Arai drum brake removal" on the Internet last night. The standard method for removing the brake is to use a special tool that consists of a large wrench head with stabilizing pins on a long bar. Because the brake is designed to withstand a significant level of torque while braking, it takes a tremendous amount of force, leverage, to get the brake loose. Without this tool, good luck getting the brake off.

There is, however, an "emergency field maneuver" I read about. This technique requires Tracy to sit on the tandem (in her normal, stoker, position) and pedal backward while I push the bicycle backward and repeatedly slam on the drum brake. This is kind of like push-starting a manual transmission car, but in reverse. With no other options until the area bicycle shops open at 10:00 a.m., we decide to give it a try on the sidewalk in front of the hostel. We finally get the maneuver down and without killing Tracy, but the brake holds fast. This is such a ridiculous maneuver that we almost crash several times because we are laughing so hard. Sorry, no video. The other great part of the whole thing is watching the locals try and figure out what we are doing. I can't believe no one calls the police. This would be fun to explain.

We make a couple of calls to bike shops after 10:00 a.m., but no one will touch the bike.

Seemingly out of options, we decide to continue our adventure with one missing spoke and a mildly out-of-true wheel. Not ideal, but hopefully we can find a mechanic down the road with the tool and skills we need.

Tracy

Today is our day off and we are planning to spend most of it getting the bike fixed, reorganizing to take off again tomorrow, and we have a lunch date. Our family friend, Emma Hawley, went to high school with our youngest daughter, Alex, and is attending summer school at Case Western University. The university is located on the east side of Cleveland in the University Circle area, about six miles from where we are. We hop on the bike (gently) to head out to lunch with Emma.

Bicycling to our lunch with Emma allows us to see more of Cleveland. The main road through the city has a bicycle lane the whole way. It is fun to see different areas of the city and travel through them by bicycle so easily. Way to go city of Cleveland and Bike Cleveland.

Peter

We get to Presti's Bakery in Little Italy a bit early because of the great roads. As we wait for Emma, a young man sitting outside asks us if we are bicycle tourists. We strike up a conversation, talk about our trip, and explain our bicycle problem. He suggests we try Cain Park Bicycles, about three miles down the road. I immediately call them and explain our problem to the receptionist – my bad – master mechanic, Madeline Gulley. She says she has worked on Santana tandems before and should be able to take care of it for us. When she asks if the brake is a bolt on or threaded, I know we are in business. After a nice lunch with Emma, we head to the bike shop.

> "Haven't been to Little Italy in decades! I have family in Cleveland. They'll love to see this."
>
> ***- Linda Sherman Marsh***

We are greeted at Cain Park Bicycle by Maddie and the shop cat,

Peter with Madeline Gulley, our brake rescuer at Cain Park Bicycle Shop in Cleveland

Bella. Maddie proposes to use a special technique, one not found in our web search, to remove the drum brake and ultimately, fix the spoke. The technique involves inserting the short end of a very large Allen wrench into a vent hole on the brake, and then levering the long end of the wrench with a metal bar down over the rear axle. Sounds scary. Maddie cautions that this could do some damage to the brake. I decide to have her go for it. We are pretty much stuck at this point anyway. Maddie takes the bike in back. Bella watches from her favorite chair.

Tracy

Bella is definitely the "shop cat" and rules the roost. She has her own chair and does not care that there is only one other chair in the place and two of us who need a seat. Peter and I take turns sitting on the other chair and of course petting Bella.

It is fun to watch Maddie and her coworker interact with their customers. They are very gracious to them all, and clear on what needs to be done to fix their bike and what it will cost. The shop is extremely busy and each customer is acknowledged and helped in a timely manner. Very professional.

Peter

I can hear Maddie struggling with the bike in the back of the shop. At one point she comes up front where we are waiting and tells me she is having trouble getting the brake loose, and asks me if I want her to try harder. I feel a bit like I am in a hospital waiting to find out if the patient will live or die. I tell her to do what she needs to do. Oh boy. Here we go. I hear pounding and grunting coming from the back of the shop again. Then, crack, followed by Maddie yelling, "I got it!" Suddenly, all is right in my world.

Our bike is back to 100 percent. We truly enjoy our return ride to the hostel. Most of the ride is on bicycle lanes that are well-designed and easy to use, even on a tandem. The tandem handles much more like a semi-tractor trailer than a personal car and is not usually our first choice as a city bike. Thanks to Maddie, Cain Park Bicycle Shop, city of Cleveland, and Bike Cleveland.

Day 55

July 25 – Cleveland to Conneaut, Ohio
87 miles (total miles 3,334)
Sunny, 75 degrees, tailwind

Tracy

We get going early, 7:30 a.m., in hopes we will not have to deal with morning rush hour traffic in downtown Cleveland. We are well-rested and the bike is in shipshape. Our personal Cleveland bicycle expert, Jacob VanSickle, has provided us with a preferred route out of town. (Apparently, the locals are not big fans of the route recommended by Adventure Cycling.) Unfortunately, we still hit rush hour on this Friday morning. The seven-mile-long route isn't too bad, though, because we are heading out of the city and are mostly riding on bicycle lanes. We are glad for our traffic-cycling experience. This could definitely be intimidating, but it isn't.

Things are going along fine until a driver, who cut off a city bus a block earlier, decides to cut us off, too. Luckily, I see her coming and warn Peter. He is able to get us stopped in plenty of time. I am not happy with her and neither is the motorist behind us. He beeps at her and gives her the evil eye.

After getting out of the city, we have several suburbs to go through, including Euclid, Eastlake, and Mentor-on-the-Lake. Navigating is tough because there are many quick turns. We also get lost in the city of Painesville (pop. 19,563). It truly is a pain, although a nice man on a bicycle helps us find Main Street and a good restaurant for lunch.

Lunch done, we have about fifty miles to go until the end of our day.

The route includes going through Geneva-on-the-Lake, which happens to be where the Spire Institute is located. The Spire Institute is a beautiful indoor track and field facility, which hosted the Big Ten Indoor Track & Field Championships a few years ago. We had the privilege of watching our older daughter, Melissa, compete as a high jumper for the University of Minnesota there. (Go Gophers!)

Our route through the city doesn't take us past the facility, but it does take us past The Lodge at Geneva-on-the-Lake, where Melissa stayed when she participated in the meet. We stop there to take some pictures to send to Melissa. It is a beautiful hotel located right on Lake Erie. We head into town, which we had not seen before, to get something to eat. It is a nice town with lots of little shops and restaurants. It is extremely busy on this beautiful summer day. We would like to stop and explore, but we are hopeful we will be back someday.

Peter

We have beautiful views of Lake Erie on and off all day.

Tracy

We make it to Conneaut (pop. 12,841) at about 6:00 p.m. We are staying at Evergreen Lake Park, a family-owned campground about three miles off route. When we register, the clerk gives us a "car pass," which is typically hung on the rear view mirror. With no rear view mirror, we hang it on Peter's seat post. The campground is a nice place and I think all the campers know we are bicycling across the country by the end of the night. Boy, news travels fast here. The other campers are very interested in our trip and we spend a fair amount of time up at the campground office talking with them.

One of the campers arrives at the campground office by golf cart, proceeds to tell me he wants to finish the trip with us, and asks if he can come along, on his golf cart. I tell him he is welcome to come, but I do not think he can keep up. He chuckles and asks me to tell him more about our trip, which we do over a couple of nice cold beers.

Day 56

July 26 – Conneaut, Ohio, to Fredonia, New York
79 miles (total miles 3,413)
Sunny, 80 degrees, tailwind

Tracy

Today is an exciting one for me. I am going to be traveling into two states I have never been in before, Pennsylvania and New York. We are also going to be bicycling in three states in one day. Very fun.

We start out in Ohio. Okay, we are only about five miles from Pennsylvania, but we are still in Ohio. Upon entering Pennsylvania, we begin biking east along the shore of Lake Erie, this time on Highway 5. We have more great views of the lake.

The largest city in Pennsylvania we travel through is Erie. We spend a fair amount of time in Erie, mainly because I get us lost. It is tough navigating with lots of turns and trails to find. Yikes.

Peter

Tracy did the best job she could in Erie, but she really never had a chance. In Erie, everything heads toward, and then slams into the lake. Once there, the congestion must either go left (west) or right (east). As the city developed, bigger and bigger roadways were built to accommodate the increasing traffic. The needs of walkers and bicyclists were seemingly abandoned to meet the needs of motor vehicles. Once the city recognized its error, they began to build sidewalks and trails. Unfortunately, these facilities are retrofits and often below standards, especially for a fully loaded tandem bicycle.

Also, the network is incomplete. Tracy was trying to navigate us on and off of residential streets, trails, commercial streets, through parking lots, under bridges, around buildings, and along busy arterial roadways, all with me yelling, "Where do I go?" It was a trying experience and exhausting. We often had to stop and ask for directions. We were moving so slowly. Tracy truly did the best job she could.

Tracy

We finally fight our way out of Erie. It is too bad we got so lost, because it would have been nice to get to know the city better.

We enter New York State, state number three for the day, about twenty miles east of Erie. We were only in Pennsylvania for forty-five miles, but it still counts. New York is our eleventh state for the trip, only three more states to go. No way.

Peter

"Welcome to New York the Empire State" the sign says. I am excited to be in a new state, until I see the road surface, that is. The city of Erie was tough to navigate, but the roads in Pennsylvania had been pretty good. The road surfaces were generally smooth and free of cracks, traffic was moderate, and sometimes we had paved shoulders to ride on. All good. But now, as I stand looking at the road at the state line, I can see this is about to change for the worse. The road on the New York side of the line has "alligator cracks" everywhere. There are tar joints aplenty, which are feeble attempts to fix the road, and large chunks of pavement are missing. This road should have been rebuilt years ago. This should be fun to ride. Not.

With no alternate route immediately available, off we go. The road is so bad I have to lock my eyes six to twelve feet ahead of the bike's front wheel and not look up. I am afraid that if I blink, we will hit a pothole or a tar joint and crash. There is a lot of summer-weekend traffic, too, which doesn't help. It is almost impossible for me to hold a straight line and the overtaking traffic doesn't seem to care. Our progress is painfully slow, and scary. "Welcome to New York" indeed.

Tracy

The traffic finally lets up a bit and the road gets better. We are in wine country now, and we bicycle past vineyards and wineries. There are few services in the area, so we stop at one of the wineries to see if they are selling anything to eat in their shop.

Peter

We are not dressed like the other winery patrons on this warm, sunny, mid-summer Saturday afternoon. It is our well-worn and sweaty biking clothes verses loafers, khakis, short-sleeved dress shirts, sundresses and high heels. We definitely stand out, and not in a good way.

Tracy

The only food they have for sale in the winery tasting room and shop is wine crackers. Figures. We decide to skip the crackers, sit outside on a picnic table and eat peanut butter and honey sandwiches. We have started carrying a loaf of bread, peanut butter and honey with us so we don't starve. Do we ever get the looks from the people coming in and out of the winery. Oh well, we had to eat somewhere and something.

Peter

Tracy emailed a guy last night who is listed in Warm Showers as living near Fredonia, New York. He accepted our request for a place to stay and gave us directions to his parents' house. Interesting. He also told us his family has property nearby with a "treehouse," and we could spend the night there if we wished. We can't pass that up. Who gets to spend the night in a treehouse?

We meet Geoffrey, a svelte, athletic-looking twentysomething, at his parents' house, an estate on the outskirts of town. We find out later that his father is a successful local businessman and Geoffrey is helping him with the business, having completed his own cross-country bicycle trip a year or so earlier. Tracy and I speculate that since Geoffrey cannot be out traveling the world himself right now, he brings the world to him via

This elaborate treehouse served as our Warm Showers hideaway near Fredonia, New York. The interior and property were just as incredible.

Warm Showers. Interestingly, Geoffrey had met the guys who started Warm Showers on a bicycle trip, before Warm Showers was even a thing. We do our laundry, shower, and then head into Fredonia for dinner at a brew pub. Geoffrey drives, we buy.

After dinner, we take a fifteen-minute drive to the property where the treehouse is located. It is off a quiet, two-lane road in the country amidst gently rolling hills, farm fields, and woodlots. They have fourteen mostly wooded acres, Geoffrey says. He turns right into a grass driveway, which is blocked by a chain with a rural fire number hanging from it. Geoffrey unlocks the chain and moves it to the side so he can drive in. Our anticipation builds. We have no idea what the "treehouse" will be. More tree or more house?

The first things we see at the end of the driveway are a wooden outhouse with sliver moons cut into the side walls, and a large fire pit with plastic, multi-colored Adirondack chairs around it. Everything appears clean and well-maintained. When we get out of the car, we see several mostly wooded paths heading off in different directions. The path to our right, which is less-wooded, leads to a huge swimming pond, complete with a diving tower and a zip line that runs from a two-story tower on one end of the pond to the other. Wow, but where's the treehouse?

We follow the path straight ahead of us down a slight hill, and then, to our right, there it is. The treehouse is much more of a house than a tree. It sits on stilts, which compensate for the steep hill it is built on, and there are mature hemlock trees growing through the rail-less deck that surrounds it. The house rises four irregular stories into the trees and is constructed of rough-sawn hemlock. The outside has several large, rectangular windows and one large round one. There are wooden lobsterpot buoys hanging about. The front door has an old ship's porthole as a window and is so heavy that it has a counterweight to help it open and close. This thing looks like something right out of *Better Homes and Gardens* magazine or *Treehouse Masters*, the TV show on the Animal Planet channel.

The inside of the treehouse does not disappoint. The first floor consists of a small living room with several well-loved chairs and a couch. The walls and beams are unfinished, rough-sawn hemlock like the outside, and the ceiling is open to the third floor. Straight past the living room is a small kitchen, followed by a staircase leading up and to the left. At the top of the stairs, on the second floor, is a small landing with a double bed where we will spend the night. The stairs continue up to a third-floor catwalk that skirts the outside walls, and is just wide enough to walk on. There are no railings. A hammock is suspended from two corner walls over the living room, three stories below. Vertigo.

The stairs continue up one more story to the crow's-nest where Geoffrey will sleep. The treehouse can sleep ten, according to Geoffrey. He tells us there was a bachelor party here several weeks ago. I asked how they keep people safe in the treehouse when the drinking starts. He smiles and says they rope off everything past the second floor. Good idea.

The light is starting to fade, so we head outside to walk the trails that crisscross the property. It feels good to stretch our legs before bed. Back inside, we turn on a few lights. There is electricity, but no plumbing. We have a couple of beers and call it a night.

Words cannot truly do this property or the treehouse justice, so let's just say that sleeping in a treehouse has been checked off our bucket list!

Chapter 11

Northeast Ups and Downs

July 27 - August 5, 2014
Total Miles 522/3,935 total

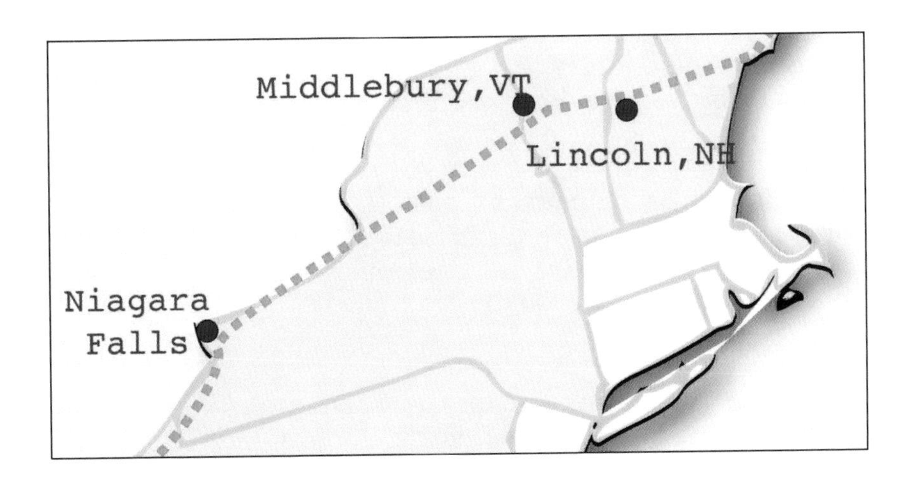

Day 57

July 27 - Fredonia to Buffalo, New York
70 miles (total miles 3,483)
Sunny and 80 degrees, tailwind

Peter

Last night it rained, but we slept like babies in the treehouse courtesy of our Warm Showers host. We want one of these.

Tracy

We get a late start today because we are at the treehouse and slept in until 8:00 a.m. We head back to our host's parents' house for breakfast and to pack up and hit the road again. We finally leave about 10:30 a.m. after thanking Geoffrey for an amazing stay. We get back on Highway 5 and head toward Buffalo. Due to the late start, we are not sure if we will make it all the way. We will decide later in the day.

We ride along Lake Erie and through more wine country with a nice tailwind, enjoying views of vineyards and the lake. Toward the end of the day, the road gets bad. There are many potholes and bad pavement right where we need to ride. The road is also narrow and there is a fair amount of traffic. It makes for a long last thirty miles.

> "We have been tracking your progress and thoroughly enjoying your commentary. You're livin' the dream. May the wind be at your back on the 'Flucke Highway' to Maine.."
>
> ***- Mike and Becky Nash***

Peter

The only bummer today was the potholes. They were bad! I didn't see much of the scenery because I was forced to concentrate so intently on the road surface, especially on the two-lane sections where there were plenty of Sunday drivers admiring the scenery. Ironic!

Tracy

We decide to continue into Buffalo (pop. 261,310), despite the roads, and enjoy a surprisingly great ride into the city on quiet streets because it is a Sunday night. We arrive about 5:30 p.m. Buffalo looks like a cool city.

Peter

We opt to stay in a hotel tonight. There is no camping in the city, and up to two inches of rain is predicted overnight anyhow. We search for a hotel online, and lucky for us, the Hyatt right downtown is one of the least expensive. On our way to the hotel, we discover why it is so cheap.

Main Street, right in front of the hotel, is completely torn up for a light rail extension project. No big deal for us on the bike, we have pushed it before. Ha.

Tracy

We check into the hotel, get cleaned up, and have dinner before wandering around downtown to check out the historic buildings. It is a very nice downtown already and the light rail will do nothing but enhance it even more.

Day 58

July 28 – Buffalo, New York to Niagara Falls, Ontario, Canada
23 miles (total miles 3,506)
Cool, low 60s, overcast and rainy

Tracy

The Hyatt has a great deal going on due to all the construction. We planned to stay a second day and explore the city, but the New York City bar exam is being held in town Monday and Tuesday. We could not get a room in the city on Monday night due to all the hopeful attorneys being in town to take the two-day test.

We head out about noon after a storm rolls through. We are heading to Niagara Falls on the Canadian side, only twenty-three miles away. Almost immediately after we leave it starts to rain, again.

Our first task is to figure out how to get across the bridge into Canada from Fort Erie. We consulted our map last night, but the instructions for crossing into Canada were confusing at best, and the addendum was no better. We decided we would just have to figure it out when we get there. Apparently, neither the Americans nor the Canadians planned very well for bicyclists to cross into their countries. How bad can it be? It is an international border, right?

Once we find where we need to be, we discover there are no bicycle accommodations on the bridge and we need to use a sidewalk. The sidewalk is not wide enough for us to ride our bicycle. We have to push it across the mile-long bridge in pouring rain, with 20 mph wind gusts hitting us from the side. To say the least, it is an eventful walk across the Buffalo/Peace Bridge. The people in their warm and dry motor vehicles, stuck in bumper-to-bumper traffic, look at us as if they think we are nuts. Who's to say who's nuts? We just laugh because it truly is quite funny.

Halfway across, we stop and admire the awesome power of the Niagara River far below. When we turn back toward the road, we are right next to a group of motorcyclists who are also getting hosed. We all laugh and give each other thumbs up.

Peter

The walk across the bridge is more like going through an automatic car wash than crossing into another country.

Tracy

Once we get across the bridge, a sign directs us to the first open lane to clear customs. Off we go, passports in hand, to the first open lane, which is actually a Fast Pass Lane. The Canadian customs agent tells us to go to the next lane. Okay. We back up the bike, and then maneuver our way into the proper lane. We clear customs with no problems.

Peter

We didn't exactly feel the love for our altruistic, non-motorized means of transportation, but it worked.

Tracy

Once through customs and into Canada, we try to follow our Adventure Cycling directions. It really looks like they are sending us onto a freeway. We do not see any other options. Just as we are getting ready to leave, a gentleman comes up to us from a customs building. Now what? He says, "You really do not want to go that way." We agree. He then directs us to a sidewalk that will lead us to a residential neighborhood and the Niagara Parkway – the very road we are searching for! We thank him and continue on our way.

The rain is starting to come down harder and we are hungry, so we stop for a late lunch in Fort Erie before continuing on to Niagara Falls. The route is along the Niagara Parkway, which has a parallel bicycle path called the Niagara River Recreation Trail. We opt to ride on the Parkway, which is in better shape and closer to the river. There is almost no traffic. We change over to the pathway when it crosses the road to the riverside. About a mile from Niagara Falls, we begin to hear a roar and see a cloud of mist rising above the water. Niagara Falls? The weather is improving and we can even see the sun.

It is a great ride along the river and exciting to come into the falls from upstream. Then, all of a sudden, we come around a bend and see the falls. Magnificent! Peter and I stop the bicycle, get off, and celebrate reaching Niagara Falls with a hug and a high-five. A couple witnesses our celebration and walks over to find out what is going on. They are from New York and are amazed that we bicycled all the way to Niagara Falls from Bellingham, Washington. They take a couple of pictures for us and wish us luck on the rest of our journey.

Yes, it's a typical tourist shot in front of Niagara Falls. But hey, we're tourists!

Peter

The Niagara River Recreation Trail has to be the best possible approach to the falls. You are along the river the entire time, it drops you right into the middle of the best views and all the excitement, and you bypass all of the motor vehicle traffic.

Tracy

Niagara Falls was one of the places we were really looking forward to seeing when we were planning our trip. It is hard to believe we have actually bicycled all the way here. It also is a sign that we are getting close to the end of our trip (approximately 750 miles to go). Some days I cannot wait to be done, and other days I do not want it to end. It has been a great adventure, but definitely a tough one. Especially lately. I am looking forward to exploring Niagara Falls and being around other people.

There are so many people around (they come in by the busloads) that we have to walk our bicycle for several miles. This is fine with us, because the views are spectacular and we want to take them all in. We are able to see the Horseshoe Falls in Canada and the American Falls in the United States.

Peter

We explore the falls area for about an hour and then continue 1.5 miles further down river to our hotel, Michael's Inn. Inexpensive, but comfortable. After a shower and hanging our gear out to dry, we walk back into town for dinner and to watch the lighting of the falls after dark. Very romantic.

Day 59

July 29 - Niagara Falls, Ontario, Canada to Medina, New York
45 miles (total miles 3,551)
65-70 degrees, partly cloudy, nice tailwind

Tracy

We decided last night to take the Horn Blower Niagara Boat Tour to the base of Niagara Falls before we leave town. We get up early and walk down Niagara Parkway to catch the boat to the falls. Our excursion leaves at 8:00 a.m. It is very fun and amazing to be this close to the falls. The water spray is like a heavy fine rain. Fortunately, we are given cheap green plastic ponchos when we board the boat. Without them, we would be soaked.

Peter

The ride is well worth it. The perspective from the river below the falls is really cool and the power of the water is truly awesome.

Tracy

After our boat trip, we head toward the Lewiston-Queenston Bridge (Interstate 190/Highway 405) for our crossing back into the United States. We are apprehensive about the crossing because the Buffalo/ Peace Bridge border crossing was not much fun and the directions on the map were incorrect. I hope that the directions are correct this time.

Here are the Adventure Cycling Association's directions: "After turning off Portage Road into the Customs building parking lot, check in with the Toll Captain. Proceed to the customs gate by crossing the westbound traffic lane, then U-turn into the eastbound traffic lane to Customs. In the U.S., you cannot walk to the plaza center. You must go thru one of the auto lanes." What?

At the Toll Captain's office, a woman tells me, "You do not have to stop at the Toll Captain's Office. Go to Customs and check in there." So off we go to Customs. But when we get there, the Customs officer tells us, "You do not have to come here. Just get in line and cross the bridge." After twenty minutes, we finally figure it out and start to cross the bridge in the car lane.

Peter

There are three traffic lanes heading back to the United States. The curb lane, where we normally would have ridden, is designated as an express truck lane and there are large trucks whizzing by in it. We are not sure where bikes belong, but we are pretty sure it isn't there. The two inside lanes are bumper to bumper with stop and go automobile traffic. We pick the right-most car lane. The stop and go traffic is too slow for us to bike in, but too fast for us to walk in. We just do our best.

Tracy

> "What an incredible adventure! I love to read your posts and enjoy hearing your highlights about how meeting different people is invigorating."
>
> ***- Steve Warner***

It takes us over an hour to ride and push our bicycle across the half-mile-long bridge. It is hot, there is no shade, and we are breathing in fumes from the cars idling around us. Not a pleasant crossing. We finally make it to U.S. Customs and re-enter the country without incident. It is amazing to me that there are no accommodations for walkers or bicyclists, not even a sidewalk. Oh well, maybe someday they will get it right.

Sixteen miles after crossing the border, we reach the Erie Canal and join the Erie Canal Trail. The trail runs along the original towpath adjacent to the canal. Proposed in 1808 and completed in 1825, the canal links the waters of Lake Erie in the west to the Hudson River in the east. The construction of a canal was proposed as early as 1768 in order to open the country west of the Appalachian Mountains to settlers and offer a cheap and safe way to carry produce to a market. However, those early proposals would connect the Hudson River with Lake Ontario near Oswego. It was not until 1808 that the state legislature funded a survey for a canal that would connect to Lake Erie. Finally, on July 4, 1817, the construction of the canal began. Two years later, the first section of the canal, between Rome and Utica, saw the beginning of commercial traffic. Use of the canal expanded as other sections were completed. When finally completed on October 26, 1825, it was the engineering marvel of its day. A ten-foot-wide towpath was built along the bank of the canal for the horses and/or mules which pulled the boats and their driver, often a young boy (sometimes referred to by later writers as a "hoggee").

The historical markers along the trail tell the story about the canal, bridges over it, and adjacent buildings. The only bad part is that the trail surface is crushed granite, and in some spots it's in bad condition. Peter is not a fan of crushed rock trails with the tandem, so this also makes it hard. He tends to get cranky when riding on these trails. The entire trail is 350 miles and we will be traveling on about 100 miles of it in total.

Peter

When I was a kid, we lived in Syracuse, New York, for several years. Every Thanksgiving, we would go for a family walk on the old Erie Canal towpath with our friends the Nelsons, Mr. and Mrs. Nelson, David, Sara, John, and Tim. (Sara is the same Nelson whose husband we met while bicycling through Washington State earlier in the trip. What an amazing coincidence.) I still remember us all walking and singing the "Erie Canal song," as we called it. The song, *Low Bridge, Everybody Down* was written in 1905 by Thomas S. Allen.

I've got an old mule and her name is Sal
Fifteen years on the Erie Canal
She's a good old worker and a good old pal
Fifteen years on the Erie Canal
We've hauled some barges in our day
Filled with lumber, coal, and hay
And every inch of the way we know
From Albany to Buffalo

Chorus:
Low bridge, everybody down
Low bridge for we're coming to a town
And you'll always know your neighbor
And you'll always know your pal
If you've ever navigated on the Erie Canal

Bicycling the towpath now, I imagine what it must have been like for the horses pulling the boats and barges along the canal. Pretty neat. I wonder if I have been on this part of the path before. Mom? Dad?

We take the path to Medina (pop. 8,065), where we start to look for somewhere to spend the night.

Tracy

There is only one hotel in town, so we decide to try something new for the night. The Historic Village Bed and Breakfast, a Victorian-style home built in 1853, is our first bed and breakfast of the trip. It is within walking distance of everything we need. The place is very nice and our hosts are great. They are even kind enough to let us do our laundry at the house.

Day 60

July 30 - Medina to Pittsford, New York
55 miles (total miles 3,606)
Cool, low 60s, cloudy and rainy

Tracy

Our day begins with a great, leisurely, breakfast at the B&B. We eat with one other guest, Doctor Z from Long Island, New York. He is in town working at a local hospital as a fill-in.

We leave Medina about 9:00 a.m. and plan to bicycle to a campground just east of Pittsfield. Our whole day will be on the Erie Canal Trail. Unfortunately, it rained hard last night and the trail is wet and therefore soft to ride on. The trail is predominately crushed granite, with asphalt sections near the towns. This type of trail is difficult for us due to our narrow tires and all the weight. We sink in and it feels like we are pulling a sack of bricks behind us. In addition, we have to get off the bike and push it through puddles. When we try to bicycle through them, the bike's back end tends to slip sideways and we risk falling. This gets old really quick.

> "You are so close to you goal now, and though I'm sure it's been challenging, you make it seem easy. I hope the last days are filled with great views and nice people!"
> ***- Barbara Ali***

The Erie Canal Trail really is an amazing bicycle and pedestrian facility, although it does get a little boring at times. It all looks the same, a path next to a canal. We are surprised there is not a lot of traffic on the canal, and we do not see much wildlife, either. We did see some tour boats that take their customers and their bicycles down the canal so they can bicycle back. Everyone seems to be having fun on the boats. Maybe we will try it sometime, when we are older. The little towns along the way and the historical aspects of the canal are interesting and definitely add to the experience.

Peter

The tandem had been jumping gears unexpectedly yesterday for part of the day. Not cool. I tried to fix the problem several times by adjusting the derailleur cable tension, but with no success. We are still having the problem today, but it isn't a big deal because I don't have to shift much on the flat trail. Tomorrow, however, we will be back on the road and in the hills again. Lots of shifting expected. We need to have things working properly by then. There is a bike shop in Brockport (pop. 8,366), so we decide to stop in and have them take a look at the bike.

The mechanic at the bike shop, more of a BMX guy than a road guy, discovers that the rear derailleur cable is frayed inside the shifter and is preventing proper shifting. He knows his stuff. Unfortunately, the shop doesn't have a tandem derailleur cable. Not to worry, we carry a spare for just such an eventuality. I inspect our tires while the mechanic does his thing and discover that the rear needs to be retired. (I love it when we literally ride the rubber off a tire.) We have a new tire (from our stash of three extras) installed and we are on our way to lunch across the street.

Dark clouds start to build during lunch, but the radar looks like the rain and storms will miss us to the north. As we eat, we spot the bike mechanic running across the street with an Allen wrench in his hand. Interesting. He bursts into the restaurant and breathlessly explains that he forgot to double check something on the bike. He bops back outside, tinkers with the bike for a minute, and gives us the thumbs up through the picture window. My kind of mechanic.

Back on the trail, it starts to rain again. It looks like we can outrun it, but no. We just keep get wetter and wetter. On the edge of Pittsford (pop. 1,365), fourteen miles short of our goal for the day, our front tire starts leaking air and goes flat. Upon inspection, I discover there is a sharp rock, probably from the trail, wedged in the tire. Bummer! We discover, after a quick Google check, that there is a bike shop only a half mile away. We decide to walk to the shop, have them fix the tire, find a hotel, take a shower, have some dinner, do some shopping, wash our clothes, clean the bike, have a beer, and go to bed. Good night!

Day 61

July 31 - Pittsford to Fulton, New York
83 miles (total miles 3,689, remaining miles 673)
Cool, 60-70 degrees, headwind and rain

Tracy

Today we start counting down the miles to our ending point, Bar Harbor, Maine. We have 673 miles to go. Unbelievable, it has gone so fast. Peter and I realized this when we were looking at the maps last night and discovered we only have Map #11 left and are halfway through Map #10. Wow. We can almost smell the salt water.

We leave a little later this morning, 9:30 a.m., to let the trail set up a bit. Thank goodness we only have fifteen more miles to go on the Erie Canal Trail. The trail is wet and the same issues as yesterday come into play, sinking in and slipping. Oh well, we make the best of it and are off the trail before we know it. It is nice to be on roads again. However, the flat roads are gone and we spend the afternoon climbing up and down hills. We also get soaked, bicycling for an hour in a rainstorm.

The route today takes us along Lake Ontario, where apple orchards abound. It looks like it will be a good crop this year. This is our third Great Lake and it is as beautiful as the other two, albeit harder to see and enjoy due to the rainy weather.

> **Blog Annoucement**
>
> *We want to let everyone know how nice it is to hear from you all, and we are glad you are enjoying the blog. Beginning late this week and into early next week, we will be in an area that will not have cell phone or internet connection. So, if you do not see a blog for a while, do not worry, we just have no service.*

Peter

The skies to the west start to cloud up about 1:30 p.m. We ride on the eastern edge of the rain for about an hour and then it hits. With no real shelter to be found, and no real idea how long the rain will last, we continue riding east in the rain, sometimes heavy, for about an hour. The rain finally relents, but the roads remain wet for the rest of the ride.

Soaked to the skin, we decided to scrap our plan to camp one more time, head to Fulton (pop. 12,536), and find a hotel. The Red Roof Inn isn't much, but it does have a working shower and it is dry. The bed may not be level, but we are tired enough to sleep almost anywhere.

Tracy

Plans are to camp tomorrow night. Hopefully the weather will be better and we will find a nice campground.

Day 62

August 1 - Fulton to Booneville, New York
77 miles (total miles 3,766, remaining miles 596)
80-84 degrees, sunny, light winds

Tracy

We get up early, anticipating a long day on the bike. Our hotel offers free breakfast with our stay and is supposed to be open for service by 6:30 a.m. We get to the restaurant at 6:30 a.m., and there is no server. I ask at the desk and a server arrives a couple of minutes later. We place our order and wait about a half hour to get our food. So much for the early start. The local Rotary Club is meeting in the room next door. It is fun to listen in on their meeting and hear about the events they have planned.

Our route today takes us along Lake Ontario to the city of Port Ontario, where we turn east and head toward the Adirondack Mountains. We see many apple orchards along the route. This must be a prime area to grow apples. We have twenty-three miles to go to Boonville (pop. 2,072). The first fifteen miles are on Osceola Road, which has many small hills. We seem to be climbing more than coasting down the backside. It definitely is burning out our legs.

Peter

It is a pleasure to, finally, ride without getting rained on today. The route climbs slightly, which tests our legs, but we are up to the challenge.

Tracy

We take a break in the small town of West Leyden, with seven miles to go to Boonville. We meet two local men at a convenience store and they tease us about the fact it is more fun, and easier, to ride Osceola Road the other direction. Now they tell us. They then tell us the last seven miles to Boonville are mostly downhill, Yay. They are right.

We roll into Boonville early because we have to do laundry before deciding which of the two local campgrounds to visit.

Peter

Fate smiles on us again.

Tracy

We head to the laundromat and see two bicyclists sitting outside. Of course, we strike up a conversation and discover they are from Kingston, Canada, and are out with a group of nine who are on a nine-day, unsupported, bicycle trip in Upstate New York. They are waiting for the rest of the group to come in. We ask where they are staying for the night, hoping they are at our campground. Instead, they are staying at North Country Manor Bed and Breakfast. The owner is allowing them to camp or stay in the B&B. For $20, you can camp, take a shower, and get breakfast the next morning. It sounds good to us and they ask us to join them. We jump at the offer. So instead of bicycling three more miles, uphill, to the closest campground, we only have to go one mile out of town to the B&B. We do our laundry, and then head out to meet up with our new friends.

We find the B&B easily, thanks to their tour director's directions, shower, and then order takeout pizza and beer with the rest of the group. We have a nice dinner, a few beers, and great conversation to fill our night. Special thanks to the Kingston Velo Club and their tour director, Hal Cain, for adopting us for the night. We had a great time. Another act of kindness.

Day 63

August 2 – Booneville to Raquette Lake, New York
52 miles (total miles 3,818, remaining miles 544)
Cooler, 70-75 degrees, partly cloudy, rain later in day (downpour)

Tracy

We get up to a nice breakfast at the B&B and say goodbye to our new friends from Canada. Shortly after leaving Booneville on Moose River Road, we come to the Black River. Unfortunately, the bridge is out and road closed signs block the way. There are no detour signs. I am having a flashback to Michigan, so I decide to walk down the hill to see how "out" the bridge is. The entire bridge has not been removed yet, and a four-foot wide concrete slab spans the river.

I give Peter a thumbs up and he walks the bicycle down the hill to look. We agree we can cross, but will need to remove the bags from the bike and take several trips across. Four feet is way too narrow for us to ride with any reasonable margin of safety. Also, the transitions at the end of the concrete slab are uneven and not rideable. Peter grabs the rear bags and walks across, while I grab the front bags and Peter follows with the bicycle, which is now easier to control. We get everything to the other side, reload the bicycle, and are on our way again.

Our first planned stop today is McKeever, seventeen miles down the road. The route is adjacent to the Moose River. It is a beautiful ride, but again, lots of ups and downs. We planned to get a snack in McKeever, but due to some road construction we miss the town. The construction is on a major bridge, which is down to one lane. We are the last ones to cross before the flagmen allow vehicles headed the other direction to go. This works out well, because the traffic going our way is held up so we do not have any cars passing us for a while.

Our route continues on the Fulton Chain of Lakes. The towns of Old Forge and Inlet are busy with the early weekend traffic. Both towns are very tourist friendly and have many services to offer. We stop for lunch in one and a snack in the other. We enjoy people watching. In the town of Inlet, the rain begins. It is just drizzling. We sit a while and then take off. The rain starts to come down harder about a mile down the road, and Peter thinks the front tire is going flat. Crap. Fixing a tire in the rain is no fun. He is really stressing out about the tire and there is nothing I can do to help. We pull over to check the tire.

As we stand on the side of the road deciding what to do, a woman who is out for a run stops and asks if we need help. Peter says, sarcastically, "Only if you have a floor pump." She equally sarcastically replies, "Well,

Peter takes a break in Inlet, New York, on the Fulton Chain of Lakes.

not on me, but I'm staying .5 miles away and there is a floor pump in the garage there you can use." Peter is embarrassed for the way he acted and apologizes to the woman. She gives us her address and tells us her name (Elizabeth) in case anyone else is at the house and wonders what we are doing. Down the road we go. We find the house and pump in the garage, and change the tube, which has a slow leak. Thanks, Elizabeth for letting us use your floor pump in the shelter of the garage.

We start up again, only to have the skies really open up on us. We get totally soaked and are cold, so we decide to look for somewhere to stay rather than continue down the road another thirty miles to Long Lake, where we had planned to stay at a campground. We make it to Raquette Lake and go into town. They are having their annual celebration and there is nowhere to stay or get out of the rain. There are so many people seeking cover.

We stop at a bar and they tell us there may be some cabins available on the other side of the lake. We hop back on the bicycle and continue down the road, homeless, cold, and wet. We stop at the first fishing camp we come to, but all of their cabins are full. Luckily, the woman at the camp is nice enough to call the next fishing camp for us. They will hold a cabin for us. No deposit necessary. We continue down the road to Burke's Marine and Cabins. Nora, the owner, is waiting for us and sends us right to the cabin to get warmed up. We can come back and pay her when we are ready. We must look really bad.

The cabin is a little, 1940s-era, lakefront fishing shack with a small living room, very small bathroom, and two bedrooms with single beds. A warm shower and a small heater soon have us warm and clean. The cabin is located on Raquette Lake and has a beautiful view of the water. It is the starting point for the annual Raquette Lake Durant Days Boat Parade, which is going on tonight. We are not able to see the parade, though. I think we missed it when we were eating dinner. They also have fireworks this evening. We hear them, but cannot see them from where we are.

Day 64

August 3 - Raquette Lake to Newcomb, New York
(Emmett's Cabin on the Goodnow Flowage)
43 miles (total miles 3,861, remaining miles 501)
Sunny, 70-75 degrees, slight tailwind

Tracy

It is a great day for a ride. The weather is beautiful. YAY! We get up and going early, even though we have a relatively short ride today. The rain has stopped, but the roads are still wet and all too soon the bicycle and we are once again wet and dirty. At least it is not coming from above. We are on our way to Emmett's "camp" near Newcomb for a couple of days.

Peter

I started training law enforcement officers in New York State about pedestrian and bicycle safety issues on a regular basis in 2012. One of my state contacts, Emmett, was constantly crowing about his "camp" upstate. He would say that I should come and stay there sometime. Apparently, he is always letting friends use it. (I eventually figured out that "camp" is New York-speak for a cabin.) He said it was on the Goodnow Flowage and simply beautiful.

I really never paid much attention to Emmitt's camp stories until this spring, when I was with him again for a training. When he mentioned his camp again, I asked if he was serious about letting us use it. I was interested if it was close enough to our route. He said, "Heck yes." I asked him for the address and immediately called it up on my phone. Sure enough, the camp was only seven miles south of our route, plenty close for a free cabin all to ourselves in the most beautiful place on earth.

Then Emmett started to hesitate. He said the camp is at the end of a long, gravel road. It isn't quite finished and is a bit primitive.

"How long's the gravel road?" I ask.

"About a mile." Manageable.

"What do you mean by 'primitive?' "

"Well, when you get inside you have to go in the basement and flip the breakers for the lights and the hot water."

Lights? Hot water? I think we will be fine.

"Oh, yeah," he says. "The beds don't have sheets on them, either."

Really? I just laughed and told him we would take it.

"Okay," he says. "The key is on the back of the cedar tree to the right in the clump of three, forty yards from the door at a thirty-degree angle. Emmett is an engineer.

Tracy

We are now very much into the Adirondack Mountains. The first town we come to is Blue Mountain Lake, a beautiful town sitting on Blue Mountain Lake, with Blue Mountain looking down on us from across the lake. We have a tough climb out of town. It is very steep for close to a mile, and then we round a bend only to have the road steepen even more for the last stretch to the top. We make it up, but are definitely out of breath at the top. From here, it is a nice downhill to the town of Long Lake.

Peter

I did some backpacking when I was in high school in the Appalachian Mountains of North Carolina and Tennessee on the Appalachian Trail and the Sierra Nevada Mountains of California on the John Muir Trail. While the mountains in the western United States tend to be much taller than the mountains in the east, the road and trail grades in the east are generally much steeper. Climbing in the mountains of the West is mostly about endurance, long climbs with manageable grades of three to six, maybe eight percent. In the East, however, while the climbs are usually shorter, they are often much steeper. These climbs are all about raw power and how long you can maintain it. We are in for a challenge with these mountains if our last climb was any indication.

Tracy

We need to grocery shop in Long Lake for food to cover our two days at Emmett's cabin, so we go a bit off route into downtown to find a grocery store. His cabin is at the end of a seven-mile ride (with the last mile being gravel and dirt), and we do not want to have to bicycle back out to get supplies. While grocery shopping, a local floatplane pilot comes up to us to talk about our trip and ask how it is going. He even offers to take us up for a flight in his floatplane the next day. He gives us his card and says if we come back to town the next day to give him a call and he will be happy to take us up. It would be cool to go up in a floatplane, but we really don't have the desire to bicycle seventeen miles back to Long Lake. It sure is nice of him to offer, though.

After a good time shopping and a nice lunch, we are both ready to hop back on the bicycle for the short ride to Emmett's Cabin. We are looking forward to a couple days off the bicycle. We need to backtrack to get back on route. When we arrive at the intersection with our route, I am not sure if we need to turn right or left. Peter asks and I tell him, "I don't know." He turns left, because we really did not have a choice at that point. He turns the corner and then immediately stops the bicycle near a gas station. He turns around and begins to yell at me.

"What are you thinking about? You need to know where we are going. Are you trying to get us killed?"

As he is screaming at me, I see a man walking over from the gas station. I am trying to calm Peter down and tell him someone is coming over and he needs to settle down. The man stops in front of me and says, "Is everything okay?" I assure him I am okay, explain what is going on, and thank him for coming over. He hesitantly walks away, but looks back several times to check on me.

I look at Peter with tears in my eyes and say, "Can we please move down the road?" I am very shocked by the whole situation. One minute ago, we were happy and relaxed, and now Peter is a raving lunatic and I am in tears. What happened? I cannot believe he has reacted so strongly to me not knowing which way to turn. He has never treated me this way before and I am hurt and embarrassed that a stranger witnessed it.

Peter

I am still really upset as we continue riding down the road, and I am trying to explain to Tracy why I always need her to know exactly where we are. Reasonable? Probably not. As I continue to talk, I continue to get more and more upset. Too upset to continue riding. I pull over to the side of the road with Tracy asking me, "What are you doing?" I get off the bike and just walk away. I can't do this anymore.

I find an old staircase cut into the side of a hill and I just start walking up. At the top of the hill, I find myself at the edge of an old cemetery. I sit down in the grass, pull my knees up to my chest, put my head on my knees, and just breathe. After about fifteen minutes, I get up, walk back down the hill and say to Tracy, "Are you ready to go?" She nods. We mount up and ride on.

This is the only time I have walked away from Tracy on a bicycle ride, either before or since.

Tracy

The rest of the ride is terrible. All I can think about is what happened and how Peter treated me. I have not said anything to him since we got back on the bicycle, except to provide the needed directions. This is tough, because I am afraid I will give him the wrong directions or say something the "wrong way" and he will go off.

We finally make it to the turnoff to Emmett's cabin. First of all, the street signs have been taken, so we are not sure if we are on the right road. We ask a motorist and he says we are. We head to our next turn and the sign, again, is gone. Thank goodness a guy comes out of his home and assures us that this is, in fact, Goodnow Road. We bicycle along this very hilly road until we hit the dirt/gravel section. We try to ride for a bit, but quickly find it is not possible. We push the bicycle for the next .75 miles.

Peter

Goodnow Road has been getting smaller and smaller as we ride, then push the bike along. We haven't seen a real road sign for miles. All we have to guide us are Emmett's directions that say things like, "Take the larger branch in the road to the left." There are signs for people's camps nailed to trees sporadically, but nothing that identifies Emmett's camp. Man, if we can't find this place, this is really going to suck. We get to another fork in the road and I have absolutely no idea which way to go. I leave Tracy with the bike and start walking down the fork to the right. After about a quarter mile the road simply ends. No Emmet's camp here.

Back with Tracy, we reread the directions for the umpteenth time. There is supposed to be a large propane tank in Emmett's front yard. Tracy looks around and spots a large grey propane tank fifty yards to our left, but no cabin. We push the bike toward the tank, more to lean the bike on it than with any hope we have arrived. I'm getting hungry. Then we spot a large, two-story, clapboard-sided building. From where we stand, all we can see are two windows on the second story and four on the lower level facing us, and a door on the right side with three rickety steps leading up to it. Could it Be? This place sure doesn't look like heaven on earth, but it is worth a try.

I slowly walk to the door. I put my back to the door, fully expecting to be disappointed, and wondering if we can pitch our tent in this guy's yard for the night, and look forty yards out at a thirty-degree angle. Oh my gosh. There is a clump of three cedar trees right where they should be. I walk to the trees and, hesitantly, run my hand around the back side of the rightmost tree. And there it is, a key. We are saved. "I got it!" I yell to Tracy.

I return to the door, carefully climb the stairs, place the key in the lock and turn it. The door opens and I walk inside.

The inside of the cabin is stunning. The ceiling in the dining room and living room to my right is open to the peak of the roof, two and one half stories above. There are floor-to-ceiling picture windows that look out on a deck and the Goodnow Flowage far below. Immediately to my left, there is a small kitchen with a sink, cupboards, refrigerator, and a stove. A grand staircase sits in the middle of the space and leads down to a basement and up to a loft. There is a bathroom with a shower and three bedrooms with beds under the loft. The loft itself is completely open and there are a couple of beds up there as well. I'm sure this place could sleep ten easily. The entire structure is constructed of massive old-growth pine logs that have had the bark removed. Incredible. There is still some finishing work to be done, but we hardly notice. We haven't had this much space to ourselves in forever, and we need it.

I carefully make my way into the basement with a flashlight and locate the circuit breakers for the electricity and hot water heater. We have lights, and soon, we will have hot water.

We are both spent, physically and mentally. The rest of our trip may be doomed, but for now, there is nothing to do but unpack, take a shower, make dinner, and get some sleep. We do these tasks in complete silence and automatically. I have no energy or will left to talk to Tracy. Sad.

I unpack the tent and hang it from the loft to dry. After a shower, I scrounge around the cabin and find a variety pack of Leinenkugel's beer, brewed in Chippewa Falls, Wisconsin. I plug in the refrigerator and set the beer to cooling. Dinner is a silent affair.

Tracy

The cabin is very nice and thankfully has lots of space. I need it. Peter and I go about our business in silence. I take a shower, make dinner, clean up the dishes, and sit down to read. Later, I take my sleeping bag and head to one of the bedrooms to try to get some sleep. I shut the door and climb in. I will sleep alone tonight.

Day 65

August 4 - Newcomb, New York

0 miles (total miles 3,861 – remaining miles - 501

Peter

Tracy and I slept in separate beds last night. We both just needed our space.

I wake up early, as I always do, and make myself a large cup of coffee which I drink alone out on the deck watching the flowage. The Goodnow Flowage reminds me a lot of northern Wisconsin, or even more like the

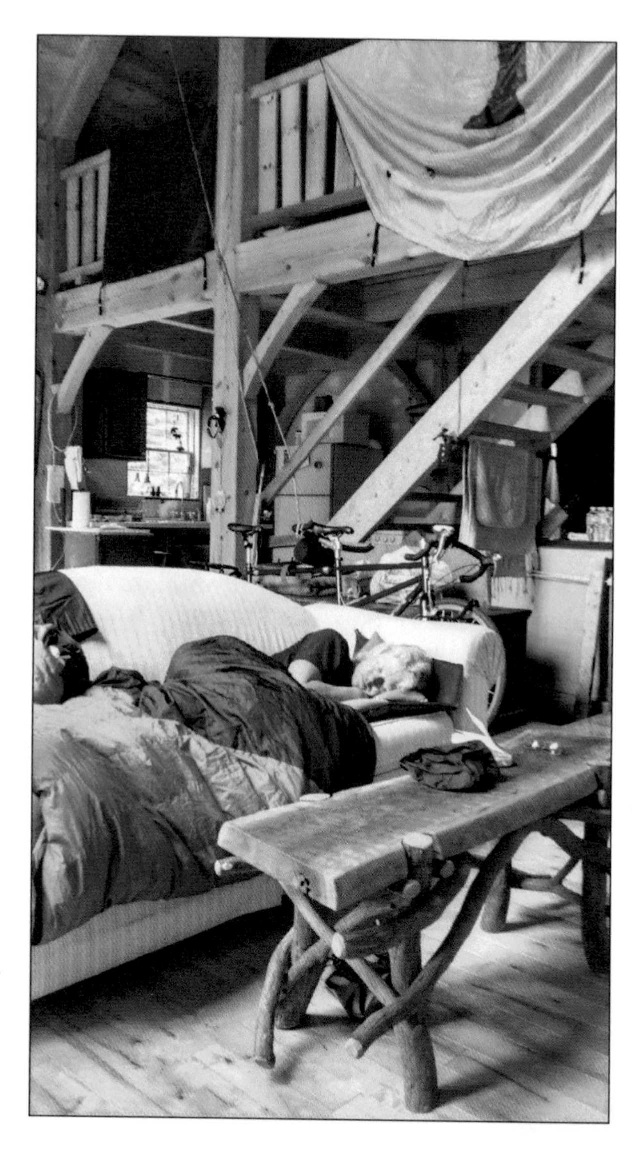

Tracy sleeps in Emmett's spectacular cabin near Newcomb, New York. That's our tent hanging from the balcony in the upper right to dry.

Boundary Waters Canoe Area in northern Minnesota. I try to think about our current situation, but I just can't do it. I make myself some breakfast and then head outside to check out the water's edge. Tracy is still sleeping.

The water is calming. Because of my forestry background, I know most of the plants and animals I can see and hear. After pushing so hard for so long, I need this.

Tracy

I did not sleep well last night, so I don't climb out of bed until 11:00 a.m. It felt great to sleep in, but upon waking I knew Peter and I needed to make a decision about the rest of the trip. I have breakfast and wander outside to check out the area. It is beautiful here and very quiet. No one is around.

Peter

Later in the day, I eat lunch and take a long nap.

Tracy

While Peter is sleeping, I think about the rest of the trip, write up my posts for the blog, work on laundry, and read my book.

We have about a week of bicycling left to get to Bar Harbor, Maine. It is hard to believe we are so close. I cannot imagine not completing the trip. Peter and I need to talk and see if we can work out a way to get to Bar Harbor without killing each other.

Peter

By midafternoon, I know I need to see if Tracy will sit down and talk. We have some big decisions to make.

"Do you want to talk?" I ask her.

"Sure," she says.

We each grab a beer and take a chair at the dining room table. I start out by telling Tracy I am sorry that this has gotten so hard and that I talked her into doing the trip. I say that we can quit if she wants to. It will take me about a day and a half to get us to a big city where we can rent a car and then we can be done.

She looks at me with this puzzled look on her face and says, "I don't want to quit. I want to finish this. You didn't talk me into anything. I wanted to do this, and I still do. Yeah, this has been hard, but I don't want to quit."

I immediately feel like a huge weight has been lifted off of my shoulders.

"You don't want to quit?"

"No."

"Okay then."

And with that, I have the answer to our problem. For weeks we have been grinding ourselves and each other down. As we both struggled to keep going, we had forgotten that our strength has always been that we make a great team. Whether it is as partners, parents, or business owners, we rock it together. I don't think either of us can do this alone anymore. But if we focus on our common goal, and build each other up and not down, we can do this.

Tracy

We talk for a long time and really listen and acknowledge each other's concerns. We discover we have the same goal, to complete the trip. Now we just have to find a way to do that in a positive manner. We agree to work as a team and not put each other down.

We have a couple of mountain passes to go over yet. Bread Loaf Pass (2,000 feet) and Kancamagus Pass (2,855 feet). These are not nearly as high as the Cascades, but we have not climbed a mountain in a while. Hopefully, we still have our climbing legs.

We are excited to complete our journey, but at the same time sad it will end. We are planning to shorten our days slightly to get into Bar Harbor on a Monday, avoiding the busy weekend.

We end the day trying to make marshmallow shots. Peter came up with this idea after seeing a Facebook post describing how to do it several days ago and finding all the needed ingredients in the cabin (marshmallows, Emmets Classic Cream Liqueur and Sabroso Licor De Café). The experiment was a bust, but we sure had fun trying. We only need one bed tonight.

Marshmallow Shots

Ingredients

6 jumbo marshmallows
Baileys Irish Cream, for filling

Directions

Stick a jumbo marshmallow halfway up a fork and toast over a burner, turning occasionally, until very toasted and warmed through.

Use another fork to help slide the marshmallow off the fork; the center should sink as it cools, making a well in the marshmallow.
-Fill each marshmallow with Baileys and serve.

(http://www.delish.com/cooking/recipe-ideas/recipes/a47791/toasted-marshmallow-shots-recipes/)

Day 66

August 5 – Newcomb, New York, to Middlebury, Vermont
74 miles (total miles 3,935, remaining miles 427)
75-80 degrees, partly sunny, rain late in day

Tracy

Today we get going from Emmett's cabin fairly early. We have a cross-country bicycle ride to finish. We must push the bicycle the first .75 miles due to the gravel road, but it goes by pretty quickly. The next six miles are hilly, but at least the road is paved. Soon we are back on route.

We stop in Newcomb, down the road three miles, for a donut and coffee/tea. When we approach the café, we see two touring bicycles leaning against the building. As we enter the café to say hello to the bicycles' owners, one of the gentlemen says, "Hello, Tracy and Peter."

We just laugh and I say, "How do you know us? The Northern Tier communication line?"

John says he had been riding with Karen and Alan, the couple from Madison, Wisconsin, that we traveled with in North Dakota. John, Karen, and Alan had traveled together for quite a while and they had told him about us. Too funny.

After eating several homemade donuts, we hop on the bicycle again and travel on Blue Bridge Road for approximately twenty miles. It is a great road that has lots of ups and downs and wonderful views. We are riding well after our rest day.

After lunch in Ticonderoga, we bicycle to Lake Champlain to take the Fort Ticonderoga Ferry across to Vermont.

Peter

The sky looks cranky to the north. The clouds are black and boiling. We can see lightning and hear thunder in the distance, and it all appears to be coming our way. The radar on my phone confirms this, and the approaching storm is big.

The ferry that will take us across Lake Champlain to Vermont is small. It only holds eighteen cars on a single open-air deck. The captain is protected from the weather in a small, elevated pilothouse and the motorists have their cars to hide in. We have nothing. After several minutes of watching the sky and the radar, we decide to go for it, hoping that one of the motorists will give us shelter if the bad weather hits while we are on the lake. It is only a seven-minute ferry ride.

Tracy

Peter and I strike up a conversation with a gentleman from Middlebury, Vermont (pop. 8,246), as we are waiting for the ferry to come. This is where we are planning to spend the night. His name is Doug Anderson, and he is the director of the local performing arts center. He gives us some good ideas on what to do in Middlebury.

After we push the tandem onboard the ferry, Peter goes to pay the ferry captain our fare, $2.00 for the bicycle, while I stay with the bike. As he approaches, the captain waves him off, saying the fee had already been paid. By whom, and why? The captain points to Doug. Doug smiles, and tips his head slightly toward us. He covered it for us. Thanks, Doug. Again, a nice thing someone did for us. What a great welcome to another state. Only three more to go. Mercifully, the storm held off.

Once into Vermont, we only have another twenty miles to go. The route is beautiful and through the mountains. Again, lots of ups and downs.

Peter

Our only real issue today is a fraying front derailleur cable. I noticed the buggered-up cable during one of our rest stops halfway through the day. The derailleur is working, but for how long? The cable is kind of like a ticking time bomb. It is going to break, but when? When it does break, I will either have to replace it – never done that before – or tie it off in one chainring, severely limiting the number of gears I will have available (9 vs. 27 or so). Not ideal in the Vermont mountains.

The ride into Middlebury is, fortunately, uneventful. Not wanting to tempt fate, we make a beeline to The Bike Center and have the cable replaced. No harm, no foul. While at the bike shop, the storm finally catches us and it starts to rain like hell. Ha. This time we are inside.

Tracy

While we are waiting for our bicycle repair, a mom and her little boy come into the shop. The boy is interested in our "double bike" and has many questions about our trip. After answering questions for several minutes, mom finally tells the boy it is time to go and asks for a business card so they can follow us on our blog and Facebook. They send me a message later in the day telling me how much they enjoyed looking at our past posts and plan to follow us to the end of the trip.

> "It was a pleasure to talk with you guys at the bike shop amidst the downpour in Middlebury (me and my 9-year-old son). We are following your blog!"

We wait out the storm and then head to our hotel, the Courtyard Middlebury, for the evening.

Chapter 12

Vermont and New Hampshire

August 6-7, 2014
Total Miles 144/4,079 total

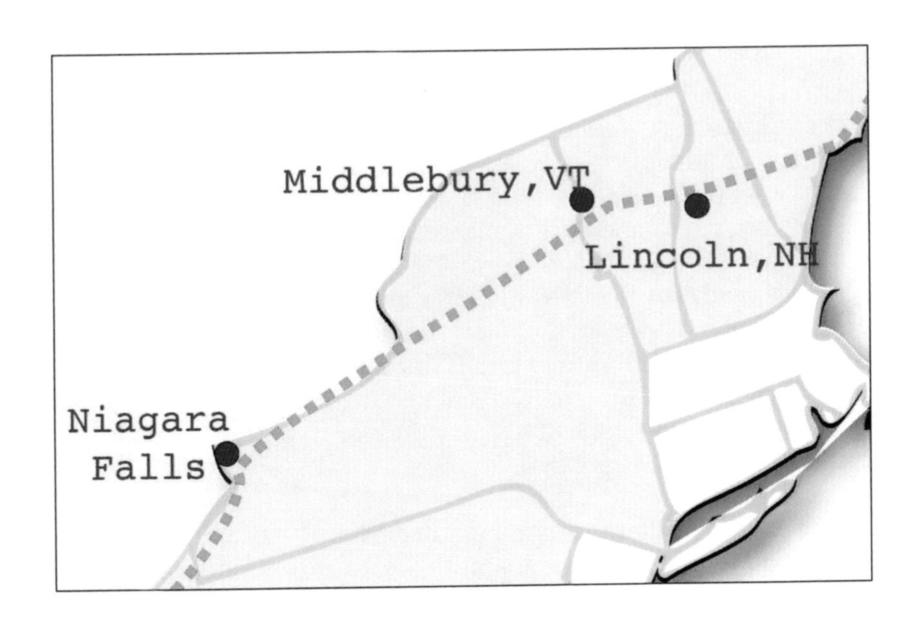

Day 67

August 6 – Middlebury to South Strafford, Vermont
75 miles (total miles 4,010, miles remaining 352)
Nice, 70 degrees, sunny

Tracy

Middlebury (pop. 8,246) is a beautiful city. They have a vibrant downtown area that is bicycle and pedestrian friendly, and effective mass transit. There is a free bus from our hotel to downtown. Last night, we planned to take the shuttle to the downtown microbrewery for a beer, and of course a glass. Unfortunately, the brewery closed early and we were not able to get there in time. Oh well, maybe next time.

We hit the road early because we have several major climbs near Bread Loaf, Vermont, including the Middlebury Gap. These are our first real climbs since the Cascade Mountains, Sherman Pass (5,575 feet) on day 5, back on June 5, and they will likely test our legs and our resolve.

The climbs are definitely tough and extremely steep. Several of the climbs have twelve percent grades. I am proud to say we did not have to push the bicycle up any of them, although we were close a couple of times.

Peter

Frankly, pushing the loaded tandem up a twelve percent grade is worse than riding up it, if we can. The extreme effort is actually worth it.

Tracy

The East Coast Mountains, while lower than the West Coast Mountains, are definitely steeper. I think I like the West Coast climbs better. We get to the top of one of the climbs and a man who is getting out of his car turns to us and congratulates us on getting to the top, and tells us we did well. I thought so, too.

We are ready for the downhill after our hard climbs. It should have been spectacular. However, the road is so steep and the pavement in such bad condition that Peter has to totally engage the drag brake and use the rim brakes to keep us slowed down enough to make sure we get down the mountain safely. Very difficult to enjoy the ride that way. Bummer.

Peter

We heard later that the extreme rains from Hurricane Sandy (2012) really did a number on the roads in this part of the country. We would agree.

Tracy

We run into the group of cyclists that left Anacortes, Washington, the same day we left Bellingham, Washington. We have been seeing them every now and then, but the last time we saw them was in North Dakota. They are having a good ride, but are definitely ready to be done. They are on a supported Adventure Cycling Association trip. A guide hauls their supplies in a van and sets how far they travel each day and where they will camp each night.

It is sparsely populated in this area and there are not a lot of places to stay, so I check Warm Showers and am able to find a home stay in South Strafford, Vermont. Our host's name is Bonna. She owns a beautiful piece of property about five miles off route in South Strafford. Bonna is a kayak tour leader and her home is totally off the grid. She uses solar and wood to heat and provide electricity for her home. She also has a yurt and tells us we can stay in the yurt or in the bedroom in her house. We choose the yurt, which is a portable, round tent traditionally covered with skins or felt. Bonna's yurt is much more than that. The yurt is located next to a rushing stream that flows through Bonna's property.

Peter

The yurt is incredibly comfortable and efficient. It is only sixteen feet in diameter, but there is a space just inside the door for boots and coats, a small kitchen area, a living room complete with oriental rug, rocking chair, couch, and bookshelves, a dining room table with chairs, and a small wood stove for heating. My favorite part is the bedroom.

In the middle of the yurt is a loft that stands about six feet tall. There is room for clothes and other storage under the loft, and on top of it is

Inside the yurt. We never would have guessed a glorified tent could be so nice.

a queen-sized bed. The head of the bed is positioned directly under a Plexiglas dome. The dome is large, five feet in diameter. With our heads only a few feet from the dome, it feels and looks just like we are sleeping under the stars.

Tracy

We can hear the stream as we drift off to sleep. Very relaxing.

Day 68

August 7 – South Strafford, Vermont, to Lincoln, New Hampshire
69 miles (total miles 4,079, miles remaining 283)
Nice early, storms midday, 70 degrees

Tracy

We received a vague message on our blog from Mark Stephany, a friend and fellow cyclist from Green Bay, back on July 30: "Peter, What is your ETA to Bar Harbor? I will send more information when I know. Enjoying all your posts!"

Last night he sent the following: "Peter and Tracy, you do a great job with your blog! Do you record all your stops or just remember all of it? Once in Bar Harbor, stop at the Thirsty Whale for lunch, good food (lobster roll) and nice selection of beer. I will have a gift card waiting for you. My brother and I have eaten there after completing the Cadillac Challenge on Mt. Desert Island and the food is good. Enjoy the last few days!"

What a nice surprise. We cannot wait to get there.

Today is another day of climbing, but with shorter climbs in the Thetford Center, Thetford Hill, and East Thetford areas.

Peter

The roads continue to be narrow and steep, but the drivers are courteous and the views are right out of a picture postcard collection.

Tracy

We enter the state of New Hampshire near Fryeburg, (yay, one more state to go), and have an enjoyable, mostly downhill ride on River Road, located adjacent to the Connecticut River. The views are great and the homes along this stretch are breathtaking.

Peter

The day started out dry, but by lunch the clouds are building ominously over the mountain range we are about to climb.

Tracy

We get caught in a hailstorm just outside of Orford. This is the first hailstorm we have experienced – another good reason to wear a bicycle helmet.

We stop in Orford for lunch and to wait out another storm that is rolling through the area. While we wait at the convenience store/ restaurant, a couple riders from the big Adventure Cycling group come in. They are staying in Orford tonight and have only bicycled thirty-five miles today. They are not happy about the short day of riding and explain they are supposed to be riding at least sixty miles a day. However, some of the group members are struggling, so the leader has decided to cut back on miles. They further explain there are many conflicts in the group (of twelve) and no one is happy.

After they leave, I tell Peter, "We are struggling and are married and love each other. I can't even imagine what it is like in the big group. I am glad it is only us."

Peter

I am glad it is only us, too. We have been doing much better as a team and partners the past three days. The first day out from Emmett's camp was tough physically, seventy-four miles with pushing the bike .75 miles, hilly terrain, a frayed derailleur cable, and rain in the afternoon, but we were fresh from our day off and handled it well all around.

The past two days have been good with great weather, lower mileage, and the end in sight helping our mood, I'm sure. I still need to watch myself to make sure I don't get upset, overreact, and take it out on Tracy. When things begin to get hard for me, I have started to ask myself what I need to do to make our team stronger instead of just reacting. This seems to be working. Yelling is never the answer. (I will reserve that reaction for when I am alone.)

Tracy

We have been a better team lately. I think talking about our issues and acknowledging that we are physically and mentally stretched helped. We now better understand each other's struggles and have the ability to acknowledge that we are doing our best, but may need help to get it right. So far, so good. I hope it will continue until we are done. The ride has become fun again.

Peter

Lunch takes longer than expected as we watch the radar and wait for the weather to clear. I really do not want to get caught in a thunderstorm up on a mountain. After about an hour, we spot an opening in the weather and decide to go for it. With thunder rumbling in the distance, we complete the fifteen-mile climb in record time and make it into Lincoln, New Hampshire, just as the sky opens up with rain, thunder, and lightning. That was close.

Tracy

We get into Lincoln (pop. 1,271) at 4:30 p.m. and bicycle through town looking for somewhere to stay. We take cover at a random hotel when the skies open up again. The hotel is full. We sit in the lobby for an hour before we can bicycle back through town to a hotel that has rooms. We stay dry, mostly.

Lincoln is located in New Hampshire's White Mountain range. The range is crossed by only two roads, White Mountain Trail and Kancamagus Highway, a designated American Scenic Byway. Part of the Appalachian Trail is also located in the White Mountains. The Mount Washington Cog Railway has been climbing to the summit of Mount Washington, the highest peak in the northeastern United States, since the 1860s. Thank goodness our route does not take us over Mount Washington.

Peter finds a brewery in the adjacent town of North Woodstock. We clean up and walk the mile to the Woodstock Inn and Brewery. The place is packed, so we decide to have a beer and our dinner at the bar. Peter sits next to a young couple from New Hampshire and we enjoy a lively conversation with them. They tell us what to expect crossing Kancamagus Pass on tomorrow's ride.

Next to me is a woman and her daughter-in-law to be. They are in town to check out the Woodstock Inn and Brewery, where the daughter-in-law is to be married in November. We also enjoy talking with them. We bid everyone farewell after dinner and head back to the hotel to do our laundry and get ready for tomorrow.

Peter

Yes, we got another beer glass.

Tracy

Kancamagus Pass, at 2,855 feet, will be our last big climb. The locals assured us the pass is not as steep as the others we have recently climbed. I sure hope so. We will find out tomorrow.

Peter

Just one more big mountain to climb then it is all (mostly) downhill to Bar Harbor, Maine, and the end of our trip (ETA, Monday, August 11, 2014).

Chapter 13

We Made It to Maine!

August 8-11, 2014
Total Miles 283/4,362 total

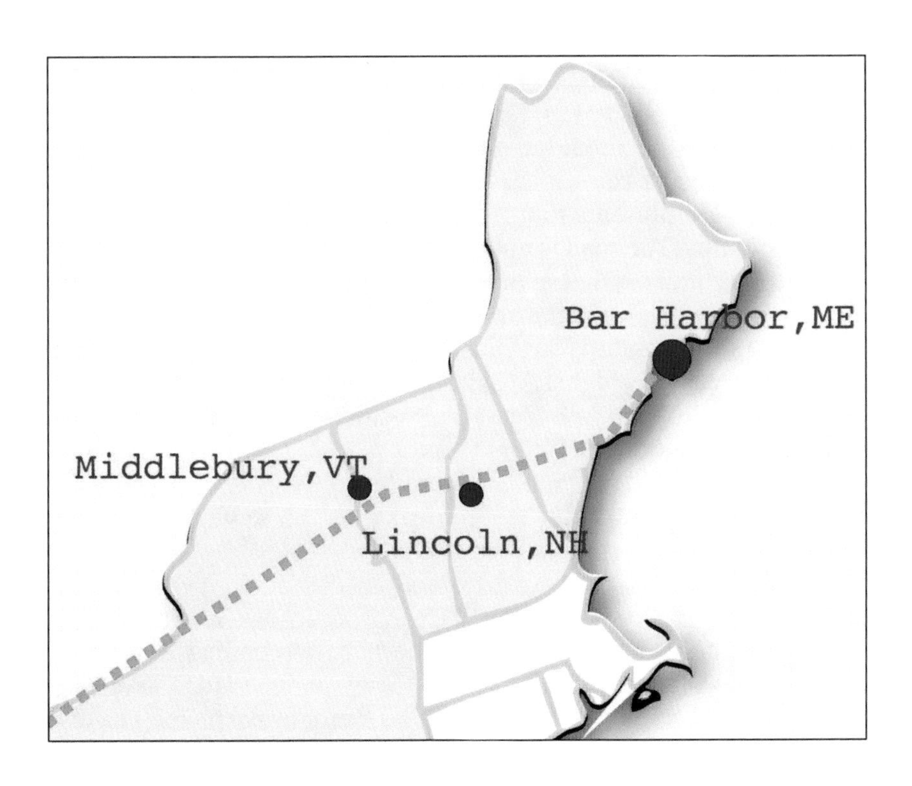

Day 69

August 8 - Lincoln, New Hampshire, to Bridgton, Maine
70 miles (total miles 4,149, remaining miles 213)
70-75 degrees, partly sunny, slight tailwind

Peter

We spent the morning reserving a rental car for our drive home from Bar Harbor, Maine.

The plan is to arrive in Bar Harbor on Monday afternoon, August 11, spend the 12th and 13th sightseeing, start driving home on the 14th, and arrive home on Saturday, August 16th. Boom!

The one-way rental process was a bit of a pain and expensive ($933.38), but with our schedules, bike shipping, and last-minute plane fares, it seemed to be the best option. It was kind of hard to deal with real-world stuff again.

Tracy

Today we face the challenge of the last big climb of our trip. We are ready for it, but still a bit nervous due to how steep the mountains have been in New Hampshire and the poor conditions of the roads.

As soon as Peter finishes reserving our rental car, we take off. We are traveling on Highway 112, Kancamagus Highway. It is in great shape and has a nice, wide shoulder most of the way, although the shoulder disappears closer to the top and, of course, the motor vehicle traffic increases. We are climbing Kancamagus Pass (2,855 feet), which is in the White Mountains. The road is not too steep (nine percent grade). It is just a long, steady climb for twelve miles to the top. The views from the top of Kancamagus Pass are amazing and definitely worth the climb.

The White Mountains are beautiful and include the Presidential Range that holds the highest peak in the northeastern United States, Mount Washington at 6,288 feet. The Presidential Range is just north of our route, thank goodness.

We head downhill for twenty-two miles to Conway. This side of the pass is in worse shape. Peter has to deal with the same bad asphalt as yesterday.

Peter

Maybe I am losing my nerve. Maybe not. Descending Kancamagus Pass is almost worse than climbing it. Once again, the road is steep and in lousy shape. I have to fully engage the rear drum brake to keep us under control almost all of the way down. I have never had the break on full for so long.

"Tracy, do you smell smoke?" I yell.

"I don't think so," she says.

I think I do. Damn, is the brake overheating? Can it overheat? I don't think so. Not worth finding out. I pull over to the side of the road to check. The brake is so hot I can't touch it, but that is normal. I check everything on the rear end of the bike and everything seems fine. We are just over 200 miles from completing our first, unsupported, cross-country bicycle trip. All we need to do now is not crash! Off we go.

Tracy

We have lunch in Conway and then head toward Fryeburg, Maine, seven and a half miles away. Unfortunately, the ride into Maine is not fun. We are riding on Highway 302/113, which is the only road to Fryeburg. There is a lot of traffic and the road is narrow. We white-knuckle it to Fryeburg and then bike an additional twenty miles deeper into Maine to end the day in Bridgton (pop. 2,403).

Bridgton is a quiet city located on Long Lake. We stay at Grady's West Shore Motel right on the lake. The room has a nice deck on the back overlooking the lake. The owner is a former police officer. Running the motel is his retirement job. Peter enjoys talking "cop" with him.

Day 70

August 9 - Bridgton to Bath, Maine
73 miles (total miles 4,222, remaining miles 140
70-80 degrees, sunny and a slight breeze

Peter

We are on the road early today, as usual. The early starts are hard (especially for Tracy), but they give us more flexibility throughout the day. Come on, sweetie, you can do it.

Tracy

Today is another hilly day. Boy, the East Coast certainly is not flat. The small, rolling hills are burning out our legs. It seems like we are constantly getting ready for the next climb.

Our first stop is in the city of Naples for coffee and a snack. We find a great little coffee shop right on Main Street across from Long Lake. The latte is Peter's second-best of the trip (the best was at the On the Fly Café in Fortine, Montana). We even see a whimsical (but real) palm tree and Old Man of the Sea statue next to the coffee shop. Peter promised me I would see buffalo on this trip. Still waiting. He did not say anything about palm trees.

The tree, statue, and people watching make the stop a lot of fun. I think we are starting to loosen up a bit. Yes, this is the same Long Lake in

Peter and the Old Man of the Sea in Naples, Maine. Our attitudes are starting to loosen up a bit as we near our Bar Harbor finish.

Bridgton, about twelve miles down the road. The lake certainly lives up to its name. It is beautiful, and well-used for recreation. Naples is very busy, definitely a tourist destination. We enjoy our stop, but all too soon have to move along.

Peter

Tracy loves palm trees. This tree is obviously a gimmick to bring tourists into the coffee shop, but it makes her happy nonetheless.

Our second break of the day is for a Coke and a moon pie at a private campground cafe on a lake. I probably won't do the moon pie thing again while biking.

After the moon pie, we are forced to go another thirty-five miles to get lunch. Normally, this wouldn't be a big deal, but the back roads in this part of the country have some short, but killer hills. After the thirty-five miles, our legs and my hands, from shifting and braking so much, are numb.

Tracy

The ride continues on hilly roads to the city of Brunswick and another bicycle shop. About five miles out of Brunswick, Peter notices the front tire seems to be going flat. (Not again!) The soft tire is making the climbs harder and the descents squirrely. We slowly make our way into town and stop on Main Street to put more air in the tire to nurse it to Center Street Cycles about two miles away.

We make it to the shop and Lee, the owner, and Peter check the tire and tube. They decide a new tire and inner tube are in order. We have the shop do the repairs; it is worth $10 at this point in the trip. We now have one tire and three tubes left to get us to Bar Harbor. We have a brand new tire on both the front and back, and should be okay until we get to the end. Let us hope so anyway.

> "You are amazing! Enjoyed following you through your lifetime adventure. Thanks for sharing with us."
>
> ***- Lynn Young Tulachka***

I ask Lee about local campgrounds while we are waiting for the repair. He tells me there are not many, but suggests one outside of Bath (pop. 9,266). I contact the campground and they have one tent site available for $70. Wow, $70 for a piece of grass on which to pitch our tent. For that, we will continue our ride to Bath and see what we find there. I bet we can find a hotel room for close to $70.

It is much later than we normally eat and Peter is getting a bit feisty. Lee recommends a local diner and we head that way for a late lunch. We ride the remaining fifteen miles to Bath. The ride is very easy and we cruise right along on the Androscoggin River Bike Path and Old Bath Road. On the way in, Peter swears he can smell salt water!

We find a room with great views for $90 at the Holiday Inn in Bath, right on Merrymeeting Bay.

Peter

We have giant scallop po' boys for dinner at a local tavern. Each po' boy has three scallops on it. While we are eating, all of a sudden Tracy wines, "Oh, no." I watch as one of her scallops falls on the table and then rolls onto the floor. She is really sad, but it is really funny to watch. I can't bring myself to offer her one of my scallops. Seriously, these are fresh giant scallops. We are getting closer to the ocean!

Day 71

August 10 - Bath to Belfast, Maine
78 miles (total miles 4,300, remaining miles 62)
70-75 degrees, sunny and a slight breeze

Tracy

Bath is a nice city located on the Kennebec River. We start our day crossing the river. The bridge is designed to accommodate all, with bike lanes and sidewalks. We plan to spend tonight in Belfast and have some pedaling to do to get there.

This part of Maine is hilly, with frequent streams and rivers to cross. Thankfully, there are small towns to explore as well. We have many fun places to stop and definitely take advantage of the experience, but at the same time we are eager to get in our miles.

Peter

The terrain continues to be hilly today, but we don't care. The adrenaline has kicked in.

Tracy

In Rockport, we reach the Atlantic coast, but due to the many twists and turns in the road, we cruise right past and totally miss the city. Oops. We continue down the road to Camden, which is also on the water. We stop for coffee and a snack, and a much-needed break.

As we are walking back to our bicycle, a couple comes up to us and asks about our trip. We discover the young man rode his bicycle across the country the summer before and he shared some of his experiences. He could definitely relate to our journey and it is fun to discover our common bond. They wish us luck and we continue down the road. I look back to give a final wave and the young man has a slightly sad look on his face, almost like he wishes it was him heading down the road. Hopefully again someday soon, my friend.

Our overnight stay tonight is at a "Cyclist Only Camp" in Belfast (pop. 6,381). It is listed on our Adventure Cycling map to contact Alex and Diane Allmayer-Beck. I reach out to Alex and he tells us we are welcome to stay.

Alex is a wonderful man and offers accommodations to bicyclists at his home. He is an avid bicyclist and motorcyclist, and feels many of the campgrounds in the area charge way too much. He decided several years ago to open his house to cyclists to help them on their way. He is a very gracious host and allows us to set up our tent in the back yard and use his shower and home as needed. Alex is five weeks out from hip surgery and doing great. He is able to bicycle now, but not as much as he would like.

After sharing a bottle of wine and some snacks with Alex, at his urging, Peter and I walk the six blocks downhill into Belfast to get some dinner and check it out. Oh, our legs felt that one. Belfast is a beautiful, historic city, patterned after the city of the same name in Ireland. It is located right on Belfast Bay. The buildings in the downtown area are amazing. It doesn't take much for us to imagine we are walking a street in Ireland. We will have to come back here someday and explore some more.

During dinner, our server tells us about a microbrewery located right behind the restaurant on the bay. Marshall Wharf Brewing Company is only open until 10:00 p.m., so we finish our dinner quickly and head that way. When we get there, the hostess tells us they are not letting anyone else in because they actually close at 9:00 p.m. on Sundays. We are bummed. Peter tells the hostess we just bicycled all the way across the country, just to come here. Wink. She looks around, steps out of the way, and tells us to go in. We have a beer and listen to a band play blue grass music, and yes, we get another beer glass. It is a nice way to end the day.

Day 72

August 11 –Belfast to Bar Harbor, Maine
62 miles (total miles 4,362, remaining miles 0)
75-80, sunny and a slight tailwind

Peter

We are only one day, sixty-two miles, 330,000 feet, from our goal, and a lobster dinner! No, I'm not a bit excited. Ha.

Tracy

This morning we are more excited than normal to get going, because today we will complete our journey. Four thousand, three hundred and sixty-two miles is a long way to ride a bicycle, and seventy-two days is a long time to be away from home, family, and friends. This has been an amazing opportunity and experience, but we are ready to be done.

We get up at 5:30 a.m. so we can be on the road by 7:00 a.m. Our host, Alex, rides out of town with us seven miles to Searsport. It is great to have an escort, because it is sometimes difficult to find our way out of a city and back on route. We will have to remember this when we host. What a nice way to make sure our guests have a stress-free ride out of town. We all stop when we reach Searsport. After a hug, a handshake, and many thanks, Peter and I continue on our way and Alex goes to find a coffee. What a pleasure to have our last day begin with another act of kindness.

The route today starts with some rolling hills and ends with some climbs near Bar Harbor. The views of the various bays are great and plentiful. We cross many bridges, with most of them in great shape and wide enough to accommodate bicyclists. Our ride is going well, so we decide to hold off on lunch until we get to Bar Harbor. We make frequent stops for snacks and eat the Cliff Bars and PowerBars we still have left on the bike. I am sick of Cliff Bars and PowerBars, and do not plan to eat any for a long time.

The traffic is unbelievably bad on Highway 3 as we get closer to Bar Harbor, and the road has no shoulder to speak of. It is late morning on a Monday and the traffic is bumper to bumper. It is a tough ride.

Peter

I had pictured this final ride into Bar Harbor and Acadia National Park, which effectively surrounds the city, as pastoral. Instead, I am finding myself fighting heavy traffic. Suddenly, I just can't take it anymore and I pull the bike to the side of the road.

> "May the conclusion bring as much satisfaction as the journey and the happiness of success linger far past the finish line."
>
> ***- Kyle Fordham***

Tracy says, "What's wrong?"

"I just need a couple of minutes," I say. I am tired, oh, so tired.

The enormity of the adventure we are about to complete has hit me with full force. And, I'm hungry. I hand the bike over to Tracy, open a PowerBar, hopefully my last for a long while, and take a seat on the curb. After a few minutes, I am ready to negotiate the traffic once more.

This happens to me again about an hour later.

"All I need to do now is get us there safely," I keep telling myself.

Tracy just keeps saying, "It's okay, we are almost there."

Tracy

We exit Highway 3 about fourteen miles out of Bar Harbor and the traffic volume drops considerably, although the shoulder of the road is still not in good shape. Peter has his hands full keeping us on the road. (We find out later that this stretch of road into Bar Harbor is being reconstructed next year with bicycle lanes. Good idea.)

Peter

Only five miles from Bar Harbor, I see a small flash of gold on the bike's front tire. I say to Tracy, "We are about to have a flat tire."

"What?" she says.

I pull over to the side of the road. I know what is in the tire even before I look. It is a carpet tack. Yup, there it is. The tire is still holding air, but I can't risk it going flat on a downhill and me losing control and crashing us out. Not five miles from the end. Reluctantly, I pull the tack out of the tire and it immediately goes flat. Nuts! We pull the bags off the front of the bike and I start to fix the flat. This is our fifth flat tire of the trip, and hopefully our last. It has to be. Right?

Tracy

I ask a nearby homeowner for a floor pump while Peter is working on the flat. He has one and loans it to me. Unfortunately, it does not have the right adaptor, so we cannot use it. Oh well, Peter has good luck with the CO2, this time, and is able to inflate the tire to 100 psi. Good enough.

Peter

We enter Bar Harbor going north on Main Street. There is a lot of traffic, but it is moving at a leisurely pace so it is easy for me to integrate the bike into the flow. The street is cute. It is tree lined and there are lots of small shops, restaurants, and motels.

Second S Street, First S Street, Hancock Street, Atlantic Avenue, where is the ocean? Derby Lane, Mt. Desert Street, Albert Meadow, Firefly Lane ... there it is!

"Tracy, can you see it?" I say.

"Yes," she says. "We made it!"

She reaches up and squeezes my shoulders. We made it!

Field Street, Cottage Way, West Street. We are at the shoreline, but up on a breakwater. How do we get to the water? I slowly turn us right on West Street as we both scan for a way down.

Then I see it. One block away is a boat ramp which leads to the water. We dismount at the top of the ramp and slowly – we do not want to slip on the algae-covered ramp and fall on our asses – roll the bike to the water's edge.

"Ready?" I say.

"Ready!"

We push the bike's front tire into the water and just let it all soak in.

Done!

Tracy

There are many people in the area, and of course the questions and comments start flying. We answer them all.

There is only one more piece of business we have to take care of. Another tradition at the end of a long bicycle ride is to lift your bicycle overhead for a celebratory picture. Well, that's all fine and dandy with a single bike, but we have never lifted the tandem straight overhead before, and certainly not with a full load. We remove the large rear panniers, the smaller front panniers, the tent, and the water bottles from the bicycle.

Peter says, "Ready?"

"Ready," I say.

Peter counts, "One, two, three."

Up goes the bike, straight overhead. Okay, now we know we can do it. Ha. We put the bike back down. All we need now is to do it again for the picture. I pick a woman, obviously a tourist like us, at random and ask her if she will take our picture. She agrees, steps back with Peter's phone and takes one shot. (What were we thinking? Bike all the way across the country and have a complete stranger take only one picture to commemorate the event. Crazy.) The picture is perfect!

We did it. Unbelievable! It was definitely an adventure, but also tough. The last several weeks were hard both mentally and physically. We are glad we did it, but are also happy to be done. What a once-in-a-lifetime adventure.

Peter

Done and done!

We made it!

Epilogue

Recovery and Return Home

August 12-13, 2014
Bar Harbor, Maine

After dipping our front wheel into the Atlantic Ocean, enjoying a lobster dinner was a requirement of arriving in Bar Harbor, Maine.

Tracy

We thoroughly enjoy our three days in Bar Harbor. It is a really nice city in which to recover: quiet, compact, easy to walk, and with all the services we need.

After dipping our front tire in the Atlantic Ocean yesterday afternoon, we backtracked a few blocks to the Anchorage Motel. The motel certainly is not fancy, but it is clean, comfortable, and affordable. We cleaned up and walked into town for a late lunch. After lunch, we explored town a bit and then headed back to the motel for a nap.

Dinner was at the Thirsty Whale, compliments of Mark Stephany. A gift certificate was waiting for us. We had a couple of local beers with our meal. It was a great way to celebrate bicycling across the country. Thanks, Mark.

We sleep in late Tuesday morning, our first day after completing the trip. We enjoy waking and dozing back off, knowing that we have nowhere to go and nothing we have to do. We have done it!

> "What an amazing accomplishment. Seems like many of us simply chase our dreams, but you caught yours. Well done!"
>
> ***- Annette Malcomson***

We eventually crawl out of bed and take inventory of our travel-weary bodies. We have each lost weight (7-10 pounds we discover later) and a lot of muscle mass, everywhere but our legs. We are otherwise unscathed. We are really hungry, though. Go figure.

We wander the streets of Bar Harbor in search of breakfast. There are many good options and we easily get our fill. After breakfast, we call Enterprise Rent-A-Car to get our rental. They pick us up at the motel and take us to their office to finalize the paperwork for the small SUV we reserved. We will be doing the rest of our touring by car.

Peter

I sure hope I can get the tandem in this thing later without completely disassembling it. Whatever, I'll figure it out.

Tracy

We head to Acadia National Park (our fourth national park) to drive the park loop. It is a beautiful place. We would love to check out more of the park, especially off the beaten path, but not this trip. There are many people in the park and traffic is quite heavy. We see lots of bicyclists riding up Cadillac Mountain and are glad we already climbed our last mountain a few days before. Everyone keeps telling us to be sure to bicycle the carriage paths in the park. I think we will pass on that as well.

Peter

We head back to the motel for a long nap.

Tracy

Of course, we must have a traditional lobster dinner. We take the twenty-minute drive over to Trenton to eat at the Trenton Bridge Lobster Pond. The young man from Enterprise recommended the restaurant.

Peter

We are lobster novices, but the employees graciously walk us through the process. We pick out two live lobsters from a huge tank and have them boiled. Good for us, bad for the lobsters. While we are waiting for our lobster to cook, we get our plastic plates and silver wear, corn on the cob, rolls with butter, melted butter, and of course, our obligatory lobster bibs. We grab a seat at one of the picnic tables on the screened-in porch behind the restaurant and wait. Shortly, our cooked lobsters arrive in a 9 x 13 roasting pan. At first, they are too hot to touch. Anticipation.

Tracy

The lobster is delicious and we enjoy the challenge of getting at all the meat. It is definitely worth the work, and yes, you do need a bib and lots of paper towel.

Peter

There is only one thing that can make fresh-cooked Maine lobster even better: bicycling 4,362 miles to get it. I may not ever have Maine lobster this good again.

After dinner, we drive back to the motel for another nap. When we wake up, we walk the four blocks to the Bar Harbor Brewing Company tap room to check it out. And, you guessed it, pick up the final pint glass of our trip.

Tracy

Wednesday we sleep in again. Yay. With a little more energy today than yesterday, we are on a mission. We eat a big breakfast, Peter gets a haircut, I get a pedicure and manicure, and we both get hour-long massages at a spa. The spa has a therapy dog, Daisy. She is a beautiful, all-white, giant poodle. Daisy can stay in the room during your massage if you want her to. Peter and I both choose to have Daisy stay with us. She is amazing. She put her head next to mine on the table and kind of leaned in so she was always touching me. The massage was wonderful and Daisy made it extra special.

Later in the day we shop, nap, shop, and nap some more before going out to dinner one last time. It is a fun way to end the trip.

Peter

I start disassembling the bike to pack it in the car after dinner and Tracy starts packing our gear for the drive home. As luck would have it, all I have to do to get the tandem in the SUV is remove both wheels and the front and rear racks. It is tight, but it all fits.

August 14-16

Bar Harbor, Maine to Green Bay, Wisconsin (by car)

Tracy

We reluctantly leave Bar Harbor in our rental SUV early on the morning of August 14. It will take us three days to travel by car what it took us about a month to bicycle. Traveling by car feels very strange.

Peter

I do not like being in the car. We are going so fast it is hard to really see anything. I can't move. I find myself constantly shifting from side to side. I can't get comfortable. Restless to bicycle again? Tracy and I had talked about doing some sightseeing during the drive, but now all I want to do is get home.

> "Your determination, perseverance and dedication is truly an inspiration. Congratulations to the both of you."
>
> **- *Marty Zeske***

Tracy to the rescue. She discovers that we are constantly crossing roads on the freeways that we bicycled days, then weeks, before. She pulls out our bicycling maps and we start to backtrack and relive the last part of our trip. It is calming and helps us pass the time.

Tracy

It is the easiest way to get back home, but not a lot of fun. Although, I do like seeing the names of communities we bicycled through and roads we traveled.

We drive as far as Syracuse, New York, spend the night and get up early the next day to continue our trip. We make it to Milwaukee, Wisconsin, the next night and spend it at my parents' house. Mom makes soup, which is delicious. It is so nice to have real homemade food and be with family again.

The next morning we leave for Green Bay and two hours later, we are home to an empty house. We forgot to let our youngest daughter know we were almost home. She was out and about and saw us driving to the airport to return our rental car. Oops. When we get back home, she is already there and says, "Thanks for letting me know you were home." Hugs all around. It is so good to see her. I did not realize how much I missed her.

Time to compare adventures. All we did was bike across the country, unsupported, on a bicycle built for two. She lived in Fiji. Ha.

Peter

Something was gnawing at me, so I turn to Tracy and say, "So, what do you want to do next?

"I don't know," she says. "But I would like to do another long bicycle trip."

"Me, too!"

"You know," I said, half kidding, "now that we have ridden west to east across the country, maybe we could go north to south. What about riding the Mississippi River?"

"We could do that," Tracy says with a smile.

Wow!

Acknowledgements

When we decided to bicycle across the country in the spring of 2014, little did we imagine we would be finishing a book about our adventure three and a half short years later. Just as our bicycling journey never would have happened without the support of many, the same is true with our book writing journey.

Jeff Ash was among the first professionals we reached out to for assistance. Not only did Jeff assure us we weren't crazy to consider writing a book, he also put us in contact with our publishers, and vouched for our trip and us. Jeff gave this project the initial shot in the arm it needed.

One of our biggest concerns about writing this book was that it had to be good. The adventure was wonderful, our presentations had been well-received, but could we translate the experience into a compelling read?

This book would never have become a reality without expertise and guidance from Mike Dauplaise and Bonnie Groessl of M&B Global Solutions Inc. As first-time authors, we knew we needed help, a lot of it, to make this happen. Mike and Bonnie provided us with the coaching, editing, publishing, and marketing expertise we needed to become successful authors. Although the book writing process is a lot of work, Mike and Bonnie have made it both manageable and fun. We truly value their professionalism, expertise and friendship.

Finally, thank you to our family, friends, and complete strangers who made this all possible.

Tracy and Peter (Fall 2017)

About the Authors

Tracy and Peter Flucke are president and vice president of WE BIKE, etc., LLC, a Green Bay, Wisconsin, consulting firm that specializes in the areas of engineering, education, enforcement, and encouragement for walking, bicycling, and healthy communities. Founded in 1993, WE BIKE does business nationally.

Tracy has held several positions of increasing responsibility in municipal government over the past thirty years. Her career includes serving as a recreation programmer, parks and recreation director, and administrator in several communities. In these roles she worked with staff, elected officials, advocates, and citizens to help create healthy and active communities through improving pedestrian and bicycle safety, mobility, and access. Tracy has a Master of Science Degree in Public Administration and a Bachelor of Science Degree in Recreation Administration.

After a successful municipal career, Tracy joined Peter in the family business to expand the company's offerings and expertise. Tracy has been an avid bicycle commuter for most of her career.

Peter is a graduate of the University of Wisconsin-Stevens Point with a Bachelor of Science Degree in Recreation and Forestry and a minor in Environmental Law Enforcement. He was a law enforcement officer in the state of Minnesota for seven years. For five of those years, he was a law enforcement ranger with the Three Rivers Park District, one of the largest metropolitan park systems in the country. Peter created one of the first police bicycle patrols in the state while at Three Rivers.

Leveraging a wealth of experience and knowledge in the pedestrian and bicycle fields, Peter has created and taught pedestrian and bicycle safety and education courses for children, adults, law enforcement officers, planners, and engineers. He has developed community pedestrian/bicycle plans, written resource guides, trained police bike patrols, and consulted on a wide variety of related topics. He was on the board of directors of the Wisconsin Bike Fed for ten years.

Peter is a nationally certified League Cycling Instructor and former coach with the League of American Bicyclists, and a Police Cyclist certified by the International Police Mountain Bike Association.

Tracy and Peter are enthusiastic bicyclists, runners, and outdoorsmen. They bring passion to their work in helping communities and citizens improve pedestrian and bicycle safety and access by looking at the world through bicyclist and pedestrian eyes. Both Peter and Tracy are experienced and well-respected presenters. They have two adult daughters, Melissa and Alexandra.

Tracy and Peter have completed three unsupported cross-country bicycle trips on their tandem: Northern Tier – 2014 (4,362 miles); Mississippi River – 2015 (3,052 miles); Historic Route 66 – 2016 (2,603 miles).